RELIGION AND THE EXERCISE OF PUBLIC AUTHORITY

In the burgeoning literature on law and religion, scholarly attention has tended to focus on broad questions concerning the scope of religious freedom, the nature of toleration and the meaning of secularism. An under-examined issue is how religion figures in the decisions, actions and experiences of those charged with performing public duties. This point of contact between religion and public authority has generated a range of legal and political controversies around issues such as the wearing of religious symbols by public officials, prayer at municipal government meetings, religious education and conscientious objection by public servants.

Authored by scholars from a variety of disciplines, the chapters in this volume provide insight into these and other issues. Yet the volume also provides an entry point into a deeper examination of the concepts that are often used to organise and manage religious diversity, notably state neutrality. By examining the exercise of public authority by individuals who are religiously committed—or who, in the discharge of their public responsibilities, must account for those who are—this volume exposes the assumptions about legal and political life that underlie the concept of state neutrality and reveals its limits as a governing ideal.

Religion and the Exercise of Public Authority

Edited by
Benjamin L Berger
and
Richard Moon

•HART•
OXFORD • LONDON • NEW YORK • NEW DELHI • SYDNEY

HART PUBLISHING
Bloomsbury Publishing Plc
Kemp House, Chawley Park, Cumnor Hill, Oxford, OX2 9PH, UK

HART PUBLISHING, the Hart/Stag logo, BLOOMSBURY and the Diana logo are trademarks of Bloomsbury Publishing Plc
First published in Great Britain 2016

First published in hardback, 2016
Paperback edition, 2018

A catalogue record for this book is available from the British Library.

Library of Congress Cataloging-in-Publication Data

Names: Berger, Benjamin L., 1977– editor. | Moon, Richard, 1956– editor.

Title: Religion and the exercise of public authority / edited by Benjamin L Berger and Richard Moon.

Description: Oxford ; Portland, Oregon : Hart Publishing, 2016. | Includes bibliographical references and index.

Identifiers: LCCN 2016005226 (print) | LCCN 2016005578 (ebook) | ISBN 9781849467155 (hardback : alk. paper) | ISBN 9781509906475 (Epub)

Subjects: LCSH: Church and state—Canada. | Freedom of religion—Canada.

Classification: LCC KE4502 .R45 2016 (print) | LCC KE4502 (ebook) | DDC 342.7108/52—dc23

LC record available at http://lccn.loc.gov/2016005226

ISBN: PB: 978-1-50992-473-8
HB: 978-1-84946-715-5
ePDF: 978-1-50990-648-2
ePub: 978-1-50990-647-5

Typeset by Compuscript Ltd, Shannon

ACKNOWLEDGEMENTS

We wish to express our thanks to the authors who contributed their knowledge, insight, and creativity to this collection and to the people at Hart Publishing for their support and expert work in bringing this volume to print. Thank you also to Rachel Devon for her superb research assistance along the way.

This collection arose out of a workshop held at Osgoode Hall Law School, York University, in the autumn of 2014. A special thank-you to Jody-Ann Rowe for her outstanding work organizing that event. We are grateful to the Social Sciences Research Council, the Religion and Diversity Project housed at the University of Ottawa, the Faculty of Law at the University of Windsor, and Osgoode Hall Law School for supporting the workshop and the collaborations that led to this volume.

CONTENTS

LIST OF CONTRIBUTORS

Amélie Barras is Assistant Professor at the Department of Social Science, York University.

Lori G Beaman is Canada Research Chair at the Department of Classics and Religious Studies, University of Ottawa.

Benjamin L Berger is Associate Professor at Osgoode Hall Law School, York University.

Faisal Bhabha is Associate Professor at Osgoode Hall Law School, York University.

Paul Bramadat is Director of the Centre for Studies in Religion and Society, University of Victoria.

Pamela E Klassen is Professor at the Department for the Study of Religion, University of Toronto.

Solange Lefebvre is Professor and Chair for the Management of Cultural and Religious Diversity at the Faculty of Theology and Religious Sciences, University of Montreal.

Jocelyn Maclure is Professor at the Faculty of Philosophy, University of Laval.

Richard Moon is Professor at the Faculty of Law, University of Windsor.

Bruce Ryder is Associate Professor at Osgoode Hall Law School, York University.

Jennifer A Selby is Associate Professor at the Department of Religious Studies, Memorial University.

Shauna Van Praagh is Professor at the Faculty of Law, McGill University.

Daniel M Weinstock is James McGill Professor at the Faculty of Law, McGill University, and Director of the McGill Institute for Health and Social Policy.

Introduction: Religious Neutrality and the Exercise of Public Authority

RICHARD MOON AND BENJAMIN L BERGER

Over the last many years a host of legal and political controversies have arisen out of the meeting of religion and the exercise of public authority. Some of the most contentious disputes have concerned the performance of public duties by religiously committed individuals. Other cases have involved public authorities struggling to account for a religiously diverse society. These issues have exposed the difficulties engendered when civic officials engage with religion—both as a fact of social life and as an aspect of their own identities—while discharging their public responsibilities.

Most familiar are the controversies that have arisen in jurisdictions around the world concerning the wearing of religious symbols by public officials. The issue has often surfaced as a question about whether teachers should be permitted to wear identifiably religious clothing.[1] But it has also arisen, in Canada—with the failed proposal for a so-called 'Charter of Quebec Values'—and elsewhere in a more general form as a controversy about whether visible or 'ostentatious' religious signs or symbols should be worn by anyone exercising a public function. The question of whether a municipal government can include a public prayer in its meetings has recently come before the courts in both the United States[2] and Canada.[3] And a range of cases have posed the question of whether, in discharging public duties, officials should be permitted to exempt themselves from functions that are inconsistent with their religious convictions. This may occur in a variety of contexts, including the performance of a same-sex marriage by a civil marriage commissioner[4] or the provision of healthcare and reproductive health services by medical professionals. The point of contact between public authority and religious commitment is a site that will continue to generate a range of legal and political controversies. The authors who have contributed to this volume provide insight into many of these issues. That is one way in which this volume is both timely and important: it offers to scholars of law, politics and religion a helpful resource in exploring these discrete but important debates.

[1] See, eg, *Dahlab v Switzerland* ECHR 2001–V 449.

[2] *Town of Greece v Galloway* 572 US (2014).

[3] *Mouvement laïque québécois v Saguenay (City)* 2015 SCC 16.

[4] *Reference Re Marriage Commissioners Appointed Under The Marriage Act* 2011 SKCA 3.

Yet perhaps more importantly, the volume also provides an entry point into a deeper examination of the concepts we use to organise and manage religious diversity—concepts such as tolerance, secularism and neutrality. The volume's focus on religion and the exercise of public authority brings to the surface the many difficulties involved in separating religious belief and practice from political action, exposing the complexity of these outwardly orderly concepts. Drawing on the insights and perspectives of anthropologists, religious studies scholars, philosophers, sociologists and legal scholars, this volume's interdisciplinary examination of the issues generated by the meeting of religion and public authority challenges our familiar ways of framing questions, encourages us to notice dimensions of these issues that might otherwise fall outside our range of vision, and pushes us to think more carefully and critically about the abstract principles that guide legal and political discussion of contemporary religious diversity.

The broad concepts that we seize upon as guides for managing religious difference express valuable ideals and provide a language for legal debate, but they also tend to paper over many of the complexities and challenges of religious difference. Two such concepts—toleration and secularism—are illustrative. 'Toleration' has, of course, a long pedigree as a philosophical ideal and legal tool in matters of religious freedom, equality and diversity. It was, for many years, the dominant concept invoked by the Supreme Court of Canada in its freedom of religion jurisprudence and anchored political discussion about how to address religious difference. And yet as cases and controversies continued to accumulate, scholarship has shown that the social experience of legal toleration is often one of exclusion and marginalisation.[5] Something similar can be seen in the concept of 'secularism', an ideal that anchors much political debate and often serves as a regulative concept in the jurisprudence, including that of the Supreme Court of Canada. The concept of secularism captures something important about a just and fair state in a context of religious diversity—that there ought to be some form of separation between state power and religion; however, broad invocations of the concept elide its various forms and the different implications of each,[6] conceal the political and historical facts that give shape to the varieties of secularism,[7] and mislead about the character of law itself.[8] An arguable consequence of that

[5] One of us has written about this at some length in Benjamin L Berger, *Law's Religion: Religious Difference and the Claims of Constitutionalism* (Toronto, University of Toronto Press, 2015). Wendy Brown has argued that toleration works precisely by *depoliticisation*—by extracting law from history and politics. See Wendy Brown, *Regulating Aversion: Tolerance in the Age of Identity and Empire* (Princeton, Princeton University Press, 2006).

[6] Michael Warner, Jonathan VanAntwerpen and Craig Calhoun (eds), *Varieties of Secularism in a Secular Age* (Cambridge, Harvard University Press, 2010); Janet R Jakobsen and Ann Pelligrini, *Secularisms* (Durham, Duke University Press, 2008).

[7] Ahmet Kuru, *Secularism and State Policies Toward Religion: The United States, France, and Turkey* (New York, Cambridge University Press, 2009); John R Bowen, *Can Islam Be French?: Pluralism and Pragmatism in a Secularist State* (Princeton, Princeton University Press, 2011).

[8] Winnifred Fallers Sullivan, Robert Yelle and Mateo Taussig-Rubbo (eds), *After Secular Law* (Stanford, Stanford University Press, 2011).

concealment has been the emergence of political claims about secularism that are at odds with principles of religious inclusion and equality.[9]

This volume is appearing just as another concept has become prominent in legal discussions of how to manage religion: the concept of state neutrality. It emerges in the jurisprudence of international courts as the foundational demand flowing from a commitment to religious freedom;[10] and here in Canada it has arguably eclipsed toleration as the central concept in the Supreme Court's approach to the management of religious difference.[11] Yet the concept of (and demand for) state neutrality has many possible meanings, and is afflicted by a certain instability. It is applied selectively or inconsistently across and within liberal democracies, reflecting the variety of postures towards religion that flow from the particularities of local political histories, cultural inheritances, and conceptions of secularism.[12] For some, the neutrality requirement is understood broadly as precluding the state from taking any position on the question of what constitutes a good society. For others, state neutrality requires an evenhandedness between religious—and non-religious—modes of life and forms of belief, but does not preclude the state from taking positions on how to pursue a just and attractive common social world.[13]

Although the Supreme Court of Canada has conceded that 'the state's duty of neutrality does not require it to abstain from celebrating and preserving its religious heritage',[14] and that 'the state always has a legitimate interest in promoting and protecting' certain 'shared values' such as equality, human rights, and democracy,[15] the Court has held that the essence of the demand for state neutrality is that it 'presupposes that the state abstains from taking a position on questions of religion'.[16] 'State neutrality', the Court has claimed, 'is assured when the state neither favours nor hinders any particular religious belief, that is, when it shows

[9] One such example is the episode involving the proposed 'Charter of Quebec Values', *Charter affirming the values of State secularism and religious neutrality and of equality between women and men, and providing a framework for accommodation requests*, 1st sess, 40th Leg, Quebec, 2013.

[10] See, eg, *Leyla Sahin v Turkey* ECHR 2005–XI 819, 44 EHRR 5; *Lautsi and Others v Italy* ECHR 2011–III 2412, 54 EHRR 3.

[11] See *Saguenay* (n 3). The theme of the ascendance of the ideal of neutrality, and its associated focus on non-exclusion rather than coercion, was noted in Richard Moon, 'Liberty, Neutrality, and Inclusion: Freedom of Religion under the Canadian Charter of Rights' (2003) 41 *Brandeis Law Review* 563. For another discussion of 'state neutrality' eclipsing 'toleration' as the court's guiding ideal, see Benjamin L Berger, 'Religious Diversity, Education, and the "Crisis" in State Neutrality' (2014) 29 *Canadian Journal of Law & Society* 103.

[12] See, eg, *Leyla Sahin v Turkey* ECHR 2005–XI 819, 44 EHRR 5; *Lautsi and Others v Italy* ECHR 2011–III 2412, 54 EHRR 3; *Dahlab v Switzerland* ECHR 2001–V 449. Richard Moon, 'Christianity, Multiculturalism, and National Identity: A Canadian Comment on Lautsi and Others v. Italy' in Jeroen Temperman (ed), *The Lautsi Papers: Multidisciplinary Reflections on Religious Symbols in the Public School Classroom* (Leiden, Martinus Nijhoff Publishers, 2012).

[13] For this view, see Bruce Ryder, 'State Neutrality and Freedom of Conscience and Religion' (2005) 29 *Supreme Court Law Review* (2d) 169; Moon (n 11); Berger (n 11).

[14] *Saguenay* (n 3), para 116.

[15] *Loyola High School v Quebec (Attorney General)* 2015 SCC 12, para 47.

[16] *Saguenay* (n 3), para 132.

respect for all postures towards religion, including that of having no religious belief whatsoever'.[17] Accordingly, the state is precluded from preferring or supporting the practices or beliefs of one religion over those of another, or favouring religious belief over non-religious belief, and vice versa.

The idea of state neutrality expresses certain important aspects of what the just treatment of religion in a religiously and morally diverse society might require. The commitment to neutrality may flow in part from the idea that religious issues should be removed from politics because of the difficulty of resolving such matters, the risk of conflict on such points, or, otherwise put, the impossibility of finding 'overlapping consensus' on questions of religion. Alternatively, the demand for state neutrality may be anchored in an inclusionary impulse linked to concerns about identity and equality. If religious belonging and belief are understood as dimensions of identity, a judgment by the state that suggests that the beliefs and practices of one group are less meritorious or true than another may be experienced not simply as a position taken on a public policy debate, but as a denial of one's equal worth, or as the marginalisation of one's religious community.[18] In these ways, the concept of state neutrality expresses important ideals.

Yet, despite its conceptual force and appeal, state neutrality is also afflicted by a number of limits, frailties, and conundrums as a governing legal ideal. For example, the courts have recognised that religious practices have shaped the traditions or customs of the community, and cannot simply be erased from the public sphere or ignored in the formulation of public policy.[19] Canadian courts have not demanded that governments eliminate religious symbols and practices from physical and social structures, some of which were constructed long ago. However, it may often be difficult to determine when the use of religious symbols or practices by that state is simply an acknowledgment of the country's religious history or of the importance of religion in the private lives of citizens, and when it amounts to a present affirmation of the truth of a particular religious belief system. Moreover, if a large part of the population is Christian, it is difficult to see how the state could not take the practices of this group into account, when, for example, it selects statutory holidays or establishes a 'pause day' from work. As long as religion remains part of private life, it is bound to affect the shape of public action. In *Chamberlain v Surrey School District*, the Supreme Court of Canada held that elected officials may draw on their religious values (or the religious values of their constituents) when making political decisions. As Chief Justice McLachlin recognised in *Chamberlain*, '[r]eligion is an integral aspect of people's lives, and cannot be left at the boardroom door'.[20]

The focus of this volume on the way that public officials must negotiate and interact with religion reminds us of the historical, demographic, and situational

[17] *SL v Commission scolaire des Chênes* 2012 SCC 7, para 32, [2012] 1 SCR 235.

[18] See ibid; Richard Moon, 'Freedom of Religion under the Charter of Rights: The Limits of State Neutrality' (2012) 45 *University of British Columbia Law Review* 497.

[19] Richard Moon, *Freedom of Conscience and Religion* (Toronto, Irwin Law, 2014).

[20] *Chamberlain v Surrey School District No 36* 2002 SCC 86, para 18, [2002] 4 SCR 710.

complexity on which the call for state neutrality floats. It reminds us that the 'state' involved in the call for state neutrality is not an abstract entity, but embodied in individuals—actors who are invested with commitments and identities, at work in particular times and settings, and called upon to discharge specific duties and respond to specific problems. Examining the exercise of public authority by individuals who are religiously committed—or who, in the discharge of their public responsibilities must account for and engage with those who are—exposes some of the assumptions about legal and political life that underlie the concept of state neutrality and reveal some of its limits as a governing ideal.

So what, in particular, does the hard look at religion and the exercise of public authority found in the contributions to this volume recover for us about the social and political realities that sit beneath the call for state neutrality?

First, through a historical and sociological examination of public officials and the exercise of public authority, a number of the chapters in this volume remind us of certain inconvenient facts about the nature, formation, and contemporary structure of the state that is expected to conform to this ideal of neutrality. Just as scholarship has shown that the language of toleration or of legal multiculturalism extracts matters from their historical and political constitution,[21] a focus on state neutrality may similarly impede a recognition of the ways in which the state has shaped itself around claims of a religious character, using metaphysical appeals and ritual performances to consolidate its boundaries, authority, and power. Pamela Klassen's chapter, 'God Keep our Land: The Legal Ritual of the McKenna-McBride Commission 1913–1916' draws this truth to our attention in a subtle way, showing how public officials charged with expanding and consolidating the nation made cosmological claims, claims that had Christian contours but drew from the particularity of this land, and that became the frame in which discussion and argument took place. These claims were, in portentous ways, in direct competition with Indigenous cosmologies, as state officials sought to clear the terrain for assertions of state sovereignty. With Idle No More and the Truth and Reconciliation Commission, we have been made keenly aware of the contemporary consequences of this project in which religion and the exercise of state authority was central. Those are some of the continuing deposits of that history of the state's involvement with religion. Yet as the chapter by Amélie Barras, Jennifer Selby and Lori Beaman shows us, these deposits are also found and felt in the experience of those living and working today in the corridors of public authority. Their chapter explores the way in which 'the workplaces of Canadian public servants are not neutral', as shown through interviews with Muslim public servants. Instead, based on this novel research, Barras, Selby and Beaman argue that many of those working in and for the state remain keenly aware of the historical Christian backdrop that shapes their workplaces. As they explain, 'Christianity is almost invariably worked-out and lived as a dimension that is constitutive of the Canadian public realm and, for these public servants, constitutive of their everyday work lives'. And so both

[21] See Berger (n 5); Brown (n 5).

historical and sociological considerations of this issue remind us of the limits of state neutrality and complicate the starting assumption of an abstract state fitted from the outset for a posture of neutrality. The state that is expected to act 'neutrally' has a particular religious history that continues to shape its day-to-day life.

Second, a focus on the challenges that surface at the confluence of religion and public authority shows that it is exceedingly difficult to maintain the dividing line between religious and non-religious matters, a distinction on which many claims for state neutrality depend. Recall that the Supreme Court of Canada has described the very essence of state neutrality as 'the state abstain[ing] from taking a position on questions of religion'.[22] And yet abstention from engagement with religious matters is not a realistic—or perhaps even desirable—ambition. The collection's focus on the actual problems and tasks with which public officials are seized makes it clear that a desire for this kind of forbearance will be consistently frustrated—that state engagement with religious claims, practices, and positions is inescapable. It turns out to be very hard to neatly distinguish 'questions of religion' from questions of political and civic moment. This difficulty—a manifestation of the instability of the private-public divide—flows from two sources: the fact of religious investment in general questions of public life, and the demographic reality of the religiously diverse world that public policy must govern.

The character of religion is that it is keenly interested in and takes positions on matters of public moment. The positions taken by the state on public matters will invariably touch on religious commitments and practices. Richard Moon's chapter examining same-sex civil marriages and the conscientious objection of marriage commissioners shows this well. As Moon explains, state neutrality in matters of religion 'depends on a distinction between civic views and actions, which must be subject to the give and take of the political process, and spiritual beliefs and practices that should be treated as personal to the individual or internal to a religious community, and should be both excluded and insulated from politics'. And yet his analysis shows that, despite the practical necessity of drawing such a distinction, religious believers will often experience state action in the civic sphere and state agnosticism or neutrality in relation to spiritual concerns as position taking in matters of religious belief. As others have argued, it is a misleading conceit to imagine that discharging the public task of administering marriage can be done without involving the state in religious questions.[23] In his chapter, Paul Bramadat invites us to look at some of the different ways in which state actors might engage with questions of religion, and in so doing, he underscores the importance of reflecting on how religious communities will receive and interpret state action. Discussing the treatment of Trinity Western University's bid for a law school, Bramadat asks us to remember that the public policy question regarding the accreditation of a law school with a discriminatory covenant is

[22] *Saguenay* (n 3), para 132.
[23] See Robert Leckey, 'Profane Matrimony' (2006) 21 *Canadian Journal of Law & Society* 1.

also—and crucially—part of a story about minority religious communities that are invested in a particular view of public life and see the state as acting on the basis of a competing liberal moral perspective.

The portion of Bramadat's chapter discussing how government officials have engaged with religious communities on questions of security and radicalisation points to the other reason that the state cannot but engage with religious views and practices: demographic facts colour the tasks that public officials must perform—with the result that the exercise of public authority will often involve a close engagement with religion. Public policy must understand and respond to a social world rich with religious diversity. This is a social and political reality that attention to religion and the exercise of public authority helps us to see better. The point comes out interestingly in Solange Lefebvre's chapter, which offers an 'insider' account of the litigation leading to the Supreme Court of Canada's decision in *Saguenay* on public prayer and state neutrality. Lefebvre shows that a court can only understand what a prayer at a municipal council meeting means in a community of diverse views on religion if it understands the character of religious ritual, and this is something, Lefebvre concludes, courts are ill-equipped to do.

There is perhaps no field of state action that demonstrates how the raw reality of religious diversity affects the tasks of public actors better than the field of education. The provision of public education in a religiously diverse society requires public officials—and foremost among them, teachers—to engage closely with religious beliefs and practices, both their own and those of their students. As Shauna Van Praagh takes us through an imaginative high school 'open house', she shows at each turn that public education involves all manner of productive encounters with and judgments about religion, religious identity, and religious practice. Public education, for Van Praagh, is an intrinsically interfaith enterprise and '[t]he relationship of religion to public law and authority in any jurisdiction at any time can be conveyed through the context of education'. Daniel Weinstock's chapter, 'A Freedom of Religion-Based Argument for the Regulation of Religious Schools', shows that because intergenerational transmission is vital to religion and religious communities, the state's role in educating children necessarily involves it in religious life. Indeed, Weinstock's provocative argument is that the state's active regulation or limitation of religious education might be an essential condition for the realisation of the religious freedom of parents because it gives them the space to parent according to their religious convictions without offending the child's right to an open future.

Finally, when we shift our attention from the state—its general character and context—to the individuals who embody the state—the public actors and officials themselves—it quickly becomes apparent that the difficulty in separating religious from non-religious matters is echoed in the challenge of distinguishing between the religious and non-religious dimensions of the individual. A number of the chapters in this volume explore the difficulties in drawing this line.

The attempt to draw such a distinction within the person, often implicit in invocations of state neutrality, can translate into a weighty demand on the individual. For public servants who find themselves acting against the background of laws and public practices that are at odds with their religious commitments, the call to separate personal religion and public responsibility can amount to a demand for an excruciating internal split, as Bruce Ryder's chapter on physicians' conscientious objections shows so clearly. Ryder explores how the physician's public service can be enmeshed with her religious identity such that the desire to distinguish between these elements, whether one views that demand as justified or not, exacts a considerable moral toll on her identity and self-understanding. Sensitivity to that fact, as Ryder shows, is important to determining how we should respond to this public policy question. Moon builds a case for the justifiability of refusing religious exemptions for marriage commissioners, concluding that a civil servant has no claim to be excused from performing the tasks associated with her position, simply because she is morally opposed to government policy, or to basic public values concerning the treatment of others in the community. Nevertheless, Moon is sensitive to the challenge of separating personal faith and civic duty and the demands this places on public servants—on their identity as both a religious person and a public actor.

Jocelyn Maclure takes up this theme in his chapter, which examines claims—made in a limited fashion in the Bouchard-Taylor commission and more sweepingly in the proposed but never enacted 'Charter of Quebec Values'—that public officials should be prohibited from wearing conspicuous religious symbols. Although he defends the need for certain forms of neutrality and circumspection on the part of religiously committed public officials, Maclure argues that a public official's neutrality must be gauged by the quality of his or her actions, not on the basis of appearance. He concludes that bans on the wearing of religious signs 'cannot withstand scrutiny at the level of political morality'. He emphasises the unacceptable costs that such a ban would place on religious believers, given the difficulty of disentangling religious belief and practice as components of identity.

Also interested in the debate surrounding public officials wearing religious symbols, Benjamin Berger asks us to consider the question from another angle: the potential losses to public life of insisting on too sharp a distinction between religion and public office. In 'Against Circumspection: Judges, Religious Symbols, and Signs of Moral Independence', Berger argues not only that such bans are indefensible in light of commitments to diversity and inclusion, but that the legitimacy and morality of some public functions could be enhanced by accepting and even encouraging a show of religious diversity among public officials. Berger's argument invites us to ask 'how much are we willing to ask of one another—of politicians, of fellow citizens, of judges—by way of interpretive creativity, flexibility, and nimbleness when met with the appearance of religion in public life?' And turning our attention to lawyers as public actors, in his contribution to this volume, Faisal Bhabha similarly asks what might be lost by an overzealous insistence on the bracketing of the religious self from one's public role in the name of neutrality. Arguing for the fruits of 'religious lawyering' and the public benefits of lawyers drawing on diverse moral and ethical resources, Bhabha challenges the assumption that we can and should distinguish, factually and normatively, between religious and non-religious actors. We see in these chapters the porousness of the boundary between individual religious life and the public life of the state and, with this, another dimension of the unstable and fraught nature of the aspiration for state neutrality.

* * *

The chapters in this volume bring to the surface the social, political and conceptual complexity of religious diversity that is otherwise concealed by organising legal and political concepts like state neutrality. They remind us of the role of religion in the historical formation and contemporary experience of the state. They suggest the inevitability of state engagement with religion, given the task of governing a religiously diverse population and the conceptual unsteadiness of the division between putatively non-religious issues and matters of religious moment. And by requiring us to recognise that the state we ask to be neutral is composed of and acts only through agents, they draw our attention to the burdens and conundrums involved in imagining a divide between the religious and non-religious *within the subject*.

The focus on religion and the exercise of public authority is thus a means of pushing us past the general concepts we employ to manage religious diversity, drawing us closer to the social facts of religious difference. It brings us close to the state and its historical and contemporary nature, as well as to the people involved and the activities that occur in the governance of a culturally plural society. In so doing, this focus helps us to recover the difficulty, paradox, and social, legal and political unruliness that characterizes modern religious diversity. For those interested in the relationship between law, politics and religion—in the struggles of religious diversity in a liberal state—this act of 'recovery' and complication is, we think, the principal value of this volume.

Paul Kahn has argued that '[e]very age has its own point of access to ethical and political deliberation. For us, that point is the problem of cultural pluralism'.[24] If this is so—and we think it is—the lessons learned and insights generated through these studies focussed on religion and the exercise of public authority have import beyond the reach of this volume, teaching us something more general about the complexity of identity, the nature of the liberal state, and the challenges of public life in a condition of deep religious pluralism.

[24] Paul W Kahn, *Putting Liberalism in Its Place* (Princeton, Princeton University Press, 2005) 1.

1

The Meaning and Entailment of the Religious Neutrality of the State: The Case of Public Employees

JOCELYN MACLURE*

There is a lively debate in academia and in the public sphere about the meaning and implications of the religious neutrality of the state. In France, neutrality requires that public officials refrain from wearing visible religious symbols when they are at work but also, according to some accounts, that parents who accompany their children on fieldtrips organised by the school, or nannies in private daycare facilities, must also refrain.[1] However, neutrality does not prevent the French state from generously funding private denominational schools, from having six statutory holidays on Christian holidays, or from employing religious counsellors in hospitals, prisons and the army. In Italy a public school may hang a crucifix on the wall, and in some American states a prayer may be said before class without infringing the religious neutrality requirement.[2] The principle of the neutrality of the state with regard to religion has widely different meanings and implications in democratic societies around the world. For instance, countries that have a (weakly) established church can move toward greater neutrality by removing the privileges of the established church or by extending recognition to other groups, while countries that are officially secular can seek to reasonably accommodate the members of minority groups who are adversely affected by norms of general application that favour the majority.

The meaning and scope of the principle of neutrality have been fiercely debated in Quebec, from the Bouchard-Taylor Commission in 2007–08, to the

* I wish to thank Sébastien Lacroix for the research assistance and editing, Dick Moon and Ben Berger for their very helpful feedback, as well the Religious Neutrality workshop participants at Osgoode Law for the fruitful discussions.

[1] For a recent philosophical discussion of these cases, see O Desmons, 'Qui doit-être neutre? L'extension du devoir de neutralité aux personnes en charge de l'enfance', *Implications philosophiques*, 25 June 2015, www.implications-philosophiques.org/actualite/une/qui-doit-etre-neutre/.

[2] See *Town of Greece v Galloway* [2014] 572 US, and *Lautsi v Italy* App no 30814/06 (ECtHR, 3 November 2009).

'Charter of Values' in 2013–14.[3] I will briefly review the recommendations of the Bouchard-Taylor Report on the implications of the religious neutrality of the state. I will then focus on the normative issue that was at the core of the public discussion during the Charter of Values debate, ie the general ban on all so-called 'conspicuous' or 'ostentatious' religious signs for public employees. I will discuss the two most convincing arguments in favour of the ban: the analogy between religious and political signs (II.B), and the 'reasonable sacrifice' and spiritual nature of 'genuine' faith argument (II.C). I will argue that neither of these arguments justifies the general ban on visible religious signs for public sector employees.

I. From the Bouchard-Taylor Commission to the Charter of Values

In February 2007 Quebec's Liberal government appointed the Bouchard-Taylor Commission to resolve the so-called 'reasonable accommodation crisis'. The debate on the recognition and accommodation of religion in the public sphere had been raging for almost a year. The Bouchard-Taylor Commission's mandate was to investigate the state of intercultural relations, take stock of how accommodation claims were managed in various milieux, organise a public consultation and make recommendations to the government. Gérard Bouchard and Charles Taylor reported that Quebec's 'common public values'—including the religious neutrality of state, and gender equality—were already substantially protected by the current institutional framework. They nonetheless argued that 'open secularism' and 'interculturalism', two of the main pillars of Quebec's citizenship regime, should be clarified and formalised. The adoption of a white paper on secularism and a policy statement on interculturalism are arguably the Report's two paramount recommendations.

Most observers agree that, following the release of the Report, the Liberal government paid only lip service to its recommendations, remaining for the most part passive. The Parti Québécois (PQ), however, seized the opportunity to assert itself as the defender of Quebec's identity and values. It promised, among other thing, to pass a 'Charter of Secularism' or a 'Charter of Quebec Values' in order to fill the alleged normative deficit regarding the regulation of religious expression in the public sphere.

The PQ formed a minority government from September 2012 to April 2014. It unveiled Draft Bill 60—entitled the 'Charter affirming the values of State secularism and religious neutrality and of equality between women and

[3] For an overview, see J Maclure, 'After the Bouchard-Taylor Commission: Religious Accommodations and Human Rights', in A-G Gagnon et José Maria Saucia (eds), *Negotiating Diversity: Identity, Pluralism and Democracy* (New York, Peter Lang, 2014) 87.

men, and providing a framework for accommodation requests'[4]—in the autumn of 2013.

Bill 60 would have:

- given formal legislative expression to the secular character and religious neutrality of the Quebec state;
- enshrined a set of interpretive principles into section 9.1 of the Quebec Charter of Human Rights and Freedoms;[5]
- codified the existing legal framework for handling religious accommodation claims within the Quebec Charter of Rights and Freedoms (section 5);
- banned the personnel of public organisations from wearing 'ostentatious' religious symbols (section 5);
- banned full-face veils for civil servants and for citizens during the provision and reception of public services (sections 6 and 7).

Despite the acrimonious tone of the debate on the PQ's legislative proposal, there was broad agreement on several oclauses of Draft Bill 60. There was a consensus following the Bouchard-Taylor Commission on the importance of clearly and explicitly declaring the secular character of the state.[6] One could hardly object to the enshrinement of the legal framework for assessing accommodation claims in the Quebec Charter of Rights and Freedoms. Chapter 5 of Bill 60 simply restated that an accommodation claim had to be derived from the right to non-discrimination or from freedom of religion, and that the accommodation measure should not generate 'excessive constraints' (that would infringe the rights of others, prevent the organisation from achieving its goals, be excessively burdensome or costly, etc).[7] Finally, the 'uncovered face' rule for the provision or reception of public services (sections 6 and 7) enjoyed wide support, and had previously been proposed by the Liberal government.[8]

All four parties in the National Assembly supported the clauses enumerated above. The only highly divisive measure was the general prohibition against wearing easily visible religious symbols for all employees of public organisations. Public bodies had—and still have—autonomy regarding the dress code of their employees. If a uniform or a particular dress code is prescribed, an

[4] Bill 60: Charter affirming the values of State secularism and religious neutrality and of equality between women and men, and providing a framework for accommodation requests.

[5] S 43 of the Draft Bill reads: 'In exercising those freedoms and rights, a person shall also maintain a proper regard for the values of equality between women and men and the primacy of the French language, as well as the separation of religions and State and the religious neutrality and secular nature of the State, while making allowance for the emblematic and toponymic elements of Québec's cultural heritage that testify to its history'.

[6] On the contested meaning of secularism, see R Bhargava, *Secularism and its Critics* (Oxford, Oxford University Press, 2004) and A Stephan and C Taylor (eds), *The Boundaries of Toleration* (New York, Columbia University Press, 2014).

[7] P Bosset, 'Limites de l'accommodement: le droit a-t-il tout dit?' (2007) 9(1) *Éthique publique* 165.

[8] Bill 94: An Act to establish guidelines governing accommodation requests within the Administration and certain institutions.

accommodation request can be presented by an employee who wishes to wear a religious garment in the workplace.[9]

II. The Case of Public Officials

The general ban on visible religious symbols, which extends to employees who are not in contact with users, was justified as a logical entailment of the principle of the religious neutrality of the state and of the corollary obligation of circumspection on the part of public employees. Public sector employees must reflect and instantiate the neutrality of public institutions, which requires, so the argument goes, that users be unable to identify the employee's religious affiliation when they are on the job. This is the argument of the necessary 'appearance of neutrality' of public employees. Citizens as individuals are free to display their religious affiliation in the private and public spheres. But as employees serving a public organisation, they must personify or embody the religious neutrality of public institutions. An employee of the state who wears a visible religious symbol might give the impression that he serves his church before the state, or that there is an organic connection between state and religion; a rule that bans the wearing of visible religious signs pre-empts the appearance of a conflict of interest. As former French President Jacques Chirac said in his 2003 speech on secularism:

> We must forcefully declare the neutrality and secularism of the public service, and that of each agent of the public, at the service of all and of the public interest, who should not display his or her own beliefs or opinions. This rule is our law, so that no citizen of France shall have reason to suspect a representative of the public authority of preferring or discriminating against anyone on the basis of personal convictions.[10]

The Bouchard-Taylor Commission recognised in its final report that the rights and obligations of public employees was one the most complex and intricate issues raised by the commitment to state secularism.[11] Secularism applies to public institutions and not to citizens, who retain their freedom of conscience at all times, as it is not a detachable module of their moral and legal personality. Secularism is a political principle by which the moral equality and freedom of conscience of

[9] See *Grant v Canada (Attorney General) (TD)* [1995] 1 FC 158.

[10] J Chirac, 'Discours relatif au respect du principe de laïcité dans la République', 17 December 2003.

[11] A young Muslim lawyer was recently hired as a trainee in one of Berlin's municipal districts, only to be told that she could not have the position when she came to sign her contract because she was wearing a hijab. Berlin, like some of the other German federated states, has a law prohibiting the overt display of religious affiliation by public sector employees. She blogged about her experience and initiated a broad public debate on the status of religion in the public sphere. See A Sauerbrey, 'Will the Burqa Be Banned in Berlin?', *The New York Times* (web), 6 July 2015, www.nytimes.com/2015/07/07/opinion/anna-sauerbrey-will-the-burqa-be-banned-in-berlin.html?rref=opinion&module=Ribbon&version=context&region=Header&action=click&contentCollection=Opinion&pgtype=Blogs.

all citizens are respected, regardless of their worldview.[12] It is not an anti-religious doctrine. It does not seek to promote secularisation, understood as the decline of faith and religious practice. However, employees are at the junction of these perspectives: they are the holders of rights *qua* their status as citizens, but they represent public authority *qua* their status as employees of public institutions.

A. The Bouchard-Taylor Commission's Compromise

The Bouchard-Taylor Commission proposed a compromise. It rejected the idea that the appearance of neutrality justifies a general ban on religious signs for all personnel in public organisations, but it recommended a ban for positions that embody, to the highest degree, the authority and coercive power of the state.

It is important, the Commission emphasised, that those who are paid by public funds show impartiality in the *exercise* of their duties. Employees must adhere to the legislative mission of the institution they serve. Their actions must not be dictated by their faith or private morality. Bouchard and Taylor asked, however, why we should think that those who wear a visible religious sign are less likely to act in an impartial, professional and loyal manner than those who do not. A Christian, for example, may give priority to his or her religious convictions without wearing any visible religious sign—think of the doctor who refuses to perform an abortion, the pharmacist unwilling to sell contraceptives, or the marriage commissioner/registrars refusing to perform a same-sex marriage.[13] Why should we think that those who display their religious affiliation are less likely to comply with their professional obligations than those whose convictions are not displayed or are less visible?[14] Why should the presumption of impartiality be granted to the latter and denied to the former?

This is why the Bouchard-Taylor Commission concluded that public employees must be evaluated on the basis of their actions. It is possible to assess the neutrality of their professional conduct without restraining a priori their religious freedom. For example, in the case of an employee who wears a visible religious symbol and proselytises at work, it is the proselytising, and not the wearing of a religious symbol, that is objectionable.

That being said, the Bouchard-Taylor Commission recommended a ban on the wearing of visible religious symbols for a narrower range of positions that embody

[12] See especially J Maclure and C Taylor, *Secularism and Freedom of Conscience* (Cambridge, Harvard University Press, 2013).

[13] Doctors and pharmacists can be exempted, under certain conditions (see Ch 8). As for marriage commissioners/registrars, the demand for accommodation in Saskatchewan for marriage commissioners who refused to perform same-sex marriages after the federal legislation on marriage was amended, was rejected. See *Marriage Commissioners Appointed Under The Marriage Act (Re)* [2011] SKCA 3 (see also Ch 9).

[14] The PQ's ban did not apply to small symbols such as a Catholic cross necklace.

the highest degree of state authority and coercive power, such as judges, Crown prosecutors, the President of the National Assembly, police officers and prison guards.[15] A greater obligation of 'circumspection' should apply to these public officers because of the nature of their positions. The removal of the appearance of conflict of interest is more pressing in their case.

There is an ambiguity in the justification offered by the Bouchard-Taylor Commission, which has barely been noticed. Two justificatory routes for the limited ban are invoked:

> Having weighed up these considerations, we believe that the imposition of a duty of circumspection to this limited range of positions achieves the best balance for contemporary Québec society. These are positions that strikingly exemplify State neutrality and whose incumbents exercise a power of coercion.
>
> Such is our conclusion. We admit that we can achieve this end by following different lines of reasoning. For example, we can deem this proposal to be the most appropriate in the context of contemporary Québec society, although it is understood that this context can change over time. Or, we can also maintain that the proposal has a more permanent character that goes beyond the current context inasmuch as it embodies the principle of the separation of the State and the churches. We do not have to decide this debate since the two lines of reasoning lead to the same conclusion.[16]

In short, the compromise recommended by the Bouchard-Taylor Commission can be justified in a contingent and contextual manner based on social acceptability, or in a more permanent and principled manner.

At the level of principles, it seems doubtful that the importance of neutrality (or the appearance of neutrality) is sufficiently weighty to justify interference with the fair equality of opportunity and the freedom of religion of the candidates for these positions. There are alternative norms and procedures that do not infringe on basic rights but which nevertheless enable citizens to have reasonable confidence in the impartiality of representatives of the authority of the state.

Consider the case of judges. The parties in a trial, and most particularly the accused in a criminal case, who may be convicted and sentenced, must have confidence in the impartiality of the judge. Can a Muslim who is a criminal defendant rely on the impartiality of a judge who wears a kippah? One of the procedures used to guarantee due process is recusal. A judge must first decide if she is able to hear a given case. If she has serious doubts regarding her capacity to conduct an impartial trial, she has the duty to recuse herself. If she fails to do so, she infringes the accused's right to a fair trial. The parties have at all times the right to make a request for recusal. Real impartiality, as the Supreme Court of Canada points out, does not require that a judge have no sympathies or opinions.

[15] G Bouchard and C Taylor, *Fonder l'avenir: le temps de la conciliation*, Final report of the Commission sur les pratiques d'accommodement reliées aux différence culturelle (Québec, Éditeur officiel du Québec, 2008) 150.

[16] ibid 151.

It requires rather that the judge be able to understand the issue and consider different points of view while keeping an open mind.[17] The partiality or impartiality of judges is embodied in their attitude towards the parties and the issues at stake, and not on the aspects of their identity. Therefore, a female justice does not have to recuse herself in order to avoid the appearance of partiality because a man accused of rape worries about her ability to judge him fairly. Furthermore, the Jewish judge in the example mentioned above would still be Jewish even if he was forbidden to wear a kippah. The judge's mind is never a blank slate.

Legal scholar Pierre Bosset recently fortified this analysis by meticulously demonstrating that the justifications offered for banning the wearing of visible religious signs by judges, police officers, teachers and elected officials would probably not withstand judicial review.[18] Since the Supreme Court generally dislikes blanket interdictions that disregard the differences between the parties affected, a precise contextual analysis of each role might be necessary to establish whether a ban on religious signs would be legally permissible in a particular case. In sum, the compromise proposed by the Bouchard-Taylor Commission, even if it is much more circumscribed and moderate than the Parti Québécois's general ban, does not stand up to critical scrutiny.[19]

In the post-Bouchard-Taylor debate, supporters of the general ban used two additional arguments to justify its legitimacy. The first rests on an argument by analogy: the religious neutrality of the state is analogised with the political neutrality of the public administration. The second seeks to show that the true faith is a subjective and spiritual experience and that the external manifestations of faith are not at the core of the right to freedom of religion. From this perspective, asking a public employee to put her religious sign away when she is on duty is imposing a 'reasonable sacrifice'.

B. The Analogy Between Religious and Political Neutrality

Defenders of the PQ's proposal had a complementary argument that involved drawing an analogy between religious symbols and political ones. It is generally thought that the state can legitimately ask employees not to express their political opinions during the exercise of their duties because the public administration must be neutral. The role of public administrators is to apply the decisions taken by the government. In the same spirit, nobody wants teachers to try to indoctrinate their students, or hospital employees to harangue patients with their political views. Some think that the same reasoning applies to religious opinions: the state

[17] *R v S (RD)* [1997] 3 SCR 484, para 35.

[18] P Bosset, 'Réflexions d'un juriste sur l'idée d'interdire le port de signes religieux aux agents de l'État' (2013) 20(70) *Vivre ensemble* 1.

[19] In our book *Secularism and Freedom of Conscience* (Cambridge, MA, Harvard University Press, 2013) Charles Taylor and I do not endorse the limited ban.

and its representatives must be neutral regarding religion. Since religious symbols have semantic content—they express a religious conviction or affiliation—it is reasonable to ban them, just as it is reasonable to ban the expression of political convictions and affiliations. The obligation of circumspection on the part of public employees would extend to visible religious signs.

This is perhaps the most serious argument for a ban on religious signs. The validity of an argument by analogy depends on the similarities and differences between the situations that are analogised. In this case, the similarities are prima facie sufficiently numerous for the argument to be taken seriously.

The argument is nevertheless unconvincing. It is true that the public administration must be politically neutral. The public administration must ensure the permanence and the stability of the state, as well as the impartial application of the law. However, if there are good reasons to separate state and religion, it is evidently impossible to separate political ideology from political power. Parties with rival political visions confront each other to gain power. If the government cannot be neutral with regard to political ideology, the civil service must be so, by contrast. As pointed out, its role is to administer the laws and policies in an impartial manner. The process of obtaining a job in the public service must depend on the merit of the candidates and not on their political allegiance. The same applies to the delivery of public services; the political opinions of civil servants and citizens should be irrelevant.

There is thus a fundamental difference between the state-political allegiance and the state-religion relationships: there is no complete separation between the state and political ideology; the government, as a crucial organ of the state, must be elected on the basis of a political programme. But the state can be independent from religion. For a civil servant or other public employee to wear a visible religious symbol does not imply that the laws have a religious grounding or that the state identifies with a religion. State employees apply laws that are politically contested before being passed, and they must be neutral regarding these controversies. Religion, however, is not a direct source in the laws' pedigree. The analogy between religious symbols and political symbols overlooks this crucial difference.[20]

Furthermore, who really feels obliged to wear a sweater that has a political slogan printed on it, or a political badge, at all times in public, including while at work? As involved citizens, we want to enjoy freedom of expression in civil society, we want to have the right to assemble peacefully and to demonstrate, to vote and to be eligible for elections, we support the freedom of the press, etc. The comparison with visible religious signs has the sole purpose of justifying a ban on

[20] I accepted the postulate that political symbols must be banned in the public sectors. However, this postulate itself must also be examined more closely. The reasons advanced appear most convincing in the case of *partisan* symbols for civil servants. But *political* symbols are not prohibited in all contexts: consider, for example, the symbols that signal membership of a union, used as a pressure tactic during negotiations. Also the obligation of political reserve of civil servants is much greater and more regulated than that of public employees such as university professors.

religious signs; its function is exclusively negative. Who really thinks that they are being kept from fulfilling their moral obligations or their conception of a worthy life because they are not allowed to wear a political badge when they are at work? Rights and freedoms, at least according to an influential philosophical theory, are intended to protect the fundamental interests of the human being construed as a moral agent.[21] If freedom of conscience and of religion are specifically protected, rather than being subsumed under the right to freedom of expression, it is because meaning-giving beliefs and commitments deserve special legal protection.[22]

In short, it is true that employees in the public sector should abide by an obligation of circumspection. Their freedom of religion is already limited when they are at work: they cannot promote their religion, their religious convictions may not dictate their professional judgment, and it is very likely that the most observant or 'orthodox' believers will not be in a position to practise their religion in their preferred fashion. For example, there is no absolute right to have a place to pray at work. It could be that the nature of a job does not allow an employee to take five short breaks to pray during the workday. It could be that the specificities of a given position do not allow an employee to leave earlier on Friday in order to get home before sunset. An employee of the state must deal with men and women. Unless numbers warrant it, it is normal for a cafeteria not to serve halal or kosher meals, etc. If an employee feels unable to accept these conditions, she self-excludes from jobs in the public sector.[23]

C. The 'Reasonable Sacrifice' Argument and the New Religious Correctness

Defenders of the general ban on wearing religious symbols in the public sector also opine that it is reasonable to demand that believers put away their religious symbols when they are at work. Religiously committed employees remain free to practise their religion in their private lives and in civil society, but their obligation of reserve requires them to abstain from expressing their religious identity when they are at work. This viewpoint presupposes that obliging a believer to put her religious symbols away when at work is at most a reasonable sacrifice. This view comes from a conception of faith that is profoundly anchored in Christian thought.

[21] See J Griffin, *On Human Rights* (Oxford, Oxford University Press, 2008).

[22] See Maclure and Taylor, *Secularism and Freedom of Conscience* (Cambridge, MA, Harvard University Press, 2013).

[23] See also J Maclure, 'Freedom of Conscience and the Charter of Quebec Values' (2014) 35(1) *Options politiques/Policy Options* 59; P Fournier, 'Les fonctionnaires sont déjà neutres', *La Presse*, 22 January 2014; S Dion, 'Signes politiques, signes religieux: une dangereuse analogie', *Le Devoir*, 5 October 2013.

The schism in Christianity caused by the Protestant Reformation in the sixteenth century encouraged a re-centring of the religious experience on the spiritual quest and the sincerity of conviction. Christians were encouraged to comprehend the word of God through their own reason and sensibility. The authority of the Catholic clergy was put in question, as was the ostentatious nature of its rituals and displays. This new approach to faith was not unknown in the Christian tradition. St Augustine, more than 10 centuries earlier, had called for religious experience to be anchored on the purity of intentions and on the dialogue with God within one's soul or conscience ('return to within yourself; truth dwells in the inner man').[24]

It is easy to understand the appeal of this vision. This form of religiosity harmonises more easily with the liberal principle of rational moral autonomy. Sociologists of religion have shown that the phenomenon of 'Protestantisation', or 'individualisation', of belief is widespread today in the West.[25]

However, there is ample evidence that many believers do not see religious rituals and symbols as mere superficial (and thus optional) external manifestations of their faith, including within Christianity. Consider the Sikh emergency medical doctor who said that he would have had no choice but to resign from his position at the McGill University Health Center had he been forced to forgo his turban.[26] Men wearing the kippah and women wearing a hijab have said the same thing. They feel they would betray themselves if they were to agree to take off their headgear. For millions of believers around the world, belief and practice are inextricable: religion is as much a belief system as it is a way of life made of ritual practices and symbols that connect them to God or to higher principles. Asking a religious person to ignore a dress code that they consider essential is the equivalent of demanding a vegetarian to put aside her ethical convictions on animal rights from nine to five.

The 'reasonable sacrifice' argument amounts to imposing a particular way of believing, or a form of 'religious correctness'. Needless to say, the acceptance of a single legitimate way of being religious would advance an impoverished understanding of freedom of conscience and religion. Living well together in a diverse society requires not only accepting religious diversity, but also different modes of religiosity. It is true that some practising religious people do not feel bound

[24] St Augustine, 'Of True Religion' in JS Burleigh (ed), *Augustine: Earlier Writings* (Louisville, Westminster John Knox Press, 1953) 262. As Richard Moon notes, '[t]he connection the Quebec government makes between wearing a symbol and promoting religion may reflect a Christian perspective on symbols and symbol wearing. While the cross and crucifix are important symbols in Christianity of the resurrection and sacrifice of Jesus, in most versions of Christianity there is no requirement that a believer wear a symbol of any kind. And so when a Christian chooses to wear a cross or other symbol, he may be seen not just as signalling a personal faith commitment but also as advertising his faith to others' (Ch 9).

[25] *cf* D Hervieu-Léger, *Le pèlerin et le converti* (Paris, Flammarion, 1999); C Taylor, *Varieties of Religion Today: William James Revisited* (Cambridge, Harvard University Press, 2002).

[26] K Gagnon, 'Signes religieux: 'Ça fait partie de mon identité'', *La Presse*, 11 September 2013.

to abide by a particular dress code. There are religiously committed and sincere Muslim women who believe that covering their hair is not mandatory. This does not authorise the conclusion that wearing a religious garment lies outside the protection of freedom of conscience and religion. The goal of freedom of conscience and religion is to allow us to determine for ourselves, within reasonable limits, what convictions and commitments give meaning to our lives. This is why the Supreme Court of Canada endorsed a 'personal and subjective' concept of freedom of religion.[27]

III. Conclusion

The principle of state neutrality in religious matters is a political battlefield in contemporary democracies. It is thought to entail, or at least to be compatible with, policies such as banning religious clothing, reciting a prayer before town hall meetings or hanging a crucifix in public buildings. Religious neutrality is an example of the open texture and conceptual indeterminateness of some legal norms. In particular, its implications for the case of a representative or employee of a public organisation are far from clear. Although positive law regarding the rights and obligations of public employees varies from country to country, I have argued that general and limited bans on religious signs cannot withstand scrutiny at the level of political morality. Public sector employees can be neutral even if they wear religious clothing. It is their acts and professional conduct, and not their mere appearance, that should determine whether they have respected their duty of circumspection. Citizens have a right to obtain public services in a fair, professional and religiously neutral way, but they don't have a right not to be exposed to the religious affiliation of public employees.[28] At the political level, the liberal state must go beyond toleration and protect the equality rights and freedom of conscience of all citizens. At the interpersonal level, tolerance can still be thought of as the civic virtue that encourages us to bear non-harmful behaviours that we nonetheless find objectionable.[29] This, I think, applies to those who feel irritation or discomfort at the sight of a public employee wearing a visible religious sign.[30]

[27] *Syndicat Northcrest v Amselem* [2004] 2 SCR 551, 2004 SCC 47.

[28] According to sociologist Guy Rocher, it is today imperative that 'respect for the religious convictions of all clienteles who have recourse to the services of public institutions financed by public funds take priority over the convictions of any personnel of these institutions'. (G Rocher, Submission to the public consultation on Bill 60).

[29] I develop this argument in J Maclure, 'Jenseits der Toleranz und zurück', *Toleranz in transkulturellerPerspektive*, Velbrück-Wissenschaft, forthcoming in 2016.

[30] I tried to show that the best public reasons in favour of the ban did not withstand scrutiny. More positive reasons can also be supplied for allowing public employees to wear religious symbols. Benjamin Berger, in this volume, argues that we ought to welcome, as a matter of a signal of judicial independence in the aggregate, the display of symbols of various identities among judges. I'm highly sympathetic to that argument, although my aim was to show that the more sophisticated justifications for the ban failed on their own terms. See Ch 2.

2

Against Circumspection: Judges, Religious Symbols, and Signs of Moral Independence

BENJAMIN L BERGER*

I. Introduction

Issues of symbolic interpretation have emerged as a mainstay of the transnational jurisprudence on law and religion. How should we understand the social and legal significance of a crucifix hanging on the wall in an Italian classroom?[1] What is the meaning and political valence of a headscarf, and how does this differ in Turkey[2] and France?[3] How should we interpret the reference to God in the Pledge of Allegiance,[4] and what is the nature, meaning, and effect—what is the phenomenology—of prayer?[5] It is this latter question about the nature and the communicative effects of prayer that was at the heart of the Supreme Court of Canada's decision in *Mouvement Laïque v Saguenay*.[6] The Court proceeded with notable confidence in finding that an individual who did not share the religious beliefs reflected in the prayer at issue in *Saguenay* would experience it as exclusionary, and as an affront to state neutrality. Given the context and the specific prayer at issue, perhaps that is so, and perhaps that effect properly dictated the outcome in that case. But apart from the 'empirical' question of how this prayer

* Thank you to the contributors to this volume, and to my co-editor Richard Moon, for their valuable comments on an early version of this chapter. I am also very grateful to Rachel Devon for her superb research assistance.

1 *Lautsi and Others v Italy* ECHR 2011–III 2412, 54 EHRR 3.

2 *Leyla Sahin v Turkey* ECHR 2005–XI 819, 44 EHRR 5.

3 See Mayanthi Fernando, 'Reconfiguring Freedom: Muslim Piety and the Limits of Secular Law and Public Discourse in France' (2010) 37 *American Ethnologist* 19.

4 *Elk Grove Unified School District v Newdow* 542 US 1 (2004).

5 *Town of Greece v Galloway* 572 US (2014). On the question of the phenomenology of prayer and its intelligibility to law, see Benjamin L Berger, 'The Legal Unintelligibility of Prayer', https://perma.cc/Q32Y-E5UK.

6 *Mouvement laïque québécois v Saguenay (City)* 2015 SCC 16.

would be perceived, there are distinct and important questions about how it could and should be interpreted. Such questions are, I suggest, always salient in cases involving religious symbols. Otherwise put, how much are we willing to ask of one another—of politicians, of fellow citizens, of judges—by way of interpretive creativity, flexibility, and nimbleness when met with the appearance of religion in public life? And who ought to bear that interpretive onus? Given a symbolically complicated social world, made so in part owing to religious and cultural difference that we seek to support and constitutionally protect, such questions seem to be increasingly exigent.

This chapter takes up these questions surrounding the interpretation of religious signs and symbols—and the interpretive possibilities that emerge when we demand more from one another in thinking about such symbols—by examining the question of judges and religious dress in the particular context of the judge's role as wielding the coercive force of the state through the exercise of criminal punishment. I advance the argument that recent debates have proceeded on a misleadingly simplistic approach to understanding the meaning of signs of religious belonging and identity in this setting and that, with this, we miss an opportunity for a deeper understanding of the virtues that we hope to find in our public officials.

In recent years, and consistent with Canadian constitutional history, Quebec has been the gravitational centre of debates and reflection in Canada about the management of religious difference in a religiously diverse society. Political and legal debates within Quebec have tended to raise, with particular clarity, issues that are salient across the country. Two recent happenings in the law and politics of religion in Quebec stand out.[7]

In 2008 Gérard Bouchard and Charles Taylor released their co-authored report arising from the Consultation Commission on Accommodation Practices Related to Cultural Difference, the 'Bouchard-Taylor Report'.[8] The report advocated a model of open secularism, one that would navigate the imperatives of regard for religious difference and the particularities of Quebec history and culture, through a more or less embracing regard for the accommodation of religious practices. The report arose from a sense of public concern about the issue of religious difference, concern generated to some extent in response to court decisions that had required the accommodation of minority religious practices. In their report, Bouchard and

[7] There are others, including issues of religious education, an issue that has found its way to the Supreme Court of Canada in the form of the cases of *SL v Commission scolaire des Chênes* 2012 SCC 7, [2012] 1 SCR 235 and *Loyola High School v Québec (Attorney General)* 2015 SCC 12. The case of *Mouvement laïque québécois v Saguenay (City)* 2015 SCC 16, which concerned prayer at the outset of municipal council meetings, in its own way raised questions of state neutrality and the appearance of religion in public life, the focus of this chapter and others in this volume.

[8] Gérard Bouchard and Charles Taylor, *Building the Future: A Time for Reconciliation* (Quebec, Commission de consultation sur les pratiques d'accomodement reliées aux différences culturelles, 2008).

Taylor urged the government to prepare a white paper on how to approach the question of religious accommodation in Quebec.

In 2013 the Parti Québecois (PQ) government took up this invitation and placed Bill 60, the 'Charter of Quebec Values', or so-called 'Charter of Secularism', on the public table for debate.[9] Although it proposed a number of amendments and initiatives, Bill 60's most controversial aspect was the prohibition that it would place on public employees wearing 'conspicuous' religious symbols. The Bill advanced a very different vision of the state relationship to religion than that urged in the Bouchard-Taylor report. Most academic and public commentators (including Charles Taylor himself) condemned the Bill's exclusionary and closed vision of secularism, and contested not only the political position evident in the Bill, but the internal consistency and rationality of the measures that it introduced. The Parti Québecois gambled and lost when they sought to place the fate of this Bill at the heart of a snap provincial election, an election that returned a devastating electoral defeat for the PQ, albeit a defeat that does not neatly or stably track support for the Bill.[10]

There seems to be a great deal of conceptual distance between the Bouchard-Taylor Report and Bill 60. They assume markedly different postures toward the accommodation of religion and the management of religious diversity in Quebec. And yet there are two notable points of convergence. First, both documents assume that the place to begin when addressing the issue of the just management of religious difference in contemporary society is with a set of claims about the nature and demands of 'the secular'. In retrospect, one might well read Bouchard and Taylor's emphasis on defining an idea of the secular as a fateful move in the road towards Bill 60, one that permitted a denatured, simplistic, and abstract claim about what secularism implies to drive a vision of religion's place in Quebec society. Bouchard and Taylor rooted their views and recommendations in an understanding of secularism, as did the Parti Québecois when the government advanced a conception of laïcité appropriate to Quebec, one that drew heavily from a particular—and arguably misleading—understanding of the nature of French laïcité.[11] Whether one creates more heat than light through seeking to deduce just approaches to dealing with religious difference from ideal concepts such as secularism is an important question; this episode in Quebec feeds

[9] *Charter affirming the values of State secularism and religious neutrality and of equality between women and men, and providing a framework for accommodation requests*, 1st sess, 40th Leg, Quebec, 2013.

[10] Many other factors were at play in the election, including stances taken about Quebec sovereignty and the perennially crucial electoral issue—the economy.

[11] Bowen shows that the conventional image of French laïcité is radically misleading in its effacing of the rich associational lives that are lived beneath the rhetoric about a single republican identity. See John R Bowen, *Can Islam Be French?: Pluralism and Pragmatism in a Secularist State* (Princeton, Princeton University Press, 2009).

my scepticism about this kind of approach.[12] Appeals to the nature and demands of such broad concepts can draw attention away from the complicated social, historical, and political facts associated with religious difference in a given society, clearing the way for policy prescriptions that—like Bill 60—have regressive and exclusionary effects.

Yet this chapter is focused on an issue that arises at a second point of convergence between these two moments in the recent history of law and religion in Quebec. Despite the normative space between the Bouchard-Taylor report and Bill 60, and although the Bouchard-Taylor report rejected a general prohibition on the wearing of religious symbols that would apply to all agents of the state, both agreed that judges—along with Crown prosecutors, police officers, prison guards, and the president and vice-president of the national assembly—should be barred from wearing religious 'signs'. In the case of Bill 60, this bar on judges wearing religious symbols was caught up in the general ban that was the focus of so much criticism. For Bouchard and Taylor, by contrast, these figures were distinctively subject to such a prohibition, and this targeted prohibition was justified by the particular character of the public duties and authority that they exercised. Bouchard and Taylor explained that in the case of other public officials, freedom of religion for these individuals, as well as the imperative of equal access to public employment, overcame any possible concern that the appearance of religious affiliation might signal an absence of state neutrality or some form of conflict of interest. For most public officials, Bouchard and Taylor reasoned, we should look to the substance of how their public duties are discharged: 'we must evaluate agents of the State in light of their acts. Do they display impartiality in the performance of their duties? Do their religious beliefs interfere in point of fact with the exercising of their professional judgment?'[13]

And yet, for Bouchard and Taylor, the balance came out differently in the case of judges, police officers, and prison guards. Although they clearly agonised over the decision, Bouchard and Taylor ultimately concluded that these individuals should be prohibited from wearing religious signs. The specific justification is of most interest to this chapter:

> We suggest that the appearance of impartiality imposes itself at the highest level in the cases of judges, police officers and prison guards, *all of whom possess a power of punishment and even coercion* in respect of individuals such as defendants, accused person and inmates, who are in a position of dependence and vulnerability. [Emphasis added][14]

Bouchard and Taylor argue that these figures should 'impose on themselves a form of circumspection concerning the expression of their religious convictions',[15]

[12] For a fuller account of my scepticism on this point, see Benjamin L Berger, 'Belonging to Law: Religious Difference, Secularism, and the Conditions of Civic Inclusion' (2015) 24 *Social & Legal Studies* 47.

[13] Bouchard and Taylor (n 8) 150.

[14] ibid 151.

[15] ibid.

a duty that translates into an obligation to not wear items that mark their religious identity. 'These are positions', the co-commissioners explained, 'that strikingly exemplify State neutrality and whose incumbents exercise a power of coercion'.[16]

It is this claim—that there is something about the public function of state punishment and coercion that justifies the prohibition on judges wearing religious symbols—that I want to explore and interrogate in this chapter. In my view, the ban proposed by both Bill 60 and the Bouchard-Taylor report fails on some rather straightforward critiques, most clearly the exclusion of particular religiously identified people (those for whom religious belonging involves outwardly identifiable displays) from key roles in the institutions of government. Prohibiting a person who will perform his duties impartially and professionally from being a judge because he wears a turban or kippah is not defensible.[17] Bouchard and Taylor were right to insist on focusing on the substance of one's conduct and treatment of others, rather than leaning on a semiotic analysis of signs and symbols in pursuit of an abstract ideal of neutrality as non-particularity, and this idea should carry through to police officers, correctional officers, and judges.

But my particular interest is in the argument from punishment and coercion. What should we make of this link between expressions of religious belonging and the judge's task of punishing? More than arguing that Bouchard and Taylor's reasoning on this point is simply unconvincing, I will suggest that it might actually be backwards—that the argument from the coercive and punishing roles of the judge might provocatively point in just the other way. Might it be that reflection on the character of these judicial tasks, and the virtues that we seek in the exercise of those functions, should actually lead us to welcome a judiciary that reflects and displays its religiously diverse nature?

The goal of this chapter is to trouble and disrupt the instinct that religion and judicial authority are best hermetically sealed from one another, offering an alternative way that we might choose to read religious symbols worn by judges. In this way, this argument should be understood, more broadly, as engaged with the set of questions raised at the outset of this chapter, questions about the burdens of interpretation in a religiously diverse and multicultural society. In exploring the specific issue of how we could and should read the appearance of religious symbols on the person of a judge, this chapter thus also gestures to this larger theme of the burdens of interpretation in a religiously plural society. Beginning with some scene-setting in the form of a brief discussion about the character of sentencing and punishment in Canada and why it is a particularly helpful entry point into a discussion about the judicial role, this chapter will take a historical excursion into the imbrications of punishment, religion, and judgment in the common law criminal trial. Having thus recovered some material that could contribute to

[16] ibid.

[17] See, eg, Jocelyn Maclure's chapter in this volume for a powerful critique of such bans on grounds of respect for identity and political morality.

a different reading or coding of the 'conspicuous' religious affiliation of judges, I will suggest that there is actually something structurally and politically appealing about markers that remind us that, in their judgments about the exercise of state power, those who stand between the will of a government and the infliction of coercive force on individuals have moral independence from the bare wishes of government.

II. Why Look to Punishment?

There is an obvious hazard involved in using sentencing and punishment as the terrain on which to explore an argument for accepting judicial displays of religious affiliation. To raise the issue will lead some to imagine judges reasoning from religious authority or justifying sentencing decisions on the basis of religious text or precept. James Whitman has touched on the way in which the peculiar version of (non-)separationism found in the United States—one in which religious institutions and public institutions are meant to be insulated from one another, but talk of religion circulates freely in political and legal discourse—has resulted in distressing examples of biblically grounded claims for greater punishment being made in US courtrooms.[18] Of course there would be much to worry about if this simplistic insertion of religion into the world of judicial punishment were the direction or thrust of my argument. But I am not offering an argument for judicial reasoning from biblical mandate, nor for the suppression of the distinctive judicial task—that of reasoning through and with publicly generated legal norms—in favour of religious moralising. I am neither sanguine in the face of the risks of injecting religion into the judicial task, nor am I complacent about the importance of the judicial discipline of public reasoning. In that sense, although I am questioning the political desirability of building too tall a wall between the character of judicial authority and the religious identity of judges, I am not squarely joining the debate about the character and content of judicial reasons in some form of rejoinder to Rawls.[19] Rather, the inquiry here is into how else the

[18] James Q Whitman, 'Separating Church and State: The Atlantic Divide' (2008) 34 *Historical Reflections* 86. On the use of religion in sentencing in the United States, see also Mark Greenlee, 'Faith on the Bench: The Role of Religious Belief in the Criminal Sentencing Decisions of Judges' (2000) 26 *University of Dayton Law Review* 2; Sanja Zgonjanin, 'Quoting the Bible: The Use of Religious References in Judicial Decisions' (2005) 9 *New York City Law Review* 31.

[19] For this kind of discussion of appeals to religion in light of the character of public reasoning see, eg, Mark C Modak-Truran, 'Habermas's Discourse Theory of Law and the Relationship Between Law and Religion' (1997) 26 *Capital University Law Review* 461; Michael J Perry, *Religion in Politics: Constitutional and Moral Perspectives* (New York, Oxford University Press, 1997); Scott C Idleman, 'The Limits of Religious Values in Judicial Decisionmaking' (1998) 81 *Marquand Law Review* 537. The frame for this debate is, of course, very much set by John Rawls, 'The Idea of Public Reason Revisited' (1997) 64 *University of Chicago Law Review* 765; Jürgen Habermas, 'Religion in the Public Sphere' (2006) 14 *European Journal of Philosophy* 1.

appearance of religion as an aspect of a judge's identity and belonging, which so troubled Bouchard and Taylor and vexes many others, might be differently coded. How else might we read it?

Why, then, select the fraught area of punishment and sentencing—the archetypal case of state coercion—as the basis for exploring these ideas about judicial authority and religious identity? Of course the answer is, in part, linked to the story told in the introduction: it was the prospect of punishment and coercion of the accused that led Bouchard and Taylor to distinguish the case of judges (as well as police and correctional officers) from other public officials, who they felt should be permitted to display religious affiliations. Punishment played, in this way, the key role in creating an otherwise unlikely convergence between these two significant policy statements on religious accommodation in Quebec.

Yet punishment offers a uniquely valuable sightline into the judicial role in Canada for reasons that have to do with the process and nature of sentencing. For most of Canadian criminal law history, criminal punishment was essentially unguided by legislation, with no statements in the Criminal Code of the purposes and principles of sentencing.[20] Choice of punishment was a quintessential example of judicial discretion, with judges left to generate their own theories and objectives of sentencing. This fundamentally discretionary approach was subject to forceful critique, with concerns voiced about consistence, predictability, and transparency. In the mid-1990s, Parliament sought to respond with a wholesale revision to the sentencing provisions of the Criminal Code. And yet the 1995 amendments did little to alter the essentially discretionary character of sentencing in Canada. Parliament offered a veritable buffet of sentencing objectives, ranging from deterrence and denunciation to rehabilitation and the cultivation of responsibility, with no indication as to which objective a judge ought to select and when, nor of the relative weighting or priority of these objectives.[21] The sentencing principles remain broad and woolly, leaving intact the substantial margin for manoeuvre available to the sentencing judge. Indeed, the legislation's newly formulated 'fundamental purpose of sentencing' underscored the deeply normative and evaluative character of the sentencing enterprise. Section 718 explained that this fundamental purpose 'is to contribute, along with crime prevention initiatives, to respect for the law and the maintenance of a just, peaceful and safe society by imposing just sanctions',[22] sanctions that pursue one or more of the listed objectives. Although precedent

[20] For an excellent brief history of sentencing in Canada, see Allan Manson, *The Law of Sentencing* (Toronto, Irwin Law, 2001) 14–29.

[21] Parliament has since offered some limited guidance in this respect, indicating in ss 718.01, 718.02, and 718.03 that primary consideration should be given to the objectives of deterrence and denunciation in cases of offences against children, and certain offences committed against peace officers, law enforcement, and other participants in the justice system. See Criminal Code, RSC 1985, c C-46, ss 718.01, 718.02, 718.03.

[22] Criminal Code, RSC 1985, c C-46, s 718.

and some legislative minima and restrictions shape the judge's range of options, the moment of punishment invites the judge to make broad judgments not just about the facts of a case and the character of an act, but about a 'just society' and the character of an offender's circumstances and life's story.

The result is that in the act of sentencing we find one of the most forceful and violent expressions of the authority of the state matched with a high degree of discretion afforded to the decision-maker. How to realise the fundamental objectives of sentencing; how to respond well, and in an individualised way, to the person that has found their way before the court; how to balance the competing interests involved in the moment of sentencing: the nature of the system is that these are matters of ineradicable and deep indeterminacy to which we accept that judges bring certain kinds of personal instincts, perspectives, and experiences. Without much by way of rule-based buffer, the whole person of the judge is drawn into an encounter with the person, responsibility, and deeds of the offender. Comforting ideas that the judge is simply a speaker of state law wither in the sentencing environment. Another way of putting this is that there is, in sentencing and punishment decisions, no plausible retreat to the conceits of legal formalism. Sentencing is one place where it is very difficult not to accept that who the judge is—the content of her conscience and philosophy of crime and punishment—matters deeply. In the moment of punishment, the clearest and most potent moment of the exercise of the raw will and coercive force of the state meets the principled but wide-ranging discretion of the sentencing judge. It is this very confluence that points, I will suggest, to why markers of religious and normative pluralism in a judiciary should be welcomed, not prohibited, or even merely tolerated.

III. A Historical Excursion

The demand for proof beyond reasonable doubt is one of the pillars of contemporary criminal law. It stands as an emblem of the modern, enlightened administration of criminal justice and, within that realm, serves as a virtual synecdoche for the rule of law. Its relationship to the rule of law flows from the imagined position that it occupies in the criminal process. It is thought that this standard of proof stands between the fearful and potentially tyrannical power of the state and the liberty of the subject, serving as a protective principle that ensures that the morally innocent are not improperly swept up in the machinery of state punishment. As we understand it today, then, proof beyond a reasonable doubt is a much-cherished but rather simple principle—a feature of modern law that serves to protect the accused from wrongful conviction.

As it turns out, the history is far more complex and interesting. This complicated history points to a very different function for the idea of proof beyond a reasonable doubt; it is a history that ties together religion, state authority, and punishment in provocative ways. In this section, I turn to this history as a means of excavating resources for thinking differently about the place that religious adherence might occupy in our picture of criminal judgment.

At the Fourth Lateran Council in 1215, Pope Innocent III prohibited the clergy from participating in trial by ordeal. This edict effectively abolished the principal means of criminal trial in England, but it also released a flood of anxiety into the criminal justice system. To be sure, trial by ordeal had been a terrible event for the accused. Whether by hot iron, cold water, or (for the higher-status accused) battle, trial by ordeal must have been a fearful process, all the more so in light of the mortal consequences of a finding of guilt. And yet it posed little concern or anxiety for those involved in administering criminal law. The logic of ordeal was straightforward enough: in the epistemology of the time, the ordeal offered a direct point of access to God's judgment as to the guilt of the accused. Concerned with the taint of blood for the clergy who oversaw these ordeals, when Pope Innocent III banned clergy participation, matters shifted entirely. Now that direct judgment from God could not be secured, criminal judgment would have to be a human matter. As James Whitman shows in *The Origins of Reasonable Doubt*,[23] this shift in responsibility after the ordeal generated deep moral anxiety, an anxiety that would be crucial to the development of the contemporary criminal trial.

Whitman explains that the act of human judgment—suddenly necessary in a post-ordeal world—was understood to be a deeply perilous and risky business. 'Early modern Christians', Whitman writes, 'experienced great anxiety about the dangers that acts of judgment presented for the soul' because 'any sinful misstep committed by a judge in the course of judging "built him a mansion in Hell"'.[24] Phrases such as 'judge not lest ye be judged', and 'they that take up the sword shall perish by the sword' rang in the ears of those responsible for judgment with a resonance and force that it is difficult to imagine today. In the case of criminal judgments, with the mortal and bloody consequences so often associated with conviction, the peril was particularly acute because, in the theological atmosphere of the time, the individual who judged wrongly was responsible for and polluted by this bloodshed, wielding the sword just as the soldier did. The stakes were high, then, not only for the accused but also for the judge, whose soul was at stake in each act of criminal judgment.

When the ordeals ended in 1215, the need to judge collided with a complex theology of doubt that had generated out of this anxiety around human judgment. A doctrine called the 'safer path' had developed in moral theology, and instructed that 'in cases of doubt, "in dubiis," one should act in such a way as to minimize the possibility of pollution'.[25] Trepidation about pronouncing judgment in the

[23] James Q Whitman, *The Origins of Reasonable Doubt: Theological Roots of the Criminal Trial* (New Haven, Yale University Press, 2008).

[24] ibid 3.

[25] ibid 117.

presence of doubt was deep. Without the moral comfort of the ordeals, other means would have to be found to manage this anxiety about judgment, and many of those techniques were the progenitors to the characteristic features of our modern criminal trial. The jury itself, Whitman explains, was one such device for the moral comfort of judges, shifting moral peril from judges to lay jurors who were placed under 'exceptional moral pressure'.[26] Jurors, no less aware of the 'safer path' than judges, were reticent to convict in the presence of any uncertainty. Over the course of the thirteenth to seventeenth centuries, however, techniques of responsibility-shifting (including the special verdict and benefit of clergy) and jury control (including, in the seventeenth century, fining and even imprisoning jurors) allowed the system to extract convictions from juries. However, in the late seventeenth and early eighteenth centuries these practices fell into disrepute. Benefit of clergy withered and jury control was abolished. And with this, jurors fell back on the safer path, reluctant to convict.

Moral theology responded to the risk that this posed to the administration of justice, and its response was the doctrine of reasonable doubt. Yes, it was a grave matter—a matter that implicated one's soul—to judge another when one had doubt. But this did not mean, this doctrine held, that you had to be concerned with any doubt whatsoever. No, your soul was safe, theologians explained, as long as you harboured no *reasonable* doubt. The origins of reasonable doubt were, thus, as a means to encourage conviction, not to discourage it. It was a device of moral comfort, not one aimed at factual proof. Whitman summarises the provocative conclusion as follows:

> the 'beyond a reasonable doubt' standard was not originally designed to make it more difficult for jurors to convict. It was designed to make conviction *easier*, by assuring jurors that their souls were safe if they voted to condemn the accused. In its original form, it had nothing to do with maintaining the rule of law in the sense that we use the phrase, and nothing like the relationship to the values of liberty we ascribe to it today. It was the product of a world troubled by moral anxieties that no longer trouble us much at all.[27]

The principal contemporary lesson that Whitman draws from this history of reasonable doubt is that, with the loss of this pervasive Christian moral frame, modern law has become comfortable—perhaps too comfortable—with judging. Indeed, he argues that '[o]ne of the features that makes our law modern is our lack of anxiety about judging others'.[28] The historical fear around judgment was an artefact of the saturation of the public and private lives of the judge and juror alike with the worldview and absolute authority of Christian moral theology. 'Modern secularization has brought the decline of the fearful religiosity of the past'.[29] Most people—including judges and jurors—no longer move in their lives trembling

[26] ibid 127.
[27] ibid 5.
[28] ibid 6.
[29] ibid 7.

with fear for the eternal fate of their souls. In many respects, release from this kind of day-to-day fear is a good thing: 'humans who no longer quake and tremble are humans who live richer lives in many ways'.[30] And yet that fear and anxiety in criminal adjudication served a function: it helped to restrain the violent hand of the criminal law. Be it in the development of demanding burdens and standards of proof or in the creation of procedural rules such as jury unanimity, this sense of moral discomfort in the exercise of criminal judgment tended historically to translate into a kind of parsimony in the use of the criminal law. Whitman concludes, harrowingly, that '[t]he larger truth is that we have slowly been losing the capacity to gaze into our own breasts and ask ourselves hard questions about when and how we have the right to punish others'.[31]

It would be a mistake to fall into nostalgia for this period in the criminal trial or to become Pollyannaish about the historical influence of Christianity on the uses to which criminal law and trial processes have been put. Yet there is significant value in the specific lesson that, in the presence of uncertainty, a due measure of anxiety about judgment is a salutatory thing. And this lesson, along with the details of the historical excursion that teaches it, points to something of structural interest for the purposes of this chapter. The story of the origins of reasonable doubt offers an example of how the meeting of religious conscience and the barest form of coercive power generated attitudes of restraint and scepticism about the uses of state power. When the seventeenth-century juror gazed into his breast, he found a source of authority in Christian moral theology that offered an important counterpoint to the raw coercive authority of the state. The salutary anxiety that Whitman identifies was produced because state punishment had to pass through the person of a judge/juror whose normative reference points could not be readily assimilated to law enforcement interests or kingly authority alone. This moral independence of the juror from the government was disciplined and controlled for centuries through mechanisms of jury control and responsibility-shifting; the story of reasonable doubt is the story of finding a way to assuage that anxiety in service of more efficient and reliable punishment. Yet it remains true that Christian theology was a force to contend with in the development of modern criminal law, forceful because it offered an alternative footing on which to stand in judgment of the rightness of an act of punishment.

One might feel as though this digression into legal history has taken us far afield from this chapter's questions about judges, religious symbols, the Bouchard-Taylor Commission, and the 'Charter of Quebec Values'. It is, however, just this structural observation—an observation about the importance of moral independence in the act of judgment—that offers the key to an alternative reading of religious symbols and the judicial role, a reading that might in fact have particular salience and appeal at the moment of state coercion or punishment.

[30] ibid.
[31] ibid.

IV. Reading Religion and the Judge

Equipped with this account from the history of the common law criminal trial, I return to the matter at hand: how to read the appearance of religious symbols on the person of a judge. The Bouchard-Taylor report reflected the instinct that there was something about the capacity to exercise state coercion—what the commissioners called 'the power of punishment'[32]—that made the case for 'circumspection' particularly strong. Consider the heart of Bouchard and Taylor's argument leading to their suggested prohibition on judges wearing items that would mark religious belonging:

> Everyone will agree that this type of situation must be broached with the utmost caution. The case of judges is probably the most complex and the hardest to decide upon. It is essential that the parties involved in a trial, especially the respondent, who may be punished, can assume the judge's impartiality. Could a Muslim respondent assume the impartiality of a Jewish judge wearing a kippah or a Hindu judge displaying a tilak?[33]

The next line of the report makes the assertion that '[t]he right to a fair trial is one of the acknowledged basic legal rights of all citizens'.[34]

Notice how this reading of the religious symbol proceeds: the symbol of religious belonging is implicated in issues of impartiality and fair trial rights. The symbol worn by one of these imagined judges is evidence of religious particularity, and this particularity translates into the possible apprehension of partiality. The protection of the fair trial rights of the accused thus requires that we ensure that there is no evidence that the judge is compromised by religious particularity. And yet with the historical excursion in hand, I think that we might imagine a very different reading of the marker of the judge's religious belonging, one that flips the argumentative valence of the moment of punishment or coercion.

Rather than tethering the religious symbol to concerns about impartiality (understood here as dependent on non-particularlity), one might choose to focus instead on the basal judicial norm of independence. Judicial independence is amongst the most fervently invoked and jealously guarded principles in the structure of our justice system. It is a commitment protected both by explicit right and by implication in the Canadian constitution.[35] Notably, most discussion of and jurisprudence about judicial independence focuses on the institutional paraphernalia of independence: security of tenure, protections around remuneration, and such. And yet the under-discussed heart of the principle is independence of mind: a kind of conscientious or moral independence. This is what the accused desires at

[32] Bouchard and Taylor (n 8) 151.
[33] ibid.
[34] ibid.
[35] See Adam Dodek and Lorne Sossin (eds), *Judicial Independence in Context* (Toronto, Irwin Law, 2010).

the moment of judgment or punishment. The accused's chief interest is not in an abstract philosophical impartiality, but rather impartiality as between the accused and his antagonist, the prosecuting authorities. The central hope is for a judge that is independent from the interests or raw will of the government. This is the foundation of the fair trial right. And if this idea of moral independence is brought into focus, the particularity of the religious symbol might designate something quite different and salutary: a marker for the existence of evaluative footings that are not reducible to the prevailing governance interests of the executive.

Both the structural logic and the practical realities of rights protection in the criminal justice system turn on the existence of a buffer, in the person of the judge, between law enforcement authorities and the subject. It is precisely at the moment of coercion—where there exists the power of punishment—that a distance between government and judge is most imperative. It is at this moment that the hope is most ardent that the authority and interests of government will not be the sole perspective from which power is exercised. And it is therefore at this moment that we might actually have the greatest appetite for the showing of religious particularity within our judiciary. The appearance of religious symbols amongst members of the judiciary can be read (and should be encouraged to be read) as a reminder that judges cannot be neatly assimilated into the apparatus of the government, functioning solely as agents of its will and authority. These symbols could be viewed as reminders of how important it is that judges have the moral independence that comes with evaluative footings that cannot be tidily identified with the perspectives of the legislature or executive.

Consider the historical case of the origins of reasonable doubt. In that story the religious conscience of adjudicators did not serve to aggravate punishment; the rule of law did not admit of that kind of effect. Rather, religion introduced a ground for scepticism and caution in the exercise of state authority through the imposition of state violence. Christianity offered resources that created a counterpoint to ideals of efficient and confident punishment. Ultimately, those cautionary principles had to find expression in the law, giving rise, as Whitman explains, to a number of the central features of our contemporary criminal trial. But the religious particularity of the judges and jurors served as an avenue through which these decision-makers achieved critical distance from the pure will of state authority, testing the will to punish against norms of justice and fairness that were not endogenous to the prevailing logic of government. That history is a rather potent expression of the idea of judicial independence and its value to a justice system.

Of course, there is nothing to assure us that the religious conviction that opens up this distance will always counsel a posture of mercy or mitigation. The moral independence that is signalled by symbols of religious belonging could instil an appetite to punish, or as a matter of outcome in a given case, align the judge with the interests and power of the government, rather than inducing scepticism about the use of criminal law. Although the historical example of the development of proof beyond a reasonable doubt is a story about religion as a force for parsimony and restraint, it would be a mistake to imagine that religious belief will consistently induce that salutary attitude. Yet in this respect we are in no different a position than we would find ourselves with a religiously committed judge whose religion does not involve symbolic displays, or with a judge inspired by otherwise-sourced political or philosophical commitments. Moreover, at a historical moment in which prevailing interpretations of the mixing of religious identity and public authority are so often negatively charged, we do well to meditate on examples of the goods—including a scepticism about state power in the context of criminal punishment—that religious commitment can bring. But what is ultimately appealing about the appearance of religious symbols within the judiciary is not a particular normative valence, but what is structurally communicated: the independence of the judge who is tasked with sitting in review of exercises of state power.

Read within these terms, consider the picture of the judiciary that is invited by the prohibition on religious symbols suggested in the Bouchard-Taylor Commission and the proposed 'Charter of Secularism'. That ban on religious symbols is not, of course a ban on symbols associated with the judiciary and the act of punishment. Symbols abound in that setting, but they are all the symbols of state authority. The coat of arms, the flag, the uniforms of public office, the 'Crown,' 'Her Majesty', the trappings of government buildings—everything that an accused meets through the process of state coercion is an expression of state authority and power. Stripped of markers of her own particularity, there is little to obviously distinguish the person of the judge from the machinery of punishment. The authority of the government and the ends of justice are too neatly aligned when all symbols and language within a justice system are those endogenous to law itself. We have never allowed the authority of law and the ends of justice to be collapsed in this way. Throughout our legal history, equity has been a structural space for the exercise of conscience that is not reducible to law alone. And through the royal prerogative of mercy, prosecutorial discretion, and the power of jury nullification, the criminal justice system has continued to depend on, cultivate, and protect ways in which justice requires that law be supplemented with assessments and evaluation from other grounds of moral and ethical judgment.[36] Manifestations of cultural and personal particularity (of which religious symbols are one example) could serve as a welcome reminder that, amongst those through whom the coercive force of the state must pass, there exist footings for just this kind of sceptical posture.[37] Viewed in this way, contemporary religious pluralism affords

[36] See Benjamin L Berger, 'The Abiding Presence of Conscience: Criminal Justice Against the Law and the Modern Constitutional Imagination' (2011) 61 *University of Toronto Law Journal* 579.

[37] For a defence of religious norms as amongst the external norms that judges, of necessity, must draw in reasoning about justice, see Mark C Modak-Truran, 'Reenchanting the Law: The Religious Dimension of Judicial Decision Making' (2004) 53 *Catholic University Law Review* 709. See also Stephen L Carter, 'The Religiously Devout Judge' (1989) 64 *Notre Dame Law Review* 932. For an influential critique of this position see Kent Greenwalt, *Private Consciences and Public Reasons* (New York, Oxford University Press, 1995).

us a symbolic cache for markers of this kind of moral independence, so central to the task of judging.

One might object that this argument suggests that we can expect greater independence or impartiality from judges who wear items that mark their religious belonging. To be clear, my argument is not that the sceptical position that I have described is somehow only possible and perceivable when religion is brought into the courtroom. My interest is not with whether a particular judge does or does not wear a religious symbol. Instead, what should be attractive to us is the appearance of various moral touchstones and resources in the aggregate picture of the judiciary, because this helps to mark the judiciary as a collegium of ethical reasoners who enjoy moral independence from the claims of government authority alone. Each judge benefits from the presence of others who manifest this particularity. The existence of a turbaned judge down the hall who is deciding a bail matter benefits the many others who wear no such symbols of religious belonging. It benefits them by association, if you will. Having, in the aggregate, a judiciary that represents a range of moral and ethical resources that may play a role within the legal discipline of hearing, arguing, reason-giving, appealing, and dissenting, reminds and comforts the public that this is not a branch that is just about the technocratic execution of legislative or executive will. With the presence of these symbols in our composite picture of the judiciary, we are reminded of the many forms and sources—some visibly marked, some not—of the sceptical, independent ground that we hope our judges will occupy. Judges are still, of course, bound to the defining practice of reason-giving through and within the law. We insist, throughout, that whatever scepticism one has can fit within and be articulated through public legal norms. And yet, though part of the state apparatus, they are not reducible to servants of government authority or command.

It seems to me that, contrary to the argument advanced by Bouchard and Taylor, this matters *most* in light of the power of punishment and aware of the risks of state coercion. Should the prevailing attitudes of the government and its exercises of state authority become unjust or excessive, a judiciary equipped with moral resources drawn from other perspectives seems a salutary thing, indeed. Might we adopt this reading of the appearance of religious symbols in the judicial setting, a reading in which the presence of such symbols comforts us by evidencing a public role as decision-makers whose resources for critiques of state power are rich and various?

V. Conclusion: Colin Westman and Michel Foucault

Over many years, Prime Minister Harper's Conservative government has marched a path of 'tough on crime' reform to Canadian criminal law. Central to that project was the revision of key elements of the sentencing regime, all of which restricted the freedom with which judges can craft sentences in pursuit of Parliament's putative will that the primary principle of sentencing be that of proportionality.[38] The Harper government introduced a spate of new mandatory minimum sentences, extinguished the use of conditional sentences for most offences, limited the credit available for pre-trial detention, and imposed higher victim fine surcharges. Although judges have responded to defence arguments on each of these points, and some of these matters have come before the Supreme Court of Canada,[39] it is the latter example—that of the new mandatory victim surcharges—that produced the most widespread and open conflict between the judiciary and the government. Judges across the country took up legal arms against this fee, some giving offenders decades to pay the fee, others ruling the surcharge unconstitutional, and some simply refusing to order the fine.[40]

Out of this controversy, Justice Colin Westman emerged as something of the public face of judicial resistance to the tough on crime agenda. He earned notoriety for taking a very public and strident stance against the surcharge, voicing his concerns through the media—an unconventional and controversial move for a sitting judge. Justice Westman, who took measures in court to evade the surcharge, denounced the government's measures, calling the surcharge a 'tax on "broken souls"'.[41] Drawing attention to the poverty, mental illness, and dislocation that so many of those who come before him suffer, and voicing his dismay at the prospect of fining these people, Justice Westman explained his actions—both in the courtroom and in the media—as follows:

> Those people in the soup kitchens I see in the courtroom, they don't have a voice. I think I have an obligation to them. These are my brothers and sisters, from a theological perspective.[42]

Quoting these words, Sean Fine, the justice reporter for the *Globe and Mail* noted: 'Justice Westman wears a Christian cross under his judicial vestments'.[43]

The theological language used by Justice Westman, and the cross sitting under his gowns, no doubt irritate some, or even appear unseemly. Justice Westman certainly received substantial criticism for his engagement with the media and for his judicial approach to the surcharge. Of Westman's conduct, Professor Adam Dodek is quoted as commenting, 'Judges cannot pick and choose which laws they like and which they do not. This undermines the rule of law and public confidence

[38] Criminal Code, RSC 1985, c C-46, s 718.1.

[39] For a recent decision of the Supreme Court of Canada declaring certain mandatory minimum sentences unconstitutional, see *R v Nur* 2015 SCC 15.

[40] See Sean Fine, 'Judges Defy Order to Impose Tories' Victim-Services Surcharge' *The Globe and Mail* (Toronto, 9 December 2013) www.theglobeandmail.com/news/politics/judges-defy-order-to-impose-tories-victim-services-surcharge/article15820100/. For example, in *R v Michael* 2014 ONCJ 360, Justice David Paciocco ruled that s 737 of the Criminal Code, which provides for the victim surcharge, was unconstitutional.

[41] Fine, 'Judges Defy Order to Impose Tories' Victim-Services Surcharge' (n 40).

[42] Sean Fine, 'The New Face of Judicial Defiance' *The Globe and Mail* (Toronto, 13 December 2013) www.theglobeandmail.com/news/politics/the-new-face-of-judicial-defiance/article15971207/.

[43] ibid.

in the administration of justice'.[44] Yet without necessarily defending Justice Westman's conduct, one can cull a more interesting and subtle lesson from this set of events, one that arguably shows a thinness in this sense of the rule of law and what might feed public confidence in the judiciary. In this case, Justice Westman's religious convictions, hidden though they were to those appearing before him, served as a lever for wedging space between the technocratic execution of the will of the government and the act of just punishment.

In his lectures on 'The Birth of Biopolitics', Foucault noted that one feature of the rise of neoliberalism was the 'anthropological erasure of the criminal'.[45] Over the course of the nineteenth century, there had been a tendency to understand crime in a way that involved the 'psychological, sociological, and anthropological problematization of the person on whom the law is applied'.[46] Foucault explains that with neoliberalism, this anthropological and individualised criminal—this *homo criminalis*—was replaced by *homo economicus*. As the market became the authoritative index of all legitimate government action, and human action was thus best interpreted through that grid of intelligibility, crime became just another form of economic action, with the criminal 'treated only as anyone whomsoever who invests in an action, expects a profit from it, and who accepts the risk of a loss'.[47]

The victim surcharge was a pristine expression of a neoliberal frame for understanding crime and the criminal. Many Canadian judges have resisted this prevailing logic of criminal justice reform and have done so without manifest recourse to religious commitments; and whatever their posture, all judges have worked within and through the law. And yet for Justice Westman, theology was a means of reintroducing an anthropology of the criminal. For this judge, religion was a resource to draw on to recomplicate the picture of crime and criminals painted by the government. Judges, through judgments about punishment and sentencing, have always done that: they have met dominant narratives about justice, crime, and society, with inconvenient facts and complicating stories. In a society characterised by deep religious pluralism, might it be that we should welcome evidence of the religious particularity of judges as enrichments of that quintessential role of the judge? Perhaps we should re-read religious symbols as markers of the moral independence of the judiciary.

[44] ibid.

[45] Michel Foucault, *The Birth of Biopolitics: Lectures at the Collège de France, 1978–1979* (New York, Palgrave Macmillan, 2008) 258.

[46] ibid 250.

[47] ibid 253.

3

Religious Lawyering and Legal Ethics

FAISAL BHABHA*

I. Introduction

For generations, lawyers in the common law tradition viewed themselves as morally neutral actors, performing a role that necessitates hyper-partisan fidelity to the client's interests coupled with personal moral indifference to the content or consequences of professional conduct. This 'gladiatorial' view of the professional role posits lawyers as players in an adversarial game that demands cunning, skill and undivided loyalty—sometimes it even requires lawyers to do things that are morally repugnant, like lying and cheating.[1]

Most contemporary legal ethics scholarship pushes back against moral neutrality and zealous advocacy as presumptive and definitive norms in the lawyer-client relationship. Current trends in ethics scholarship offer an array of models of moderate and mindful professionalism. These tend to be concerned with the lawyer's role as an agent for justice, holding the key to accessing rights and ensuring the rule of law, and capable of effecting positive redress for clients' claims of harm, unfairness, or structural injustice.[2] Balancing client interests with a concern for justice manifests by lawyers taking into account the public interest. Contemporary lawyers work towards promoting a high standard of integrity in the profession[3] both through individual ethical conduct, but also through the

* The author acknowledges the dependable research support of Simmy Sahdra, and is grateful to Bruce Ryder, Kiran Kang and the volume's editors for helpful comments.

[1] See eg, Daniel Markovits, *A Modern Legal Ethics: Adversary Advocacy in a Democratic Age* (Princeton, Princeton University Press, 2008) (defending the traditional zealous advocate role, and characterising loyalty as requiring lawyers to cheat and lie).

[2] See eg, William H Simon, *The Practice of Justice: A Theory of Lawyers' Ethics* (Cambridge, Harvard University Press, 1998) 138 (critiquing the 'dominant view' of the lawyer's role as zealous advocate and asserting that 'lawyers should take those actions that, considering the relevant circumstances of the particular case, seem likely to promote justice').

[3] See Trevor Farrow, 'Sustainable Professionalism' (2008) 46 *Osgoode Hall Law Journal* 51, 63–71 (summarising the conventional approach, and outlining a reconstruction that accounts for interests beyond those of the client).

profession's efforts to represent and serve all sectors of society. Today, this also means promoting access to lawyers by performing pro bono work, engaging in public legal education, and engendering respect for human rights and corporate accountability within the organisations that lawyers serve.[4]

This broader understanding of the role lawyers play in society acknowledges that lawyers are not empty vessels or simple technicians, but in fact are moral actors, whether they admit it or not.[5] This becomes evident when 'neutral' professional action causes or contributes to negative consequences. As scholars have noted with respect to the notorious US cases of Abu Ghraib and Enron[6] (the lessons of which apply equally to all legal transactions): when clients behave criminally or dishonestly and the lawyer participates in, discovers or suspects it, the posture of partisan loyalty and moral neutrality can seem dangerously thin. Loyalty has necessary limits, at least partly because lawyers who fail to call out client dishonesty or illegality become complicit, if not liable. Individual lawyers' moral failings taint the entire profession.[7]

Thus, it must be accepted as a premise that the lawyer's work is never morally neutral. If that is the case, then what moral framework governs, or should govern, lawyers' professional conduct? Formal ethics rules are rather general in their prescriptions and proscriptions. They offer some clarity with respect to certain stipulated offences (such as unauthorised practice, fraud, crimes and illegality) and articulate duties that speak to general ethical aspirations (such as practising with candour, honour and integrity). However, the rules rarely provide clear conclusions with respect to the factually complex situations that arise in everyday law practice. The gap between what the rules say and what actually occurs necessitates that lawyers evaluate the moral values and interests at stake in any given situation, whether they do so consciously or unconsciously.[8]

[4] See Federation of Law Societies of Canada, Model Code of Professional Conduct (October 2014), ss 2.1-1, 2.1-2, 3.2-2, 3.2-7, 3.2-8, 5.1-1, 5.1-2, 5.1-5, 5.6-1, 5.6-2, 6.3, 7.2-1, 7.3-1, 7.3-2, online: http://flsc.ca/wp-content/uploads/2014/12/conduct1.pdf.

[5] Robert K Vischer, 'Legal Advice as Moral Perspective' (2006) 19 *Georgetown Journal of Legal Ethics* 225.

[6] Vischer (n 5) 8–18 (noting the failure of government lawyers to adequately integrate moral considerations in their 2002 legal opinions relating to the treatment of prisoners in the war on terror. Torture and mistreatment of detainees in Iraq and Guantanamo were later established: 'The problem does not lie with the legal merits of the advice given or the professional context in which the attorneys plied their wares; rather, it lies with the amoral construct into which inescapably moral advice is forced, and the stark consequences of failing to bring that moral dimension to the surface of the attorney-client dialogue'.) See also Vischer (n 5) 7, 17–26 (commenting on the 2001 collapse and bankruptcy of the Enron corporation due to perilous and illegal profit-making practices by management: 'Lawyers from Vinson & Elkins were so enmeshed in Enron's management culture that their legal advice became tailored to supporting the maximization of share price, to the exclusion of other considerations more in keeping with the company's long-term interests'.)

[7] *R v Murray* (2000) 48 OR (3d) 544 (SCJ) (criminal lawyer concealed 'smoking gun' evidence then faced criminal prosecution for obstruction. He was found not guilty due to the lack of *mens rea* given confusion in ethical practice concerning a professional duty to hide or disclose incriminating physical evidence in criminal prosecution.)

[8] See Farrow (n 3) 72–74.

How lawyers incorporate personal moral decision-making into their professional role is a question of general interest. This chapter focuses on one particular mode of integrating morality into the practice of law: religious lawyering.[9] The first part will be primarily descriptive, drawing focus on the core features of religious lawyering and some of the tensions in professional ethics. Next, it turns to examine the context of public contestation around religion in public life. From these experiences, it outlines legal and political factors that inform whether lawyers should integrate religious values in professional life. Specifically, it considers whether there are features of Canadian legal education, lawyer regulation and/or public law, which present unique concerns or reservations about religious lawyering in Canada. This is set in the context of a proposal for an evangelical Christian law school at Trinity Western University (TWU) in British Columbia, the first of its kind in the country. The debate around the institution's controversial application for accreditation provides a useful case study to weigh the arguments for and against the blending of religion and law practice. The chapter concludes by encouraging a style of practice for both religious and secular lawyers that seeks to produce a model of sustainable professional integrity and reduce the strain of at least some of the identified tensions in professional life. This means prioritising mindfulness, critical self-reflection, planning and deliberation as mechanisms to foster the healthy integration of personal and professional norms, and avoiding ethical conflicts.

II. The Religious Lawyering Movement

The concept of religious lawyering emerged in legal literature in the 1970s. Thomas Shaffer developed a vision of being a Christian lawyer in reference to emerging normative discourse on legal ethics and professional responsibility.[10] He sought to reform the inherited posture of 'moral indifference' and declared that religious faithfulness requires 'that a lawyer imagines that she is first of all a believer' from a 'community of the faithful'.[11] Moral indifference could not hold for a lawyer who begins from a position of faith. For the Christian lawyer, Shaffer

[9] Briefly, a word about evidence is warranted. In Canada, there has been little research and writing about religious lawyering movements. Faith-based lawyer and law student organisations have existed for some time, as have interfaith groups within the profession. Without a doubt, there are religious lawyers in Canada, but there is little evidence of a movement. It is an unfortunate absence that there is a gap in empirical research on the role of religion in the lives of Canadian lawyers. Given that this chapter offers no such data, it is difficult to make any definitive factual claims about religious lawyering in Canada.

[10] Thomas L Shaffer, *On Being a Christian and a Lawyer: Law for the Innocent* (Provo, Brigham Young University Press, 1981). See also Joseph Alligretti, 'Christ in the Code: The Dilemma of the Christian Attorney' (1988) 34 *Catholic Lawyer* 131.

[11] Thomas L Shaffer, *American Lawyers and Their Communities* (Notre Dame, University of Notre Dame Press, 1991) 198.

explained, the individual's lawyer identity is secondary or subservient to her status as a believer and as a member of a community of faith. Describing Christian lawyering, Timothy W Floyd has explained that

> we are called to live our faith in all of our activities and in all aspects of our lives. God cannot be compartmentalized into the religious sphere of our lives while being irrelevant in our work lives. We simply cannot relegate our obligations to God and neighbor to the 'nonlawyer' parts of our lives.[12]

Religious lawyering scholarship diversified beginning in the 1990s as a multi-faith movement began to emerge. Lawyers from a variety of traditions, including Baha'i, Buddhist, Hindu, Jewish, Muslim and others, began to contribute to discussions around religious identity, faith and legal practice.[13] By the end of the decade, religious lawyering in the US had 'become a full-fledged movement drawing upon a sizeable and significant body of scholarship, and attracting the attention of a growing number of lawyers and judges'.[14] In an oft-cited article, Sanford Levinson sought to identify the 'Jewish Lawyer' within constructions of professional identity.[15] He outlined five modes of being a Jewish lawyer that covered the diversity of American Jewish experience. This pluralist paradigm for considering the ways in which religion intersects with lawyers' professional identity is a particularly useful template for mapping modes of harmonising religious identity with professional conduct. What follows is my reconstruction of Levinson's paradigm into a 'non-sectarian' taxonomy of modes of religious lawyering.

The first mode includes all persons who are both religious (within a particular faith tradition) and who are lawyers. Such lawyers may, to varying degrees, consciously or not, bring religion into their professional life. In one sense, this category amounts to a simple head count. However, it can in fact be surprisingly complicated to accurately determine the number of members of any particular faith group, depending on how membership is determined. This heading includes the broadest possible spectrum of faith adherents/group members.

The second mode represents religious lawyering as an expression of social and political solidarity. It describes those who feel a high degree of membership in and loyalty to a religious community, regardless of the strength of their personal commitment to faith per se. Such lawyers may build up their client base within their faith or cultural community, take on causes of common concern, and

[12] Timothy W Floyd, 'The Practice of Law as a Vocation or Calling' (1998) 66 *Fordham Law Review* 1405, 1409.

[13] Russell G Pearce, 'Jewish Lawyering in a Multicultural Society: A Midrash on Levinson' (1993) 14 *Cardozo Law Review* 1613; Jerome Hornblass, 'The Jewish Lawyer' (1993) 14 *Cardozo Law Review* 1639; Azizah Y al-Hibri, 'Faith and the Attorney-Client Relationship: A Muslim Perspective' (1998) 66 *Fordham Law Review* 1131; Thomas E Baker and Timothy W Floyd (eds), *Can a Good Christian be a Good Lawyer? Homilies, Witnesses, and Reflections* (Notre Dame, University of Notre Dame Press, 1998).

[14] Russell G Pearce, 'Forward-The Religious Lawyering Movement: An Emerging Force in Legal Ethics and Professionalism' (1998) 66 *Fordham Law Review* 1075.

[15] Sanford Levinson, 'Identifying the Jewish Lawyer: Reflections on the Construction of Professional Identity' (1993) 14 *Cardozo Law Review* 1577.

develop formal associations grounded in faith and/or community with a view to representing community perspectives at the bar and in the public. This lawyer feels a strong personal identification with the similarly identified client and the issues, but religion per se does not enter the workplace in any material way.

The third mode operates when religion enters the legal workplace but neither shapes the lawyer's practice nor puts any burden of accommodation on the internal norms of ordinary practice. Under this mode, the lawyer's religion may impact on things such as choice of holidays or some aspect of professional attire, but does not directly influence the manner of the lawyer's practice or the quality of his or her services. Religion is, as it were, neutral in respect of professional conduct. For such a lawyer, the fact of personal religious identification does not equate with reliance on religious norms in the lawyer's judgment or advice. This type of religious lawyer segregates morality based on roles in order to keep personal religious ethics and professional ethics categorically separate. This type of lawyer does not necessarily believe that following professional rules over personal morality is a sin. Rather, this lawyer accepts and respects the legal system as good, and likely views the preservation of the administration of justice as morally a good thing. As such, conflict of professional and religious norms is unlikely.

The fourth mode of religious practice is represented by the tiny minority of religious lawyers who choose to practise exclusively or substantially within their own religious community. According to Levinson, such lawyers' personal morality is most likely to align with clients' and with the norms of the particular legal system in which they operate. Thus, for Levinson, there presents little risk of tension in the professional role.[16]

Under the fifth mode, religion is similarly a 'constitutive aspect' of the lawyer's general approach to legal practice, regardless of the practice setting or client. This mode is the characteristic of the devoutly religious lawyer who offers his or her professional services to the general public. For this religious lawyer, who is faith-driven, religious identity supersedes professional identity. Thus, this type of religious lawyer must find personal accommodation between religious norms and the demands of practice, which can, at times, present an irresolvable tension.

It is worth noting that this modified Levinson catalogue contains modes that are not mutually exclusive; a lawyer may display characteristics of two or more at the same time, or at different times depending on circumstances. The first three modes overlap considerably, and the fourth mode applies to few if any lawyers. It is the fifth mode that tethers the form and content of legal professionalism to a personal and spiritual identity and mission. It is this mode that is primarily implicated in the questions at issue in this chapter.

[16] It is not manifestly evident that the mere fact that clients, lawyers and the institutional setting are all Jewish means that there will be little tension with religious and professional morality. On the contrary, religious ethics can be as indeterminate, and as deeply contested by adherents, as professional ethics questions are among lawyers. What is unique about this tension is that there are two axes of potential tension: (1) between religious and professional ethics, and (2) between different religious interpretations of how to be an ethical lawyer. Even a religious lawyer practising in a religious context can be expected to struggle navigating between competing identities and roles.

III. Religion: Part of a Lawyer's Ethical Role?

The question that has animated much of the literature exploring the intersection of faith and professional identity has been whether there is any space for an individual lawyer's faith to positively influence her professional practice. The conventional approach would hold that a lawyer is duty-bound to banish personal religious conviction from any role in professional decision-making and conduct. However, from a religious lawyer's perspective, the question gets things backwards, by presupposing that the professional calling is not itself shaped and influenced by one's religious identity and values. Indeed, the very decision to enter the law can be deeply personal and moral. This is true for the religious lawyer but also for many non-religious people who infuse their professional role with a moral commitment to justice, to values, or to cause communities, which are in many cases as devotional as faith commitments. Yet, despite the values that a career in law practice promises for many, beginning in law school prospective lawyers encounter the self-effacing pressures of legal education and professional acculturation.[17] Meaningful personal identities, including religious beliefs and practices, come under scrutiny, raising questions about the religious person's belonging in a secular rule of law system.[18]

Traditional professional ethics compel lawyers to relegate faith to the personal (ie non-professional) sphere while falsely maintaining the irrelevance of faith to professional behaviour and decision-making.[19] Early scholarship by religious lawyers responded to the exclusion of religion from professional identity by developing religiously normative accounts of professional responsibility that rooted their moral obligations as lawyers in religious principles and doctrine. Christian lawyering sought to resolve the internal tension between Christian values and the secular values of legal professionalism. The project was important not only to refute the idea within legal professionalism that personal morality was an obstacle to professional conduct but also to prove wrong those members of faith communities who claimed that a good Christian could never be a good

[17] See Brenna Bhandar, 'Always on the Defence: The Myth of Universality and the Persistence of Privilege in Legal Education' (2002) 14(2) *Canadian Journal of Women and the Law* 341; Valerie Fontaine, 'Progress Report: Women and People of Color in Legal Education and the Legal Profession' (1995) 6 *Hastings Women's Law Journal* 27; Margalynne Joan Armstrong and Stephanie Wildman, 'Teaching Race/Teaching Whiteness: Transforming Colorblindness to Color Insight' (2008) 86 *North Carolina Law Review* 635.

[18] Noting the lack of empirical evidence on the issue, Professor Dwight Newman has written: 'I think that those who are honest with themselves will recognise many ways in which Canada's secular law schools are significantly unwelcoming to those of different religious faiths…'. See Dwight Newman, 'On the Trinity Western University Controversy: An Argument for a Christian Law School in Canada' (2013) 22(3) *Constitutional Forum* 1.

[19] Thomas E Baker and Timothy W Floyd (eds), *Can a Good Christian Be a Good Lawyer?: Homilies, Witnesses, and Reflections* (Notre Dame, University of Notre Dame Press, 1997) 1408–09.

lawyer.[20] The goal of religious lawyering, then, is to reconcile the dual mission of faith and professionalism within a single, integrated professional identity (what has been dubbed a 'calling' or 'vocation'),[21] rather than a compartmentalised mutually exclusive set of selves.

For many religious lawyers, their faith will form a part of their identity in a manner that is unlikely to ever conflict with their role as lawyers. For the faith-driven subset of religious lawyers, faith is more than a deeply held, invisible set of values that can be set aside while the diligent professional dons his lawyer cap. For these lawyers, faith will both compel and shape their very professional identity. Indeed, there is a big difference between religion determining 'whether [a lawyer] will go to work on a given day' and the extent to which faith will affect 'the very way that a lawyer relates to his clients'.[22] For the faith-driven religious lawyer, faith is the source of inspiration and normative understanding of every aspect of the role of lawyering. This means that the faith-driven religious lawyer will respect secular professional rules to the extent that they conform (or do not conflict) with the lawyer's faith-based normative framework. However, where there is conflict, the lawyer will not compromise on a matter of faith. In such circumstances, the lawyer's duties to the client remain ongoing, but an irresolvable conflict between a client's need and a lawyer's conscience may create an actual conflict of interest that necessitates measures to replace representation while ensuring no adverse impact on the client's interests.

Thus, while the faith-driven religious lawyer will prioritise lawyering within the bounds of faith, this lawyer will also prioritise ensuring compliance with formal professional rules to limit risk and avoid encountering situations that will present conflicts with personal values. When played out in practice, this amounts to a kind of internal negotiation between the personal and professional self. This may drive some into highly specialised practice within religious communities. But for many, the avoidance of tension between religious morality and professional responsibility is a lifelong pursuit. Maintaining an active and informed awareness of how to navigate this tension and avoid ethical crises is thus critical for the faith-driven religious lawyer.

IV. Confession, Communion and Contestation

A religious lawyer is not simply engaged in a personal struggle to reconcile faith and professional obligations. The personal struggle often occurs in conditions that

[20] See Floyd (n 19), 1409 ('I have known people who assert that a person of faith should not or cannot be a lawyer. In their view, the legal system is too corrupt and worldly for a Christian to be able to participate'.)

[21] See Floyd (n 19).

[22] Levinson (n 22) 1604.

are similarly experienced by others. Indeed the religious lawyer's experience in practice is often shaped and reinforced by the positions of conscience of others similarly oriented: 'Religious lawyers do not function as atomistic conscientious objectors opposing the unitary leviathan of the profession. Increasingly, the profession itself seems more properly viewed as a host of competing and contrasting subcommunities of lawyers, and many of these subcommunities are explicitly religious in nature'.[23] To be a religious lawyer is often not simply to be a religious person who practises law, but rather to be part of a community of religiously identified professionals who develop parallel norms and ethics within the practice of law. Religious lawyers navigate between their membership in the broader legal community and the sub-community of faithful practitioners, where many meaningful allegiances lie. These sub-communities are more than friendly or spiritual networks; they generate new normative visions of what it means to be a lawyer. The potential contributions of religious sub-communities to general principles of Canadian legal ethics is yet under-explored. Greater exploration and integration of these perspectives could lead to more meaningfully pluralistic understandings of the professional role.

Legal pluralism acknowledges that law functions in society in layered textures, with multiple normative systems, formal and informal, operating alongside one another giving rise to a multiplicity of presumptively equal sets of rules and visions.[24] The peril of pluralism is that religious lawyering movements undermine the posture of professional uniformity that Canadian law societies continue to project and institutionalise through accreditation and regulation. According to some, the law societies behave like 'little Caesars eager to expand their powers to regulate to the social values of lawyers in Canada' in ways that stifle religious freedom.[25] If this critique is true, it presents a challenge in the increasingly pluralistic world of Canadian lawyering. Indeed, the reality of contemporary Canadian lawyering is that the conflict between personal values and professional ethics is one potentially faced by lawyers well beyond the faith-driven subset. Any lawyer who infuses a personal moral perspective into their professional identity will experience to some degree a similar conflict with role morality. This could impact any variety of individual lawyers and in particular those whose very idea of legal professionalism is interwoven with extra-legal or pluralistic normative commitments.

Consider 'social justice' lawyers, clinic lawyers, criminal defence lawyers, union lawyers, feminist lawyers, disability rights lawyers, racial justice lawyers, and so on. For many lawyers within these professional subgroups, the conception of their moral self is tied to a vision of professional role. The connection to a

[23] Robert K Vischer, 'Heretics in the Temple of Law: The Promise and Peril of the Religious Lawyering Movement' (2004) 19 *Journal of Law & Religion* 427, 432 ('Heretics').

[24] See Sally Engle Merry, 'Legal Pluralism' (1988) 22 *Law & Society Review* 869, 870 (defining legal pluralism as 'a situation in which two or more legal systems coexist in the same social field').

[25] Raj Sharma, 'Let Trinity Western University Have its Law School' (Summer 2015) 40(2) *Law Matters* 38–39.

community of like-minded defenders of particular norms and values is integral to such lawyers' job performance and professional well-being. While the analogy to religion may not apply neatly, the point is that for many lawyers, religious and non-religious, mediating between deeply held personal and professional commitments will present both the possibility for deeply fulfilling work and the perpetual risk of ethical peril. One of the roles of sub-communities can be to provide support networks and common ways of understanding issues from a shared perspective to avoid peril and maximise personal and professional enrichment.

It should be clear by now that the fact of ethical tension alone cannot defeat the desire for religious lawyering. Also there is no reason to assume that a faith-driven religious lawyer is any more likely to encounter ethical tension in professional dealings than a morally motivated non-religious lawyer. It is, however, necessary to consider the other side of the coin: if we allow that personal morality (including religious morality) can and should enter the arena of professional ethics, then we must also acknowledge that it will perform some function in that arena. The question, then, is whether that function will necessarily threaten or detract from the professional role.

It is quite likely that religious lawyers can help settle difficult questions in professional ethics and construct a counter-dominant normative account of lawyering. In this way, they are not dissimilar to the radical lawyers that emanated from the new left movement of the late 1960s.[26] Lawyers working for social justice began from a position of critique and scepticism about power. They adopted an ethic of practice that is centred on remediating structured hierarchies and inequalities, which seeks to promote a moral vision of the ideal society, and which challenges the dominant moral-neutrality model of role-defined lawyering. For social justice lawyers, moral neutrality equals complicity with power. Like religious lawyers, social justice lawyers see lawyering as a means to serve and support a community and a cause as part of a process of social engagement political activism and personal transformation.[27] Group or collective identification is an important aspect of both religious movements and social justice movements. Indeed, scholars have noted that the existence of an identifiable group identity is a precondition for effective social action.[28] Such identity has also been shown to be critical in mobilising lawyers as activists.[29] It stands to reason that whether religious or secular in nature, a lawyer whose professional ethical framework is

[26] See eg, Michael Blazer, 'The Community Legal Clinic Movement in Ontario: Practice and Theory, Means and Ends' (1991) 7 *Journal of Law & Social Policy* 49, 54–58 (tracing the origins of poverty lawyering in Ontario).

[27] See generally Shin Imai, 'A Counter-pedagogy for Social Justice: Core Skills for Community Lawyering' (2002) 9.1 *Clinical Law Review* 195.

[28] See eg, Scott A Hunt and Robert A Benford, 'Collective Identity, Solidarity, and Commitment' in David A Snow, Sarah A Soule, and Hanspeter Kriesi (eds), *The Blackwell Companion to Social Movements* (New York, Blackwell, 2007) 433–57.

[29] Corey Shdaimah, 'Intersecting Identities: Cause Lawyers as Legal Professionals and Social Movement Actors' in Austin Sarat and Stuart Scheingold (eds), *Cause Lawyering and Social Movements* (Stanford, Stanford University Press, 2006).

shaped by an extra-legal moral value system will likely gravitate towards others who are similarly oriented within the profession.

An effective movement will identify issues of common concern to members of the group and enable them to rally together to overcome obstacles or systemic forces that obstruct the realisation of the collective ambition. The 'insider' lawyer translates deep knowledge of the community in the advice and services she provides, while also offering a meaningful possibility for community empowerment in law by representing the law to the members of her community from a 'dual insider' (and thus more credible) perspective. This can have potentially positive impact for communities on the fringes and can increase the reach of access to justice. It also begins to put meat on the bones of what diversity in the profession really means.[30]

V. Taming the 'Heretics in the Temple of Law'[31]

It appears that concerns about *whether* lawyers should bring religion into their professional identity are now largely settled.[32] The issue that remains is *how* and *to what extent*? This arises at a time when the traditional conception of the amoral, zealous advocate is no longer viewed as the necessary, let alone universally desirable, model of lawyering. This turn to ethics, public values and personal judgment has produced a culture of professionalism that draws focus to the content of the individual lawyer's character and tendency towards integrity. The question that arises, then, is whether and how (in a qualitative sense) this contemporary professional culture can be accommodating of, or influenced by, religious values. To answer this question, it is necessary to consider whether there is any reason to exclude religious values from the moral sources that lawyers may draw from in their individual professional practice. It is also necessary to consider the collective element of religious professionalism. The case study of a proposed religious law school in British Columbia provides the context to reach some cautious conclusions about the place and role of religious lawyering in the Canadian legal landscape.

At this point, it is worth returning to the modified Levinson approach and focus on the harm that could potentially flow from allowing 'heretics in the temple of law'.[33] That is, what threat do the strongly identified, faith-driven lawyers present

[30] See generally Faisal Bhabha, 'Towards a Pedagogy of Diversity in Legal Education' (2014) 52 *Osgoode Hall Law Journal* 59 (exploring the meaning behind 'diversity' as a norm in legal education and in the profession).

[31] See Heretics (n 23).

[32] Russell G Pearce and Amelia J Uelmen, 'Religious Lawyering's Second Wave' (2006) 21 *Journal of Law & Religion* 269, 274 (describing the first wave as addressing the question 'whether or not lawyers should bring religious values to bear on their professional work').

[33] See Heretics (n 23). The epithet is Robert Vischer's, but the meaning is the author's in this context.

to contemporary legal practice. It appears settled that softer modes of religious lawyering identity can be, and are, comfortably accommodated within existing models of professional responsibility under doctrines of diversity, pluralism and anti-discrimination. Under each of the first three modes of religious lawyering, the lawyer's religious identity either exists separately or converges with the lawyer's professional identity. Religion may colour and flavour aspects of the lawyer's personality, character and style, but it never supersedes and rarely if ever conflicts with professional obligations. However, in the stronger form of religious lawyering, whereby religion forms a 'constitutive element' of the lawyer's identity, religion dominates. It is this mode of religious lawyering that turns lawyers into heretics and can galvanise members of a differently oriented community to seek to create separate, safe spaces for their members. This desire is what fuels the development of networks, organisations and ultimately institutions based on bonds of faith.

VI. Towards a Faith-Based Law School?

If religion has the capacity to mobilise people as individuals and to come together as communal units with shared identities, values and aspirations, then it should come as no surprise that religion will inspire individuals within the profession to 'come out' and self-identify as religious lawyers. In 1978, the Christian Legal Fellowship (CLF) was incorporated, with an express commitment to the 'conviction that the vocation of law is a calling from God'.[34] CLF describes itself as being dedicated to

> uniting Christians involved in the administration, practice, teaching and study of law … motivating them to advocate for justice and religious freedom, informing the Christian community about legal issues affecting them, and by advocating a Biblical Judeo-Christian worldview of law and Justice in the public sphere.[35]

If members of faith groups come together in communion, organise and grow as communities, it is not surprising to expect that their vision will inspire the foundation of faith-based institutions for prayer, study, arts and culture, charity and more. Indeed, the Evangelical Free Church of America founded a private Christian college in Langley, British Columbia in 1962. It was accredited as a university in 1979 and became Trinity Western University (TWU) in 1985. TWU offers a wide variety of undergraduate and graduate degree programmes to about 4,000 students each year.

TWU was at the centre of litigation in the 1990s as a result of a decision by the British Columbia College of Teachers (BCCT) to refuse to accredit TWU's

[34] Christian Legal Fellowship, 'About Christian Legal Fellowship' www.christianlegalfellowship.org/index.cfm?i=15718&mid=1000&id=391475.

[35] ibid.

education programme because of the University's Community Standards policy. The policy required students to refrain from 'sexual sins' such as premarital sex, adultery, homosexual behaviour and viewing pornography. The BCCT had a statutory mandate to establish teaching standards with regard to the 'public interest' and determined that TWU's sex policy was not in accord with the public interest. Consequently, the BCCT determined that TWU graduates were not adequately prepared to teach in the province's public schools. In a precedent-setting decision in 2001, the Supreme Court of Canada ruled that the BCCT did not have the authority to discriminate against TWU in exercising its power to regulate teachers in British Columbia.[36] The court ruled that there was no rational basis to find that faith-educated teachers should be presumed unable to perform at a suitable standard for the public school classroom. TWU was vindicated.

In June 2012, TWU submitted a proposal to the Federation of Law Societies of Canada (Federation) and the British Columbia Ministry of Advanced Education to open a faith-based law school beginning in September 2016.[37] In a letter dated 20 November 2012, the Canadian Council of Law Deans, representing the top administrators from law schools across the country, condemned the proposal, citing TWU's controversial 'community covenant', which restricts all students' sexual activity to within the bounds of traditional Christian marriage.[38] The Council's President, Dean Bill Flanagan of Queen's Law, wrote that the covenant discriminates against LGBT students in a way that is 'fundamentally incompatible' with the core values of Canadian law schools and an equal society. According to the Council, 'to admit a new law school that has a policy that expressly discriminates on the basis of sexual orientation is something that is very troubling for us'.[39]

After the proposal was passed in December 2013, criticism grew to a chorus of public outcry, lobbying and pressure within various institutional settings to oppose TWU on the basis of its community covenant.[40] In April 2014, Ontario's law society (LSUC) ruled that TWU law degrees would not be recognised in the

[36] *Trinity Western University v British Columbia College of Teachers* [2001] 1 SCR 772.

[37] 'Proposal for a School of Law at Trinity Western University' (Trinity Western University Proposal June 2013) http://twu.ca/news/2013/proposal-for-a-school-of-law-at-twu.pdf.

[38] The Community Covenant is a modified (and according to many, improved) version of the Community Standards policy at issue in the TWU teachers case.

[39] Letter from Bill Flanagan, President, Canadian Council of Law Deans to John JL Hunter and Gerald R Tremblay, President, Federation of Law Societies of Canada (November 20, 2012), www.ccld-cdfdc.ca/images/reports/CCLDnov20-2012lettertoFederation-reTWU.pdf.

[40] Commentators on both sides of the issue traded jabs in the press. In support of TWU, see Jonathan Kay, 'The Case for Trinity Western University's Christian Law School' *The National Post* (Toronto, 23 January 2013) http://news.nationalpost.com/full-comment/jonathan-kay-the-case-for-trinity-western-universitys-christian-law-school; John Carpay, 'A Free Society Should Tolerate a Christian-based Law School' *Vancouver Sun* (Vancouver, 21 January 2013) www.vancouversun.com/life/free+society+should+tolerate+Christian+based+school/7851191/story.html; Faisal Bhabha, 'Let TWU Have Its Law School' (SLAW online 24 January 2014) www.slaw.ca/2014/01/24/let-twu-have-its-law-school/. For the case against, see Ruby and Chan (n 72); Heather Gardiner, 'Law students oppose TWU law school bid' *Canadian Lawyer Magazine* (21 March 2013); Elaine Craig, 'Law societies must show more courage on Trinity Western application' *The Globe and Mail* (Toronto, 18 December 2013) http://www.theglobeandmail.com/globe-debate/law-societies-must-show-more-courage-on-trinity-western-application/article16023053/.

province.[41] The next day, Nova Scotia's barristers' society (NSBS) similarly ruled that TWU would not be accredited in the province unless law students were exempted from the University's 'discriminatory' sex policy.[42] Later that year, the British Columbia law society (LSBC) reversed its previous decision to recognise TWU.[43] All three law society decisions are, at the time of writing, subject to court challenge.

The case against accreditation for TWU law school rested on one or both of two broad claims: the first was that a religious law school that places religious doctrine above human rights cannot produce sufficiently ethical lawyers; and the second was that accrediting a religious law school that excludes on the basis of protected grounds amounts to law society complicity in discrimination against members of affected groups who seek to join the legal profession generally. The first claim relates to the concern with what I have earlier described as 'faith-driven lawyers'. These lawyers present the biggest risk to the limits of accommodating difference within the norms of legal professionalism. Common concerns centre on the unknowns: how do we know that religious lawyers will not discriminate against clients and potential clients whose circumstances do not accord to the lawyer's moral or religious outlook? How do we understand and apply standards of competence when dealing with inaccurate or corrupted interpretations of the law based on religion? Can lawyers who put faith in God or religious affiliation above all else be trusted to uphold the principles of professionalism as prescribed in governing instruments? Will they be able to keep from imposing their religion on others? Are they able to respect human rights? Indeed, many worry that TWU will produce lawyers who harbour anti-gay sentiment, are more likely to discriminate against LGBT, and will work to undermine the normative force of the Charter and human rights. Two prominent human rights lawyers called TWU 'bigoted' in the national press for espousing the religious view that homosexuality is a sin.[44] Although the Supreme Court of Canada rejected this characterisation in the BC Teachers case, the objectors to TWU's law school have built their case on the assumption that faith-based exclusions that adversely impact members of LGBT communities amount to homophobic bigotry, though not apparently anti-Semitism or Islamophobia, despite the fact that the Covenant is no less exclusionary (and is possibly more so) towards Muslims, Jews, and indeed all non-Christians than it is towards members of LGBT communities.

[41] Convocation voted to reject the accreditation of TWU by a vote of 28 to 21 with one abstention, following two days of debate, which were webcast to the public and the profession. See 'Trinity Western University (TWU) Accreditation', www.lsuc.on.ca/twu/.

[42] Following an extensive debate on 25 April 2014, at which every member of the 21-member Council spoke, the members voted 10-9 in favour of the conditional approval. See 'Council votes for Option C in Trinity Western University law school decision', http://nsbs.org/news/2014/04/council-votes-option-c-trinity-western-university-law-school-decision.

[43] On 31 October 2014, the BC Benchers decided not to approve a proposed law school at TWU after administering a referendum among BC lawyers on the issue. See 'Trinity Western University: proposed law school' (28 August 2015) http://www.lawsociety.bc.ca/page.cfm?cid=3912.

[44] Clayton Ruby and Gerald Chan, 'A law school at Trinity Western University will impose a queer quota', *The National Post* (Toronto, 29 July 2013) http://news.nationalpost.com/full-comment/clayton-ruby-and-gerald-chan-a-law-school-at-trinity-western-university-will-impose-a-queer-quota.

The second claim against TWU relates to concerns that a self-selected association of faith adherents within a private institution should be permitted to perform the important function of gatekeeping to the legal profession while showing contempt for basic tenets of Canadian public law.[45] Moreover, even if private religious institutions are not bound by the Charter and anti-discrimination statutes the law societies may owe a duty to promote human rights when exercising statutory authority to determine who is ultimately permitted to join the legal profession. In other words, if a law school excludes members of equality-seeking groups, law societies may be concerned about appearing to condone or even comply with exclusionary practices.

The courts have now split in two completely different directions on these questions. In a January 2015 judgment,[46] a judge of the Nova Scotia Supreme Court determined that the Barristers' Society (NSBS) decision to condition the licensure of TWU graduates on the university changing its admission policy was improper and exceeded its authority. Several months later, in a July 2015 decision, a three-member panel of the Ontario Divisional Court reached the opposite conclusion in a review of the LSUC's decision not to recognise TWU degrees for licensing in Ontario. The court ruled that TWU's community covenant would erect barriers for potential LGBT and women lawyers in the province.[47] The divergence in the decisions stems from their respective focus in identifying the relevant issue of moral/legal concern: in Nova Scotia, the court was concerned with the abuse of administrative power to exclude a group of minority Christian lawyers exercising constitutional rights; in Ontario, the court was concerned with the abuse of religious freedom to exclude members of historically disadvantaged LGBT communities from attending religious institutions. The cases are ongoing, and the issue will no doubt require further appeal(s).

VII. A Faint Prayer: Advancing Harmony and Equality (at the Same Time)

Implicit to TWU's assertion that the public values of freedom and equality justify TWU's accreditation was an assumption that law societies have a duty to accommodate evangelical Christians, *as a normative community*, within the

[45] See Heather Gardiner, 'Law students oppose TWU law school bid', *Canadian Lawyer Magazine* (Toronto 21 March 2013) www.canadianlawyermag.com/legalfeeds/1376/law-students-oppose-twu-law-school-bid.html.

[46] *Trinity Western University v Nova Scotia Barristers' Society* [2015] NSSC 100.

[47] *Trinity Western University v Law Society of Upper Canada* (2015) ONSC 4250 (Div Ct) [10] (reaching the conclusion that if the LSUC were to recognise a TWU degree for accreditation purposes in Ontario, this could amount to discrimination because of TWU's effective exclusion of LGBT students through its discriminatory admissions policy; ie, the LSUC would effectively be creating additional barriers to entry for prospective LGBT members of the profession).

profession. By this logic, opening a law school at TWU would create space for evangelical Christians to thrive in a law school environment uniquely tailored for their community's needs. By definition, such an institution would exist not for the general public, but for the benefit of a self-identified segment of the population. The Nova Scotia court heard evidence from a number of witnesses and concluded that for evangelical Christians,

> religious faith governs every aspect of their lives. When they study law, whether at a Christian law school or elsewhere, they are studying law first as Christians ... They gain spiritual strength from communing in that way. They seek out opportunities to do that. Being part of institutions that are defined as Christian in character is not an insignificant part of who they are.[48]

A community's desire to have a private institution to serve their unique faith-based needs seems logical enough. However, it falls into peril when it runs up against a competing claim. In the TWU case, the concern is that enhancing equality for the group (evangelical Christians) necessarily creates barriers for others (LGBT, and others). It is not implicitly clear that the connection between one group's desire to be included in the profession and another group's experience with exclusion from the profession are necessarily related. But in the Ontario Divisional Court decision, it appears that the discriminatory treatment of LGBT by a religious group provided greater justification for the state to discriminate against the religious group.[49]

Constitutional law does not generally apply substantively to the opinions and actions of religious institutions.[50] Under statutory human rights, 'special interest organisations' are exempted from prohibitions on discrimination.[51] This is not just a shield from review; it is also a substantive right without which it would be near impossible for members of protected groups to effectively identify, organise and commune with one another. This begs the question, if the reason for the discriminatory treatment of a religious group is based on a lawful exclusion that is itself the exercise of substantive human rights, should the law societies not defer to the statutory exemption when exercising their statutory powers?

It has become fashionable to exaggerate religion as a source of danger and diminish its potential as a source of good.[52] When the reaction to the TWU proposal

[48] ibid [230]. The Ontario Court heard similar evidence and reached the conclusion that, while 'Evangelical Christians are a religious subculture in Canada', there was no evidence of a religious obligation to 'study at a law school that only permits the presence of evangelical Christian beliefs and only permits the attendance of those persons who commit to those beliefs'. See *TWU v LSUC* (n 47) [10], [78].

[49] See *TWU v LSUC* (n 47) [115]–[119] (balancing between the interests of LGBT and women, who are excluded from TWU and the interests of TWU itself).

[50] See *Reference re Same-Sex Marriage*, [2004] 3 SCR 698 [58]–[59] (clarifying that religious officials would not be compelled to perform same-sex marriages and that religious institutions cannot be forced to provide same-sex services notwithstanding the conclusion of the Court).

[51] See Ontario *Human Rights Code* s 18.

[52] See generally Sam Harris, *The End of Faith: Religion, Terror, and the Future of Reason* (New York, WW Norton, 2004); Richard Dawkins, *The God Delusion* (London, Bantam Press, 2006); Daniel

followed that predictable pattern,[53] it was not manifestly clear why there was such a rush to condemn the religious law school. For TWU's staunchest defenders, the impulse to negativity was evidence of anti-Christian bigotry and stereotyping.[54] A more fair-minded approach to TWU's proposal might have also considered the body of scholarship documenting the positive impact of religious law schools in the United States, where many have flourished for decades. Newman cites evidence that religious law schools have been found to increase the accessibility of legal education to students who may not fit in well at other law schools. Research also shows that Christian and Jewish law schools offer a surprising diversity of approaches to integrating religion in the life, classroom and administration of different schools.[55] A further benefit of religious law schools is that they open up the possibility of engagement with new forms of legal scholarship. Faith-based legal scholars can bring unique perspectives that enrich scholarly debates.[56] Faith-based scholars can also offer a distinctive, values-based engagement with legal thought that secular scholars have often struggled to do.[57] They can create bridges for exchanges with secular scholars. They also offer the possibility for intra-religious dialogue, providing a site for valuable dialogues between different types of religious scholars and lawyers, including those who are not necessarily faith directed (modes 1–3 in the Levinson taxonomy).

At a certain level, one might have expected the proposal for a new kind of law school to be welcomed within the Canadian legal academy. An uncompromised spirit of academic freedom and intellectual curiosity would relish the possibility of incubating innovative forms of teaching and scholarship regardless of whether all of its content or spirit have universal appeal. It appears counter-intuitive that an academic community that declares commitments to values of diversity and pluralism would reject out of hand the possibility of inclusion for an evangelical take on legal education. Yet, in a series of measures, the Canadian Council of Law Deans acted to thwart the possibility that TWU would ever become a full member of the small community of Canadian law schools.[58] The Council's

Dennett, *Breaking the Spell: Religion as a Natural Phenomenon* (New York, Penguin Books, 2006); Christopher Hitchens, *God Is Not Great: How Religion Poisons Everything* (New York, Hachette Book Group, 2007).

[53] See Elaine Craig, 'The Case for the Federation of Law Societies Rejecting Trinity Western University's Proposed Law School Program' (2013) 25 *Canadian Journal of Women and the Law* 148.

[54] Emma Teitel, 'The false debate over Trinity Western' *Maclean's* (Toronto, 30 April 2014) www.macleans.ca/authors/emma-teitel/the-false-debate-over-trinity-western/ ('TWU president Bob Kuhn has so far framed the case against accreditation as anti-Christian bigotry').

[55] Newman (n 18) 2 (noting that Cardozo law school at Yeshiva University creates a Jewish environment that accommodates Orthodox and observant students, while not increasing the content of Jewish law in the curriculum).

[56] ibid 2–3 (citing evidence of positive value in scholarly work that brings to bear faith-based perspectives).

[57] See ibid 3 (and the sources he cites).

[58] Dwight Newman, 'The desperate campaign to thwart a Christian law school' *The National Post* (Toronto, 21 January 2014) http://news.nationalpost.com/full-comment/dwight-newman-the-desperate-campaign-to-thwart-a-christian-law-school ('Desperate campaign').

discomfort with TWU's position on LGBT inclusion would be uncontroversial if TWU were a public institution bound by the Charter. However, for a private university that is established as a religious institution, equality principles may require more carefully tailored means than an outright ban to achieve any pressing objective of distancing the public actors from otherwise discriminatory practices within the university. The Ontario Divisional Court ruling concluded that, although the LSUC breached TWU's freedom of religion, it was justifiable because any harm was negligible in comparison to the harm of TWU's exclusion of aspiring LGBT lawyers.

It is widely accepted that creating 'safe spaces' is an important tool for promoting equality. If a private, black-focused law school in Canada were proposed it would likely (hopefully) be welcomed broadly.[59] That is because, among other things, it would offer a space where a self-identified community of teachers, scholars and students who have a sense of shared history, identity and destiny, could work and learn together in a self-empowered setting. Many of the views propagated in the law school may not be of interest or enjoy support within the legal academy or in the profession. The school's particular pedagogical assumptions and frameworks may even oppose settled legal doctrine. This is precisely the point of ensuring spaces for minority perspectives to be cultivated, ideally for the benefit of both minority community members and broader academic inquiry and law reform. If there is a case for treating any differently the affirmative aspirations of groups protected by religious equality as compared to those of racial equality, it has not been made. Absent evidence-based conclusions about actual harm caused by private religious education, negative assumptions deserve to be treated suspiciously, especially where they confirm a stereotype.

VIII. Integrity: Towards an Undivided Self

It is worth returning to the question of how to assess the role of the faith-driven lawyer in professional life. A reasonable approach would concern itself not with evaluating the merits of the lawyer's ethical motivations or beliefs, but rather with tracking the substantive consequence produced by the lawyer's conduct. This does not mean that the moral merit of a lawyer's conduct is absent or purely subjectively determined. It does suggest that assisting lawyers with different moral outlooks to find common cause is as valuable as enforcing a set of universally held public values. Consider by way of example the legal aid clinic setting. This environment may attract a lawyer who is personally and professionally motivated by an anti-poverty ethos and who determines to make a career in the service of that

[59] In fact, there has already been an initiative to establish an Inuit-focused law school in the north. See www.akitsiraq.ca. Similarly, a women's law school or LGBT law school likely could be justified on equality principles.

secular mission. The same job may attract a faith-driven lawyer who is motivated by a religious duty to perform charity and expects to view her job as 'God's work'. From a legal ethics perspective, the two are not differently situated in any meaningful way. They both seek work that will enable them to play a particular kind of lawyer role (a 'zealous advocate' for the poor), which are similarly infused with moral commitments, even if the particular motivation differs. The question for religious and secular poverty lawyers alike is this: how successful are you at building a practice (or obtaining employment) in a context in which personal-professional moral conflict is less likely to occur?

Perhaps we can call this an aspiration towards an ethic of sustainable integrity. Integrity is the primary and governing characteristic of professionalism, as provided in the Federation of Law Societies of Canada's Model Code.[60] Yet, the Model Code does not actually define integrity. The dictionary defines it as the quality of being honest, fair and incorruptible as well as the state of being complete, undivided and whole.[61] This definition appears to include both expectations around behaviour (fair and honest dealings) and assurances about a personal moral framework (completeness, wholeness). For many religious lawyers, faith is an integral part of what makes them whole and complete.

Integrity is usually measured on the basis of the lawyer's record of past conduct from which one's general reputation is earned. Also, part of the meaning of integrity is how one is perceived by others, in moral terms. *Is she a good person? Is he trustworthy?* Perhaps integrity can therefore be measured not only in moral terms, but also in pragmatic terms. For instance, by the degree to which the lawyer plans and develops practices and habits designed to proactively produce the kind of professional integrity required by an ethical practitioner. It might also mean structuring law practice not only to avoid harm and demonstrate candour and honesty, but also to avoid creating or entering situations that attract a risk of harm or nurturing conditions that incentivise dishonesty.

This approach is called sustainable because the point is not just to demonstrate integrity when facing challenges or resolving a crisis. Rather, it seeks to minimise risk, interpersonal conflict and personal moral strife by getting ahead of any tension that may arise between loyal advocacy and personal morality in the representation of a client. Recall for a moment our example of the secular and religious poverty lawyer, mentioned above, who made professional decisions based on personal conscience in the hope of finding in the legal clinic the kind of practice that satisfies their moral baselines. These are good examples of working towards individual sustainable professional integrity. Sustainable integrity envisages creating conditions that not only ensure ethical compliance, but which also promote personal ethical peace and harmony. Individuals who join a profession of public importance, such as the legal profession, understand that they must act

[60] Model Code (n 4) s 2.

[61] 'Integrity' (Merriam-Webster Definition) www.merriam-webster.com/dictionary/integrity.

positively to ensure ethical conduct. Sustainable integrity is a valuable instrument for religious lawyers to practise mindfully, with diligence, care, introspection, prudence and humility. By avoiding conflict through careful practice management, religious lawyers should aim to establish not only that their religion poses no threat to their professional conduct, but also that it can strengthen their professional integrity. In doing so, they can develop a valuable model of ethical lawyering for the religious and non-religious alike.

IX. Conclusion

For the person of faith, the idea of morality rooted in God or the supernatural, coupled with the absence of an explicit moral code in prescribed law, provides an occasion to marry the normative with the positive in the lawyer's understanding of law and law practice. The law does not demand that a lawyer proclaim any particular faith, but also does not require a muting of personal religious conviction. Thus, for the religious lawyer, faith does not necessarily present a crisis or a threat to professionalism. In fact, it can offer the possibility of a meaningful and self-fulfilling professional life that allows lawyers to serve clients in ways that accord with their faith-based commitments. Self-fulfilment is a not a goal unique to the religious lawyer. The desire to harmonise what motivates one's desire to practice law with what and how one practises law must be a near universal goal.

It may be too much to expect that the prospect of a religious law school in Canada would contribute constructively to advancing the cause of diversity and pluralism, or that it would create excitement about new research and scholarship directions. If TWU were to plan a curriculum that is boldly experiential and otherwise pedagogically innovative and sound, it would be difficult to discredit, notwithstanding the controversial covenant. Indeed, if faith-based religious educators can demonstrate through the use of both secular and religious analytical and discursive modes how to engage across difference and to communicate between religious and secular norms in mutually beneficially ways, they will not only prove their harshest critics wrong, they just may establish themselves as trailblazers in Canadian legal education.

4

Managing and Imagining Religion in Canada from the Top and the Bottom: 15 Years After

PAUL BRAMADAT

I. Introduction

In this chapter I reflect on what I have learned during a little over 15 years of observing and working with opinion-makers struggling to engage meaningfully with religion in their work. A decade and a half ending in October 2015 with the electoral victory of the Liberal Party of Canada, were rather action-packed years in both religion and politics, largely due to the arguably epoch-making events of 9/11 in 2001. These were a tumultuous 15 years during which some of the events took place not just on formal political stages, but also on what we might call informal discursive stages. Those engaged in these discussions employed distinctive approaches to religion. The two sections below reveal differences between what we might consider 'top-down' versus 'bottom-up' management of tensions between religious communities and ostensibly secular institutions. By top-down, I have in mind those forms of management, interaction, or 'governmentality' that putatively directly reflect the interests of a particular government department, political party or leader, whereas bottom-up forms of management are more diffuse and are subject to less control from a single (state or private) entity. The top-down approach evident in the cases concerning radicalisation seems to reflect a view of religion that is more liberal and inclusive; this might surprise people concerned with the tendency among federal and provincial political leaders to 'securitise' some ethnic and religious groups.[1] The bottom-up case study concerning the law school proposed by Trinity Western University indicates that it would be naïve to assume that even apparently well-intended public or professional discursive processes will necessarily produce creative results or will be carried out in ways

[1] Paul Bramadat and Lorne Dawson (eds), *Religious Radicalization and Securitization in Canada and Beyond* (Toronto, University of Toronto Press, 2014).

that comport well with a certain kind of open secularism or a commitment to equality one finds in the Charter.[2]

I should observe at the outset that the outcomes of the two approaches or styles of engaging difficult religious claims and issues are not necessarily indicative of consistent trends in either kinds of approach. That is, it is not the case that relatively direct (top-down) governmental interactions with religion always reflect a significant level of openness and tolerance.[3] Nor is it the case that the indirect public management of religion will necessarily be less inclusive.[4] Moreover, my primary interest in this chapter is to reflect critically on the nature and direction of influence (top-down, as opposed to bottom-up); I am less intrinsically concerned with the subject matter itself (religious radicalisation as opposed to the religious management of human sexuality).[5] While the cases in question might interest those curious about the differences between top-down and bottom-up approaches to the management of religion (especially those forms of Christianity and Islam deemed to be problems for a liberal society), the conclusions I draw may seem counter-intuitive to some readers.

II. Top-Down: Working with the State

By way of a preamble to the first set of cases, I would like to propose that inasmuch as Canadians think about their government(s) at all, most assume both that governments act in coherent, systematic ways, and that governments govern those not in government. This is not the place for a full discussion of these claims, though

[2] Lori Beaman, 'The Missing Link: Tolerance, Accommodation and … Equality' (2012) 9 *Canadian Diversity* 16; Lori Beaman, 'Deep Equality: Moving Beyond Tolerance and Accommodation' (2012) *Impetus Magazine*. www.luthercollege.edu/university/academics/impetus/winter-2012-impetus/deep-equality-moving-beyond-tolerance-and-accommodation.

[3] This will be evident to observers of the government's efforts to ban women from wearing the hijab at citizenship ceremonies. Jason Kenny, the Minister of Citizenship and Immigration had instituted this ban in 2011, but it was determined to be in violation of the Charter. In March 2015, Stephen Harper vowed to appeal the court's decision. See *Ishaq v Canada (Minister of Citizenship and Immigration)* 2015 FC 156. See also Douglas Quan, 'Harper Appeals Court Ruling that Struck Down Ban on Wearing Niqab During Citizenship Oath' *National Post* (Toronto, 9 March 2015) www.news.nationalpost.com/news/canada/harper-appeals-court-ruling-that-struck-down-ban-on-wearing-niqab-during-citizenship-oath.

[4] This is clear from the broad distaste for anti-Semitism that has become entrenched in Canadian public life as a result of what might be considered bottom-up consensus-building and historical changes. While anti-Semitism thrives on the Internet and in the minds of some Canadians (see eg, 'Information Handout on Religion, Racism, Intergroup Relations and Integration Results' (Canadian Race Relations Foundation, April 2014) www.crr.ca/en/news-a-events/404-articles/24974-january-2014-survey), it is anathema in public and political discourse, whereas it was once (relatively) uncontroversial for social leaders to utter anti-Semitic claims. See Irving M Abella, *A Coat of Many Colours: Two Centuries of Jewish Life in Canada* (Toronto, University of Toronto Press, 1990).

[5] I have used the sociological 'ideal types' of top-down and bottom-up, but neither context is entirely horizontal or vertical. Nonetheless, there is value in considering the different norms of expression and powers of coercion that characterise each setting.

I suspect they reflect broad public assumptions. Although the wisdom of concentrating power in the Prime Minister's Office over time has been debated at length,[6] the following examples suggest that departments within the government sometimes operate at cross-purposes to one another and in a manner that seems out of keeping with the image the government is trying to promote. As such, we need to pay attention to the limitations of these widely held assumptions.

Consider the following scenarios that reflect this internal diversity and reveal 'the government's' complex interactions with religion, and scholars of religion. In 2007 I was contracted, along with Scott Wortley, a criminologist from the University of Toronto, to write a report on religion and youth radicalisation. Wortley and I determined that some members of religious minority communities did engage in discourse tilting in the direction of violence construed in religious terms. However, members of Christian groups also voiced what might be described as radicalised or proto-radicalised sentiments (regarding the illegitimate nature of the secular state, or the failings of one or another Canadian foreign policy). We concluded, not very surprisingly, both that further research was necessary and that the implications of our findings were limited since many racialised and radicalised groups by 2007–08 presumably knew they were being monitored by the state (and therefore would probably be less likely to be demonstrative about their convictions on-line), whereas Christian radicals (or radicals-in-waiting) might have more confidence in their on-line anonymity.

In this chapter I am interested not in elaborating on our quite modest findings[7] but rather in reflecting on a revealing comment made to me during the preliminary discussions I had with a number of senior officials of this department. As we were discussing the particulars of the contract—timeline, budget, partners, methodology—I sought clarification of the government's interest in this issue. One key person in these initial conversations replied:

> Okay, basically, we want you to write something that we can give to the right-wing members of the RCMP and CSIS when they are freaking out about Muslims and religious diversity. So, when they are nervous about minorities, we can take your study and plunk it down on their desk and say 'Here, read this'.

The colleague went on to say that many people in her department were worried by the way Canadian security agencies and other federal departments tended to frame Islam as particularly problematic. They were confident that they would be able to use the conclusions Wortley and I would reach to challenge the status quo approach to Muslims evident in other departments and agencies within the government. In other words, in addition to being of possible interest to the

[6] Michael Harris, *Party Of One: Stephen Harper and Canada's Radical Makeover* (Toronto, Penguin Random House, 2014); Donald Savoie, *Governing from the Centre: Concentration of Power in Canadian Politics* (Toronto, University of Toronto Press, 1999).

[7] Paul Bramadat and Scott Wortley, 'Religious Youth Radicalization in Canada' (2008) 6 *Canadian Diversity* 47.

broader academic and non-academic public, they wanted our study to alter the opinions of people in other areas of the government. In some sense this comment about the dual purpose of the research project crystalises insights I have received from colleagues in other government departments.

Of course I emphasised that Wortley and I were bound to follow the methodological and analytical norms of the academy, though I did speculate that their hunch—that we would find very limited evidence of Muslim, or for that matter, Christian, youth radicalisation on-line—was probably accurate. Important to note, here, is the underlying rather optimistic understanding of religion at work; religion was framed as something good Canadian multiculturalists should celebrate, as something that is essentially what insiders say it is: a benevolent force that only wreaks havoc when it has been 'hijacked' or otherwise distorted by non-religious actors. In other words, the project would be scholarly, but also part of what one might consider a larger liberal 'advocacy' agenda.

Contrast this to the approach at work when I was contracted to work with another colleague, the University of Waterloo sociologist of religion, Lorne Dawson. Just as in the previous case study, the diverse conclusions reached by the 13 authors in the book we produced are not of particular interest to me in this chapter.[8] Instead, I want to note that in the several months of discussions about the possibility of organising a major interdisciplinary research project on 'religious radicalisation and securitisation' the government representatives were enthusiastically supportive of our academic freedom. This openness continued even several months into the project when it became clear to everyone involved that several of the contributors[9] were likely to articulate strong criticisms of the Conservative government in their chapters. Although some might argue that the notion of 'religious violence' often obscures the real political and economic sources of religiously-justified mayhem,[10] members of our team and representatives of the government departments that supported the formation of our team, approached the phenomenon as a practical matter of significant concern for people interested in protecting public safety. We might call this a 'critical realist' position on religion and religious violence.

In these cases, one sees in particular the tension between 'advocacy' and 'critical realist' approaches to religion. In the first case described above, the department championed a form of research partially because they believe it is inherently

[8] See Bramadat and Dawson, *Religious Radicalization* (n 1). In *Religious Radicalization and Securitization in Canada and Beyond*, researchers grapple with the ways radicalisation might develop within particular communities and in particular social contexts. Our focus was on Canada, but France, the US, the UK, Japan and India were also considered. This project was funded by Public Safety Canada and Defence Research Development Canada.

[9] See chapters by Peter Beyer, Paul Bramadat, Uzma Jamil, and Edna Keeble in Bramadat and Dawson (n 1).

[10] William Cavanaugh, *The Myth of Religious Violence* (New York, Oxford University Press, 2009); *cf* Ian Reader, 'Beating a Path to Salvation' in Bramadat and Dawson (n 1).

worthwhile, and partially because they sought to correct what they perceive to be the excessively critical or suspicious attitudes, largely toward Islam, that are found in the wings of the state more obviously associated with security. In the second case, the departments—or at least the components of the departments with which Dawson and I worked on this project—championed a form of research both because they perceive it to be inherently worthwhile and because they acknowledge (wisely) that none of the other organs of the state will be able to address religious radicalisation and securitisation effectively in the absence of a sound research base.

I share these two cases not by way of criticising or exonerating 'the government' or any of the senior policy-makers with whom we worked on these projects. I offer an account of these scenarios strictly to provide some sense of the diversity of approaches one finds within the federal government—a form of diversity that both reflects and perhaps engenders the tensions that exist between different departments. Although Canada's Conservative government strove—as did its predecessors—to convey a singular image of itself to the public, in truth, there is no 'government' in the singular, unified sense. This is not a banal post-modern axiom, but rather an expression of the diversity one sees between (even otherwise unified) sectors of the same government.

These expressions of 'top-down' management of religious diversity occurred under the aegis of a Conservative federal government involved in violent overseas military operations, and deeply concerned about so-called 'home-grown' radicalisation, especially among Muslim youth. Although these concerns characterised the political operating conditions under which these two contractual arrangements were negotiated and carried out, the results in both cases were arguably supportive of a liberal, inclusive agenda. In theory, one might attribute these outcomes to the actions of atypical or rogue liberals operating stealthily in departments that answered to a Conservative government. However, these operatives also required, and received, the approval of their own supervisors to go ahead with the projects; moreover, although the government has a track record both of silencing researchers in other fields of practice[11] and of ignoring research it finds unpalatable,[12] it did not approach these projects in the same manner. So, while it is not the case that the government necessarily tolerates—not to mention funds—all forms of criticism of its policies, it also does not squelch all forms, either.

[11] Pallab Ghosh, 'Canadian Government is "Muzzling its Scientists"' *BBC News* (Vancouver, 17 February 2012) www.bbc.com/news/science-environment-16861468; Melissa Mancini, 'Science Cuts And Muzzling In Canada: How Conservatives Reshaped A Discipline' *Huffington Post Canada* (Toronto, 30 April 2013) www.huffingtonpost.ca/2013/04/30/science-cuts-muzzling-canada-conservatives_n_3112348.html.

[12] Jeffrey Simpson, 'Americans Get Tough on "Tough on Crime" Policy' *The Globe and Mail* (Toronto, 9 May 2015) www.theglobeandmail.com/globe-debate/americans-get-tough-on-tough-on-crime-policy/article24330216/.

III. Bottom-up: Trinity Western University: How, Why, When, and Whether to Say No

By the time this book is published, this case will have received even more attention by the Canadian courts. Here, I use the conversations we have witnessed thus far as an opportunity to assess the cut and thrust of public and professional discourse. In particular, I am interested in the public and political furore concerning the proposal by Trinity Western University (TWU) to establish a law school, and both the subsequent refusal of the Law Society of Upper Canada (LSUC) in April 2014 to accredit graduates of TWU's proposed law programme in the province of Ontario, and the October 2014 decision of the Law Society of British Columbia (LSBC) to reject the law school.[13] TWU's programme had previously received the approval of the Federation of Law Societies of Canada's Approval Committee and the government of British Columbia, but a complex series of more or less simultaneous public and professional debates in British Columbia, Ontario, and Nova Scotia resulted in formal rejections of the law school. In December 2014, TWU's lawyers submitted to the Supreme Court of British Columbia a notice of civil claim against the LSBC. In July 2015 the Ontario Divisional Court upheld the LSUC's earlier decision.[14] If TWU's legal team is successful in an appeal to the Supreme Court of Canada (since they are likely to seek a hearing), the negative assessment of the law societies may well be overturned. Nonetheless, the university's request to launch a law program has been rejected by enough peers—with the LSUC and BCLS representing the largest 'markets' for English-speaking lawyers—to make it, at least for now, seem to have a rather unlikely future. Although the situation is in flux, the general observations I wish to make below remain relevant to the argument I am advancing about top-down as opposed to bottom-up deliberations.[15]

[13] For the LSUC announcement, see 'Treasurer's Statement Regarding Vote on TWU Law School' (*Law Society of Upper Canada*, 10 April 2014) www.lsuc.on.ca/newsarchives.aspx?id=2147485737&cid=2147498273. For the LSBC announcement, see 'Proposed TWU Law School Not Approved for Law Society's Admission Program' (Law Society of British Columbia, 31 October 2014) www.lawsociety.bc.ca/page.cfm?cid=3997&t=Proposed-TWU-law-school-not-approved-for-Law-Society%E2%80%99s-admission-program.

[14] See *Trinity Western University v Law Society of Upper Canada* 2015 ONSC 4250, 126 OR (3d) 1.

[15] As it happens, in 2015 the Attorney General of Canada entered the debate. This is an interesting intrusion of a vertical juridical discourse into legal and professional discourses that had so far been more horizontal (at least at the level of the Ontario and British Columbia law societies' debates). The Attorney General's factum contended: 'While discrimination on prohibited grounds in the practice of law in Ontario should not be tolerated, the LSUC went too far and issued a disproportionately broad remedy to not accredit the TWU Law School that was unnecessary in the circumstances. Instances of discrimination on a prohibited ground can be effectively dealt with by the LSUC on an individual basis without the need to infringe an entire group's freedom of religion'. *Trinity Western University v Law Society of Upper Canada* 2015 ONSC 4250, 126 OR (3d) 1 (Factum of the Intervener). Given that the appeal against the LSUC concerns a professional association under the aegis of provincial legislation, it is unusual for the federal government to involve itself in this manner, and at this stage of the deliberations.

The core dilemma for those opposed to the law school is the fact that all students at TWU must, as part of their admissions process, agree to a 'community covenant' that (among other things) commits them to abstaining from 'sexual intimacy that violates the sacredness of marriage between a man and a woman'; moreover, under a subheading of 'Healthy Sexuality', prospective applicants read that according to the covenant, 'sexual intimacy is reserved for marriage between one man and one woman'.[16] These moral assertions may not distinguish TWU from other evangelical or fundamentalist Protestant contexts, but many detractors contended that the covenant: a) discriminates against individuals engaged in lawful sexual activities, b) is not in keeping with the ostensibly secular professional standards governing other law programmes and legal societies in Canada, and c) is contrary to the spirit and the letter of the Charter of Rights and Freedoms that protects same-sex relationships.

My interest here is not to defend a particular stance on the covenant, sexuality, or marriage.[17] Instead, I am interested in determining whether any lessons can be learned from the diffuse debates that have taken place with regard to TWU's proposal. Arguably, the professional and public discourse around the debates has demonstrated problematic understandings of religion, religious convictions, religious documents (such as covenants), and religious communities that are emblematic of relatively 'bottom-up' debates involving religion; in this sense, we may learn similar things from these deliberations that we learned from the debates that occurred with respect to the prospect of a Shariah-based arbitration system in Ontario,[18] a context I discuss below. My mixed feelings about these problematic features grew out of lengthy and productive conversations with lawyers associated with both sides of the matter, a special debate held at the Centre for Studies in Religion and Society at the University of Victoria (at which a number of scholars working on issues related to the case were asked to share their perspectives) in the summer of 2014, and my observations of the debates I followed among lawyers and within public discourse.

Although a number of different arguments were presented on both sides of the debate, and indeed although the LSUC vote of 28-21 in favour of rejecting TWU's proposed law school suggests a significant minority of Benchers supported TWU's proposal, there arguably emerged in both the LSUC context and in the broader society a mostly negative consensus among academic, political, and

[16] See Trinity Western University, 'Community Covenant Agreement', http://twu.ca/studenthandbook/twu-community-covenant-agreement.pdf. TWU's proposed law school already has its own webpage. See Trinity Western University, 'Proposed School Of Law', www.twu.ca/academics/school-of-law/.

[17] In the interest of full disclosure, I do not embrace the views of sexuality the covenant appears to enshrine. Indeed, for several years before and after same-sex weddings became legal (2005), I used to perform such rituals for lesbian and gay friends, students, and colleagues. So, I have some personal commitments on this issue that make it unlikely that I would express misgivings about the political, legal, and public debates occurring around TWU's proposed law school.

[18] Anna C Korteweg and Jennifer A Selby (eds), *Debating Sharia: Islam, Gender Politics and Family Law Arbitration* (Toronto, University of Toronto Press, 2012).

public figures. The consensus was certainly not homogenous: some disagreed with TWU's proposal because they feel the covenant is homophobic; some felt the proposal could not be accepted because it violates the Charter; some felt the law school would violate the inherently or implicitly secular nature of Canadian law schools; some felt that regardless of their own feelings about same-sex relationships, the mandatory covenant is a private matter for TWU to manage.

Space does not permit a thorough exposition of the arguments made for and against TWU's proposal, but selected comments on both sides should capture the key claims, and the tone. In the LSUC's quite sober statement on their decision, the treasurer wrote: 'The decision was a difficult one. It was arrived at carefully and respectfully, by a process that began in January of this year, and has been transparent, open, and fair'.[19] Jeremy Webber, Dean of Law at the University of Victoria commented:

> Indeed, one can't help wondering if the special antipathy that exists to same-sex relations … is as much a product of social prejudice as of religious injunction. If so, does it deserve the level of respect that is being requested? In the end, TWU is asking that the law societies acknowledge a program that bars validly married gay and lesbian people from its classes simply because of their sexual orientation. [I]f it wants public recognition for its law degree, it cannot pursue a discriminatory admissions policy. Accreditation must be conditional either on the offending provisions being removed, or on TWU making its covenant optional, not compulsory.[20]

The tone and content of other legal critics were more passionate. Frances Mahon, of the Out On Bay Street group, commented that 'For me, as a gay person and as a lawyer working on this case, the decision of the Law Society [of Upper Canada] is incredibly important. It suggests to me they chose to be on the right side of history'.[21] LSUC Bencher Howard Goldblatt contended that 'I cannot accept that it's in the public interest to accredit a law school that wants to control its students in the bedroom', while Bencher Julian Falconer personalised the rhetoric by saying: 'To my 13 year old son, who will not read these transcripts today, but [will] five or 10 years from now, I say to him, "I will do the right thing, I will vote against accrediting TWU"'.[22]

By contrast, the TWU insider's interpretation of the professional and public consensus that developed around the proposal is captured well in Janet Epp Buckingham's comments:

> I really felt that the lawyers [of the LSUC] were sitting in judgement of our religious beliefs and then deciding that our graduates were unworthy to practice law in the

[19] 'Treasurer's Statement' (n 13).

[20] Jeremy Webber, 'Opinion: Religion vs Equality: Issue of Accreditation of TWU's Law Program is Complicated' *Vancouver Sun* (Vancouver, 8 April 2014) www.vancouversun.com/life/Opinion+Religion+equality/9715430/story.html#sthash.6SxJC75Z.dpuf.

[21] Jacques Gallant, 'Barring Evangelical Law School's Graduates "Not Reasonable", Argues Federal Government' *The Star* (Toronto, 14 May 2015) www.thestar.com/news/gta/2015/05/14/barring-evangelical-law-schools-graduates-not-reasonable-argues-federal-government.html.

[22] Yamri Taddese, 'LSUC Says No to TWU Law School' (*Canadian Lawyer* and *Law Times*, 24 April 2014) www.canadianlawyermag.com/legalfeeds/2056/lsuc-says-no-to-twu-law-school.html.

> province of Ontario … We really felt that … [they were] wishing to impose a different view of what our community covenant should be or what the sexual practices within our community should be … We really felt that the lawyers … dealt with this from an emotive and very personal perspective of their own interpretation of sexual morality and we didn't feel that that was appropriate.[23]

Chris Selley of the *National Post* remarked: 'Most of the opposition to TWU Law isn't based on legal technicalities, but precisely on the notion of "sending a message". And to the extent the popular debate does include questions of law, most interveners seem to take it as read—as Judge Campbell puts it—that "equality rights have … jumped the queue to now trump religious freedom"'.[24] The Evangelical Fellowship of Canada asserted that: '[L]aw societies that have voted not to accept TWU law graduates have overstepped their mandates … such decisions violate the religious freedom of TWU and its graduates'.[25] Bruce Clemenger, the EFC's President, argued that:

> The Canadian Charter of Rights and Freedoms does not apply to TWU since it is a private institution. However the Charter, which protects individuals and groups from the state, does apply to governmental or quasi-governmental bodies like the [Nova Scotia Bar Society, which voted to reject TWU's proposal]. Government bodies cannot impose beliefs nor can they coerce private institutions to conform to the beliefs of others about sexuality and marriage.[26]

I have no interest in persuading readers that one or another outcome of these votes is preferable; moreover, my expertise and interest are not in the procedural particularities governing the LSUC and LSBC processes. However, whenever one sees a 'pile-on' effect in professional or public discourse, and whenever one hears responses such as Epp Buckingham's (in which the word feel/felt was used in every sentence), we should reflect critically on what we might make of the consensus that did emerge, and of the often quite inflammatory rhetoric in which it was couched.[27] Although the debate occurred in the public and professional arenas and was not constrained by a hegemonic rhetoric of governmentality that would presumably characterise a formal government response, what do we witness in the more open contexts in which the TWU consensus was forged?

[23] See Sun News interview: www.youtube.com/watch?v=Umf8DnzHuGo.

[24] Chris Selley, 'Those Opposed to TWU Law are Being Awfully Picky about Which Civil Rights They Believe In' *National Post* (Toronto, 30 January 2015) www.news.nationalpost.com/full-comment/chris-selley-those-opposed-to-twu-law-are-being-awfully-picky-about-which-civil-rights-they-believe-in.

[25] The Evangelical Fellowship of Canada, 'Trinity Western University School of Law', www.evangelicalfellowship.ca/TWUlaw. Interestingly, in this respect, the 2014 EFC position echoes the argument made in the factum submitted by the Attorney General of Canada in May, 2015. See *Trinity Western University v Law Society of Upper Canada* 2015 ONSC 4250, 126 OR (3d) 1 (Factum of the Intervener).

[26] Bruce J Clemenger, 'Organizations Free to Maintain Religious Identity: Reflections *on TWU v. Nova Scotia Barristers' Society*' (Evangelical Fellowship of Canada, 4 February 2015) www.evangelicalfellowship.ca/NSBS2015.

[27] See Faisal Bhabha, 'Let TWU Have its Law School' (*Slaw*, 24 January 2014) www.slaw.ca/2014/01/24/let-twu-have-its-law-school/.

I would like to suggest that although the actors involved in the TWU debate both in the public and professional realms were, by definition, not constrained by a single authority (as one might expect or imagine in the scenarios described in the first section), the consensus that emerged among the majority of the lawyers who weighed in reflects what we might call a selectively closed secularism that precludes a more creative and open secularism that is, in general, a more characteristic feature of recent political and public discourse in Canada.[28]

The limits of space do not permit a full discussion of this matter in these pages, but the simplest way to exemplify some of the shortcomings in what became the dominant position is to identify three particularly problematic features.

A. Conceptual Ossification

We might begin by wondering about how well we understand the broader historical trajectory of which TWU is a part. Protestant fundamentalists often speak of their values and perspectives as though they reflect ancient biblical or in any event 'fundamental' norms and dogmas. However, in fact the fundamentalist movement (if indeed one wishes to place TWU in this category, rather than in the broader evangelical category) only coalesced in North America in the early decades of the twentieth century as a kind of protest against a society in which their views had become subject to the derision of urban educated liberals.[29] As a result of the influence of a great many forces—from higher biblical criticism to Marxism, Freudianism, secularisation, civil rights, and the increasing latitude of women—evangelicals and fundamentalists saw and responded to the deterioration of the conservative Protestant consensus, habitus, beliefs and practice that had been for so long intractably bound up with

[28] See Lori Beaman and Peter Beyer (eds), *Religion and Diversity in Canada* (Leiden, Brill, 2008); Paul Bramadat and David Seljak, 'Between Secularism and Post-Secularism: A Canadian Interregnum' in Bruce J Berman, Rajeev Bhargava and André Laliberté (eds), *Secular States and Religious Diversity* (Vancouver, UBC Press, 2013); Micheline Milot, 'Co-Vivendi: Religious Diversity in Canada' in Paul Bramadat and Matthias Koenig (eds), *International Migration and the Governance of Religious Diversity* (Montreal, McGill-Queen's University Press, 2009); Richard Moon (ed), *Law and Religious Pluralism in Canada* (Vancouver, UBC Press, 2008); Shauna Van Praagh, 'View from the Succah: Religion and Neighbourly Relations' in Richard Moon (ed), *Law and Religious Pluralism in Canada* (Vancouver, UBC Press, 2008). Open and closed forms of secularism were introduced into Canadian intellectual and public discourse mainly through the work of philosopher Charles Taylor (2007) and also the public engagement process that led to the so-called 'Bouchard-Taylor report' (2008) in which Taylor and sociologist Gérard Bouchard sought to provide both an overview of and some possible solutions to the dilemmas facing Quebec society. Both forms embrace many of the conventional values and norms of secularism, but open secularism promotes a more conciliatory approach to those with an interest in expressing their religious beliefs and living out their cherished practices in the public realm.

[29] Nancy T Ammerman, 'North American Protestant Fundamentalism' in Martin E Marty and R Scott Appleby (eds), *Fundamentalisms Observed* (Chicago, University of Chicago Press, 1991); Paul Bramadat, *The Church on the World's Turf: An Evangelical Group on a Secular Campus* (New York, Oxford University Press, 2000); George M Marsden, *Understanding Fundamentalism and Evangelicalism* (Grand Rapids, Wm B Eerdmans Publishing Co, 1991).

American society.[30] The point is that their movement and most of its respective literature—covenants and the like—are only about a hundred years old. The covenant is thus a product of a community that is using the decidedly contemporary theological, legal, moral, and human rights language available to it to articulate values and practices in the wake of the loss of whatever culture wars might have been waged in Canada over the last few decades.[31] The covenant might be understood in part as an elegy, a *cri de coeur* of a religious minority in a now hegemonic cultural context they experience as hostile to some of their deepest convictions.[32]

It is true that on this front, TWU's own rhetoric and that of the covenant's detractors converge: both act as though the covenant reflects timeless and non-negotiable features of a certain Christian identity. Nonetheless, it behoves us to consider:

a) the changes that have been made in Trinity's covenant since the university was founded in 1962; for example, their covenant once forbade alcohol and dancing;
b) the on-going conversations, often *sotto voce*, among the university's faculty members and students, many of whom question its content and would like to see it made voluntary;[33]
c) the fact that all non-married, non-heterosexual, non-monogamous sexual activity is problematised or forbidden (ie, premarital, extra-marital, polygamous, as well as same-sex sexual activities), so that the covenant has been written with a view toward protecting the university from charges of singling out LGBTQ relationships and communities for special exclusion; whether or not this covenant would survive a challenge based on the Charter or any

[30] Ammerman, 'North American Protestant Fundamentalism'; on parallel Canadian developments, see John G Stackhouse Jr, *Canadian Evangelicalism in the Twentieth Century: An Introduction to its Character* (Toronto, University of Toronto Press, 1993).

[31] See Jonathan Naymark, 'The Emergence of a Canadian Culture War' *Huffington Post Canada* (Toronto, 7 September 2011) www.huffingtonpost.ca/jonathan-naymark/canada-culture-funding_b_893119.html.

[32] Unfortunately for TWU, this particular minority is closely associated with historical power so in public (and political) discourse they do not resemble other minority communities in terms of their inherited privileges, habitus, or likely future social or economic outcomes.

[33] I offer just two illustrations of this internal conversation: Lindsey Mayhew, the editor of TWU's newspaper *Mars Hill* (and so presumably not a marginal member of the TWU community), wrote an opinion piece in *The Province* newspaper, with the title, 'TWU student says harmful covenant must evolve'. In this article, she wrote: 'In my experience at Trinity, gay students are entirely welcome, and so it baffles me why … the administration insists upon stubbornly keeping an antiquated contract as it is. The covenant is an ever-evolving document; students used to not even be allowed to dance on campus!' See Lindsey Mayhew, 'TWU Student Says Harmful Covenant Must Evolve' (*The Province*, 12 June 2014) www.blogs.theprovince.com/2014/06/12/lindsey-mayhew-twu-student-harmful-covenant-must-evolve/. As well, in February, 2015, TWU hosted 'Building Bridges: A Conversation on LGBT Christians and the Church' in which two gay Christians, Justin Lee and Ron Belgau engaged in a respectful conversation with one another and with audience members at a large public gathering held at TWU and opened by TWU's president. See: www.vimeo.com/121196444.

provincial human rights code, it is clearly written with these documents in mind.[34]

The covenant and its authors are products, rather than independent, of contemporary historical trends. This does not guarantee that the changes will be applauded by liberal or secular individuals, not to mention law societies; nor that the changes will occur as rapidly as the dominant society or law societies (or I) might wish. However, if one had to characterise the 'direction' of the changes that have been evidenced both at TWU and indeed in other evangelical organisations (such as the Inter-Varsity Christian Fellowship)[35] over the last several decades, one would have to say that they seem to be moving in a generally liberal direction (or at least away from any fundamentalist mooring). If the university's public and legal defence of their position has demonstrated intransigence, it is important to bear in mind Berger's observations about how appearing before the law, or becoming in that sense a subject of the law, has the tendency to 'induce fundamentalism' by establishing a discursive arena in which participants are—almost—required to present themselves in auto-caricatured manners.[36]

B. Beyond Yes vs No?

The simultaneous debates that occurred in public and professional arenas generally culminated in calls for a 'yes' or 'no' response to TWU's proposal. Of course, TWU also sought such a tidy confirmation. One possible alternative way to imagine how the conflict over TWU's law school might have developed (under different political and legal conditions) can be found in the public, political, media and legal maelstrom around the proposal of the Islamic Institute of Civil Justice in Ontario to offer Sharia-compliant family law tribunals. In response to that controversy, the former Ontario Attorney General, Marion Boyd, was asked by senior members of the Ontario government to study the issue(s) involved in this case and to make recommendations to the government. Her report (2004) was thorough and based on extensive consultations with stakeholders. She offered 46 recommendations to address the public and legal concerns she had heard during her research and public engagement process.[37]

[34] It is beyond the scope of this chapter to expand on these factors, but these would be the obvious directions in which a complete analysis of the TWU covenant controversy would move.

[35] Bramadat, *The Church on the World's Turf* (n 29).

[36] Benjamin L Berger, 'Inducing Fundamentalisms: Law as a Cultural Force in the Domain of Religion' (2012) 9 *Canadian Diversity* 25; *cf* Lourdes Peroni, 'The European Court of Human Rights and Intragroup Religious Diversity: A Critical Review' (2014) 89 *Chicago-Kent Law Review* 663.

[37] See Marion Boyd, 'Dispute Resolution in Family Law: Protecting Choice, Promoting Inclusion: Executive Summary' (December 2004), www.attorneygeneral.jus.gov.on.ca/english/about/pubs/boyd/executivesummary.pdf. This is not the place for a thorough analysis of this debate (see Korteweg and Selby, *Debating Sharia* (n 18)).

I mention this episode simply to illustrate that it was possible for Boyd, even in an extremely complex and politically sensitive case, to propose a 'yes, with provisos' response to this particular minority. However, after spending a tremendous amount of time and energy fulfilling her mandate the premier and his advisors determined (probably accurately) that the public was not in favour of allowing Muslims to use the 1991 Arbitration Act, even though Jewish and Christian groups had used this Act, without attracting much attention, for a decade. In response to this political mood, the government seized the opportunity to reject or massively constrain 'faith-based' arbitration. The point here is that Boyd's 'yes, with provisos' was transformed through the logic of political opportunism and public discourse into a rather blunt, and to some, quite alienating, 'absolutely not'. Of course, no doubt some Muslim women and men are currently making use of Sharia-informed formal and informal family legal practices, but without the state oversight or safeguards that might have been possible within her provisos.

The report's 'yes, with provisos' elicited both virulent Islamophobia as well as a rather smug form of closed secularism.[38] One wonders how a detailed set of provisos might have been received by TWU,[39] given the fact that the public participants in the debate had framed the covenant's supporters not as articulating a comprehensive moral vision that sought to safeguard evangelical community convictions against the more permissive practices and principles of the dominant society (which would be how TWU's supporters would explain their stance), but as violating basic moral intuitions and human rights discourses that are inviolable parts of all decent liberal democracies.

C. Honesty Makes the Best Policies

I have considered the fact that religion in this debate has been framed as a non-negotiable or static social force even though religion is no more a fixed or stable entity than is law. Moreover, I have suggested that this is a function of the way the interaction between religion and the law is usually understood both by legal actors and by religious communities themselves, as a competition in which there

[38] Bramadat and Seljak, 'Between Secularism and Post-Secularism' (n 28); Gérard Bouchard and Charles Taylor, *Building the Future: A Time for Reconciliati* on (Quebec, Commission de consultation sur les pratiques d'accomodement reliées aux différences culturelles, 2008); Anna Korteweg and Jennifer Selby, *Debating Sharia* (n 18).

[39] When the Nova Scotia Barristers' Society originally rejected TWU's proposed law school (April 2014), it did appear to propose something approaching a 'yes with provisos'. Unfortunately the proviso was that they alter the nature of the covenant, and so the proviso was deemed too extreme. Moreover, in January 2015 the NS Supreme Court ruled that the NSBS had no authority to deny accreditation. See *Trinity Western University v Nova Scotia Barristers' Society* 2015 NSSC 25, 381 DLR (4th) 296. See also See Sheema Khan, 'What York University Forgot: Gender Equality is Not Negotiable' *The Globe and Mail* (Toronto, 10 January 2014) www.theglobeandmail.com/globe-debate/what-york-university-forgot-gender-equality-is-not-negotiable/article16278726/.

will need to be a winner and a loser, and in which it is the duty of law to serve as a neutral manager of this determination.[40] This dominant understanding of both law (*qua* referee) and religion (*qua* stable producer of timeless beliefs and practices) not only leads to overly fixed views of religion,[41] but also insufficiently critical perspectives of our own institutions and history.

Consider some well-known deeply problematic examples. First, the implicit or explicit quotas that constrained the admission of Jews to universities—including law schools—in Canada are now fairly well known.[42] Over time these policies and norms were ultimately changed. Second, legal and medical discourses about homosexuality have improved dramatically over the decades, with homosexuality being transformed from a capital crime into an example of 'gross indecency' and then finally decriminalised in 1969 (but only removed from the *Diagnostic and Statistical Manual of Mental Disorders* in 1973). The treatment of and policies related to LGBTQ students and faculty in many universities have been markedly improved.[43] Some of these changes have just begun in the last few decades, and indeed some (such as changes in the protections offered to transgender individuals) have really only entered the public debate in earnest within the past few years. Finally, the shift from a race-based 'quota system' to a more neutral 'points system' as the means by which potential immigrants are assessed led to a sea change in Canadian society—but only took legal effect in the late 1960s.[44]

When lawyers join politicians and other members of the social elite to reject a code of sexual morality that the dominant society considers to be out of keeping with other professional societies, and that might exclude a very small number of LGBTQ applicants (who for some reason might wish to enter an academic environment they know in advance is not friendly to their sexual preferences), it would be best to bear in mind how recently Canada's major institutions—of medicine, law, higher education, government—formally espoused views of sexuality, physical ability, ethnicity, race, class, gender, and citizenship that now strike us as profoundly illiberal.

The social and political changes that have made our institutions more welcoming of members of minority communities occurred only after long debates within these institutions, legal challenges from outside of them, and parallel changes in the national and international cultural arenas made certain laws, policies, and practices seem intolerable to the dominant society. These institutions and

[40] Benjamin L Berger, 'Law's Religion: Rendering Culture' (2007) 45 *Osgoode Hall Law Journal* 277; Berger, 'Inducing Fundamentalisms' (n 36).

[41] Winnifred Fallers Sullivan, *The Impossibility of Religious Freedom* (Princeton, Princeton University Press, 2007).

[42] Gerald Tulchinsky, *Canada's Jews: A People's Journey* (Toronto, University of Toronto Press, 2008).

[43] Given the evidence of surveillance of members of the LGBTQ community until very recently, some might say that true equality is still in the future. See Gary Kinsman and Patrizia Gentile, *The Canadian War on Queers: National Security as Sexual Regulation* (Vancouver, UBC Press, 2009).

[44] Ninette Kelley and Michael Trebilcock, *The Making of the Mosaic: A History of Canadian Immigration Policy* (Toronto, University of Toronto Press, 2010).

government departments were permitted to provide their respective services in the midst of their own transformations. In other words, even when their serious shortcomings were obvious to many people within them, and even when they ran afoul of the emergent or established powers, they were allowed their continued existence as an instance of 'yes, with provisos'.[45] The argument for such leniency (with provisos, of course) would not need to be rooted in Charter-derived rights to contravene this or that public interest, but rather possibly in a sense of what approach is most likely to lead to lasting forms of social change.

One might well observe that there were no other options but to employ a 'yes, with provisos' approach with, for example, our medical schools, immigration regime, or law schools, since there were no alternative service providers available once the proverbial tide (on, say, same-sex marriage or racial quotas) had turned. However, these changes did not occur even within these institutions—and even within similar examples of the same category of institutions (say, all hospitals)—all at once. Across our society the progressive drift in our institutions has been discontinuous, or perhaps segmented. In some cases—some religiously affiliated hospitals, for example—religious principles and policies continue to exist awkwardly alongside of secular ones, even when the state provides the funding, legitimation, and regulation of the institution. In other arenas, we tolerate discriminatory laws and policies (eg, section 93, the constitutional guarantee of state funding (only) for Roman Catholic schools in Ontario) largely because many people have become used to them and the labour and political costs involved in changing the constitution are deemed to be too severe.

The list of arrangements by which we permit some institutions, or provinces, to act in discriminatory ways may be shrinking, but remains long; this fact should humble us. The situation on the ground is both mixed and in motion, and it is demonstrably not the case that in order for a new institution to be allowed by the state and professional organisations to provide a social good it is self-evident that it must conform immediately to the norms that have imperfectly shaped our institutions over many decades, or else liberal society can 'absolutely not' support the proposal. In practice, the expressions of discrimination and injustice that attract attention are not always those that harm the most people,[46] just as political shifts are often out of keeping with empirical reality (eg, the 'get tough on crime' agenda, in a society in which crime rates are dropping). However, such episodes are revealing indictors, nonetheless, of the nightmare scenarios that plague us as individuals and societies. If federal and provincial governments,

[45] Exactly what sorts of 'provisos' might have been attached to a 'yes' in this case would need to be determined with the same kind of care that Marion Boyd demonstrated in her study.

[46] Consider the controversy that erupted in 2014 over a York University student's request to be exempted from an in-person seminar component of an on-line course due to religious convictions prohibiting casual gender mixing. See Sheema Khan, 'What York University Forgot: Gender Equality is Not Negotiable' *The Globe and Mail* (Toronto, 10 January 2014) www.theglobeandmail.com/globe-debate/what-york-university-forgot-gender-equality-is-not-negotiable/article16278726/.

lawyers, scholars, journalists, activists, or other members of civil society adopted the same tenacious approach to all entrenched forms of discrimination as many have toward TWU's covenant, a wholly different (and perhaps much improved) society would emerge. In reality, although social, political and legal processes are underway to change some or many of the above examples (section 93, etc.), these processes are slow, discontinuous, and often invisible.

Why do some proposals from some minority communities receive more attention or generate more negative consensus than others?[47] Why do some principles inspire urgent debates and yes-or-no decisions, whereas others are thought to require lengthy deliberations and mutual patience? Surely many lawyers and other participants in the broader debate made their decisions on the basis of sound and sincere legal and moral reasoning, perhaps out of opposition to any form of discrimination, or out of solidarity with sexual minorities. Nonetheless, it is worthwhile to reflect upon additional forces at work behind the psychological or social scenes in the energies devoted to defeating TWU's proposal, rather than addressing other pressing social dilemmas.

I raise this not to suggest that it is inappropriate to discuss or even to oppose vehemently the TWU proposal itself or the view of sexuality contained in it. Rather, I think it is wise to perform a genealogy on the debate and our respective roles therein. By way of an illustration of some of the symbolic 'work' being performed by some participants in the TWU debate, it might be interesting to consider the comment of a British Columbia lawyer who voted against supporting TWU's proposal:

> I think [the 74% negative vote of the LSBC] might have been an act of rebellion against the horror many of us feel about the role of Harper's brand of religion in running the state. We were given an opportunity to draw a line in the sand [against Harper] and [we] drew it. [Personal correspondence.]

This is more or less consistent with what *National Post* writer Chris Selley, quoted above, meant when he referred to the sense in which the 'opposition to TWU Law' is mainly a matter of 'sending a message'. Of course, this reveals a difficult dilemma for the lawyers and other participants in public discourse who sought to send a message to TWU, conservative Protestants, or Stephen Harper himself: as Winnifred Fallers Sullivan succinctly put it in her reflections on the US Supreme Court's decision on *Burwell v Hobby Lobby*, 'You cannot both celebrate religious freedom and deny it to those whose religion you don't like'.[48]

[47] See Myer Siemiatycki, 'Contesting Sacred Urban Space: The Case of the Eruv' (2005) 6 *Journal of International Migration and Integration* 255; Janet McLellan and Marybeth White, 'Social Capital and Identity Politics Among Asian Buddhists in Toronto' (2005) 6 *Journal of International Migration and Integration* 235.

[48] Winnifred Fallers Sullivan, 'Religious Freedom in the United States: The Impossibility of Religious Freedom' (*The Imminent Frame*, 8 July 2014) www.blogs.ssrc.org/tif/2014/07/08/impossibility-of-religious-freedom/.

IV. Conclusion

In this essay I have used my direct experience as a researcher working with government agencies as well as my more removed experience as an observer of a particular political and legal controversy to make some broad observations about the ways religion is managed and imagined by opinion makers in contemporary Canada.

The first two case studies I described as indicative of a 'top-down' approach to religion, inasmuch as in both cases my colleagues and I were contracted directly by representatives of the federal government. Those who have very limited exposure to government representatives often over-simplify the interests at work within a given government. While government colleagues have an interest in working with academics in an effort to provide a given state or department with specific and often rather technical answers to particular problems (eg, mining, infrastructure needs, de-radicalisation 'best practices', etc.), they also have an interest in correcting or championing certain perspectives they observe both in the broader society and among other government departments. Advocacy and critical realist perspectives with regard to religion co-exist in tension, even within governmental regimes interested in presenting a united front. In the case of the two projects in which I was involved, this top-down approach resulted in inclusive and critical interpretations of the phenomena the scholars involved were asked to address.

In the final case study, which I described as reflective of a 'bottom-up' direction of influence, we see the long trajectory of a dilemma as it is resolved through the machinery of public and professional discourses, debates, votes, and currently, legal appeals. This debate gave us a chance to observe a complex interplay of social and political forces. In my view, the dominant rhetoric among many opinion-makers, as well as the final decisions from the British Columbia and Ontario law societies, seem to make it difficult to tell more complicated truths about the fluidity of religion, social and personal change, the history of Canadian institutions, and the operation of political and cultural power in our society. In this sense, we might consider this an expression of a kind of comparatively closed secularism, and an obstacle to what Lori Beaman extols as deep diversity.[49]

Although in practice top-down and bottom-up approaches are not completely distinct, it is arguably the case that one can see in any given controversy a preponderance of one approach over the other. Moreover, neither approach is necessarily more likely than the other to produce particular social goals (eg, liberal, conservative, progressive, radical). My interest in this chapter has been to observe, most specifically, that although one might imagine that religion might be handled more creatively within relatively horizontal arenas in which professionals and other

[49] Beaman, 'The Missing Link' (n 2); Beaman 'Deep Equality' (n 2).

social leaders are not constrained by the more concentrated and vertical political vectors of control, in fact, in these cases it was actually the latter forum in which one can arguably see greater evidence of liberal inclusivity. More broadly, though, the analysis above suggests that the way we manage religion reflects habits of mind and cultural practices that are passed down to us by our families, friends, and colleagues, and that are imagined to be more fixed than they actually are.

5

God Keep Our Land: The Legal Ritual of the McKenna-McBride Royal Commission, 1913–16

PAMELA E KLASSEN

In this chapter, I argue that the public exercise of authority depends on civic—and therefore contested—performances of storytelling, ritual, and law.[1] The story at the centre of my argument is a founding myth that the Canadian nation continues to tell about itself: namely, that Canada is a 'resource-rich' territory. I focus on how this story of the resource-rich nation was elaborated and enacted through the 'legal ritual' of the 1913–16 Royal Commission on Indian Affairs for the Province of British Columbia, popularly known as the McKenna-McBride Commission.[2] A federal-provincial Commission constituted in the wake of the persistent refusal of British Columbia to consider Indigenous land claims via other legal rituals, such as petitions or court cases, the McKenna-McBride Commission effectively ended federal government support for a legal solution to land claims. Another effect in the wake of the travelling band of Commissioners who visited 'Indian reserves' across the province, however, was the uniting in 1916 of Indigenous nations into the Allied Indian Tribes of British Columbia, in order to continue their land claims struggle.[3]

[1] See also: P Klassen, 'Fantasies of Sovereignty: Civic Secularism in Canada' (2015) 3 *Critical Research on Religion* 41. I thank Benjamin Berger and Richard Moon, as well as the participants at the Religion and Public Exercise of Authority Workshop and participants in the Resource Cultures SFB 1070 at the University of Tübingen for their very helpful comments and critiques of this argument. I also thank my student Russell Turner for his insightful reading of the Commission transcripts, and my research assistant Magdalene Klassen.

[2] PA Winn, 'Legal Ritual' (1991) 2 *Law and Critique*, 207; the documents of the Commission are available at the website of the Union of British Columbian Indian Chiefs, 'Our Homes are Bleeding—Digital Collection', www.ubcic.bc.ca/Resources/ourhomesare/.

[3] See especially: H Foster and BL Berger, 'From Humble Prayers to Legal Demands: The Cowichan Petition of 1909 and the British Columbia Indian Land Question' in AR Buck, BL Berger, and H Foster (eds), *The Grand Experiment: Law and Legal Culture in British Settler Societies* (Vancouver, UBC Press, 2008); RM Galois, 'The Indian Rights Association, Native Protest Activity, and the "Land Question" in British Columbia, 1903–1916' (1992) 8 *Native Studies Review* 1.

In a British imperial context, Royal Commissions have been civic 'theatres of power' in which the Crown exercises its public authority by listening to its people in ritually and legally circumscribed settings and then recording these conversations in lengthy documents.[4] As geographic historian Cole Harris has shown, the transcripts of the McKenna-McBride Commission display an imperial and capitalist 'ideology of land on which colonialism (the actual taking up of land and dispossession of its former owners) depends. One might equally say that imperialism constructs particular kinds of knowledge and representations of land by means of which colonial dispossessions proceed'.[5] One such imperial representation is the exhaustive print—and now digital—culture of the transcribed conversations of the McKenna-McBride Commission. At the same time, these texts are also a repository of century-old narratives and voices of both 'Indians' and 'white men' that can be read anew with different stories, laws, and rituals in mind.[6]

The story of Canada as a resource-rich nation is one that Canadians hear regularly, told by politicians, journalists, and those in the resource extraction industry; it is also an old story, told from the beginnings of European presence on the land they named North America.[7] Not a myth in the sense of a 'lie', the resource-rich story is certainly an ideology of land, but it is also what I call a 'cosmology of land': a set of stories, logics, and practices for organising and understanding the world that value land (and water) in relation to underlying principles of transcendence or divinity.[8] This Canadian story may not have had the blunt doctrinal force of the US idea of 'manifest destiny', but both have been grounded on what Robert J Miller has called the 'rituals' and 'Christian god' of the Doctrine of Discovery, which justified European claims of ownership over Indigenous land.[9]

All cosmologies of land depend on cultural underpinnings, including structures of authoritative knowledge about the origins of the world and human responsibility for it. A capitalist cosmology of land, for example, understands land and water as the site of 'natural resources'. Minerals, fossil fuels, wood, fish, etc are there to be extracted from the earth and waters, for people to sell as commodities.

[4] A Ashforth, 'Reckoning Schemes of Legitimation: On Commissions of Inquiry as Power/Knowledge Forms' (1990) 3 *Journal of Historical Sociology* 1; O Frankel, 'Scenes of Commission: Royal Commissions of Inquiry and the Culture of Social Investigation in Early Victorian Britain' (1999) 4 *The European Legacy* 20.

[5] C Harris, *Making Native Space: Colonialism, Resistance, and Reserves in British Columbia* (Vancouver, UBC Press, 2002) 48.

[6] I draw the categories of 'Indian' and 'white men' directly from the Commission transcripts; I continue to use these categories when they are used in the sources. Otherwise, I use the terms Indigenous and settler.

[7] See also: JE Chamberlin, *The Harrowing of Eden: White Attitudes toward Native Americans* (New York, Seabury Press, 1975).

[8] See also: M Sahlins, 'The Sadness of Sweetness: The Native Anthropology of Western Cosmology' (1996) 37 *Current Anthropology* 395.

[9] RJ Miller, 'American Indians, the Doctrine of Discovery, and Manifest Destiny' (2011) 2 *Wyoming Law Review* 329, 340, 348.

A more recent, contrasting example is the 'Keep it in the Ground' movement, which argues in favour of leaving fossil fuels in the earth and figuring out how to live without them. This challenge to the resource extraction story is oriented by a cosmology of land that considers leaving such resources undisturbed in the earth to be a wise investment and an ethical practice for a world facing climate change.[10]

Cosmologies of land undergird the very norms, laws, and practices that turn land into 'territory': land that is owned, or 'under the jurisdiction of a ruler, state, or group of people'.[11] Colonial contexts are marked by an uneasy coexistence of territorial practices, in which Indigenous peoples continue to practise their own cosmologies of land in the midst of colonial assertions of ownership.[12] For example, in northwestern British Columbia, Indigenous peoples have long asserted and transferred the collective ownership of territory through rituals of feasting and the bestowing of names within clans.[13] At the same time, in their petitions to the King, their audiences with the Pope (in the case of Catholic Indigenous peoples from southern British Columbia), and their testimonies to the McKenna-McBride Commission, they persistently authorised their unceded title to their lands with recourse to a God who they claimed in common with the 'white man'; a common God who had given them the land, animals, and waters. Sometimes, Christian missionaries, lawyers, and missionaries who were also trained lawyers, assisted them.[14]

These Indigenous cosmologies of land literally 'took place' at the same time as colonial practices of territorialisation, which were themselves based in part on a Christian story of a God who gave the earth to Adam.[15] Named the 'Dominion of Canada' at its founding in 1867, Canada invented a new political entity in order to assume its place within the British Commonwealth, by borrowing from the biblical passage of Psalm 72: 'And He shall have dominion from sea unto sea'.[16] If we look carefully, we can find cosmologies of land within both Indigenous and settler discourses: federal and provincial government claims of 'Crown Land', government

[10] 'Keep it in the Ground' *The Guardian*, www.theguardian.com/environment/series/keep-it-in-the-ground; see also: N Klein, *This Changes Everything: Capitalism vs. The Climate* (New York, Simon & Schuster, 2014).

[11] 'Territory, n.1,' *OED Online* (Oxford University Press), September 2015.

[12] See also: L Benton, *A Search for Sovereignty: Law and Geography in European Empires, 1400–1900* (Cambridge, Cambridge University Press, 2009); JE Chamberlin, *If This Is Your Land, Where Are Your Stories?: Finding Common Ground* (New York, Random House, 2004); TM Li, *Land's End: Capitalist Relations on an Indigenous Frontier* (Raleigh, Duke University Press, 2014).

[13] See especially: D Cole and I Chaikin, *An Iron Hand upon the People: The Law against the Potlatch on the Northwest Coast* (Vancouver, Douglas & McIntyre, 1990); CF Roth, 'Goods, Names, and Selves: Rethinking the Tsimshian Potlatch' (2002) 29 *American Ethnologist* 123; VR Napoleon, 'Ayook: Gitksan Legal Order, Law, and Legal Theory' (PhD Thesis, University of Victoria, 2009).

[14] See also: Galois, 'The Indian Rights Association' (n 3); Foster and Berger, 'From Humble Prayers to Legal Demands' (n 3); M Harvey, 'Story People: Stó:lo-State Relations and Indigenous Literacies in British Columbia, 1864-1874' (2013) 24 *Journal of the Canadian Historical Association* 51; Harris, *Making Native Space* (n 5).

[15] See also: Harris, *Making Native Space* (n 5), 49; T King, *The Truth about Stories: A Native Narrative* (Toronto, House of Anansi Press, 2003); T King, *The Inconvenient Indian: A Curious Account of Native People in North America* (Toronto, Doubleday Canada, 2012).

[16] HV Nelles, *A Little History of Canada* (Toronto, Oxford University Press, 2004), 114.

'land grants' to both settlers and corporations (including railways), kinship-based inheritance, land transfers internal to clans, institutions or corporations (including within churches), and real estate purchases.[17] As in the Canadian anthem, 'God keep our land' has long been a refrain of both Indigenous and colonial claims to territory.

I. Legal Rituals as Public Performances of Authority

As a dominant cosmology of land in North America, the idea of the resource-rich nation requires the continual exercise of public authority via story, law, and ritual to keep stable the cultural underpinnings of its claims to territory and extraction. Whether through laws that encode 'mineral rights' or governments that press the message that the extraction of such minerals is vital to national wellbeing, the stories and 'legal rituals' of resource extraction are undergirded by religious warrants. Borrowing from Peter A Winn, I use the phrase legal ritual to denote 'legal events' that are performances that do not simply refer to, but actually constitute the law, and thereby the authority of the state. As Winn phrased it: 'legal rituals are concrete, visible sets of symbolic acts which give life to social institutions'.[18] For Winn, the concept of legal rituals allows for what we might call a provincialising of Western law, and its supposedly 'rational' grounding:

> Industrial societies have more clearly demarcated the natural world from the social world, and are more likely to understand the natural world through scientific concepts and technology. However, ritual remains important in industrial societies in the creation and maintenance of social institutions, and to orient and relate people to one another in the context of these institutions. Among these institutions, of course, are law and religion.[19]

Bringing together the concept of the legal ritual with the story of Canada as a resource-rich nation, I would go further to argue that rituals of state power have also done the work of 'industrialising' society. Demarcating the natural from the social has been central to both the ideology and the cosmology of land on which capitalist and colonial resource extraction depends.[20] Turning nature into resources allowed for the flourishing of one vision of social and political life, at the expense of an Indigenous cosmology of land.

The legal ritual of the McKenna-McBride Commission expressed and effected the social institution of colonial property ownership and the social imaginary

[17] See also: PE Klassen, 'Mentality, Fundamentality and the Colonial Secular; or How Real Is Real Estate?,' in R Braidotti, B Blaagaard, and E Midden (eds) *The Postsecular Condition* (London, Palgrave Macmillan, 2014).

[18] Winn, 'Legal Ritual', 219.

[19] ibid, 210; see also: D Chakrabarty, *Provincializing Europe: Postcolonial Thought and Historical Difference* (Princeton, Princeton University Press, 2000).

[20] See also: JS Youngblood Henderson, 'The Context of the State of Nature' in M Battiste (ed), *Reclaiming Indigenous Voice and Vision* (Vancouver, UBC Press, 2000).

of resource extraction through symbolic acts rooted both in the state and religion. By religion, here I mean a form of authoritative knowledge that appeals to a transcendent or ancestral root as its legitimising principle.[21] In the case of Canadian Royal Commissions, and the longer British tradition of which they are a part, Christianity has been the religion undergirding the state's authority. We can see this in an 'ambient' sense in the use of the Bible to swear in witnesses to an inquiry.[22] But the legitimation provided by Christianity goes much deeper than the oath; the 'Royal' authority ascribed to a commission signals a sovereign power based on the divine right of monarchs, even if such divine rights are largely forgotten today.[23]

The testimonies of the McKenna-McBride Commission reveal Indigenous witnesses who were aware that they were participating in a legal ritual that combined political and religious power. In addition to frequently invoking the King, the Government, and God, they also sought to shape the pacing and the rhetorical style of the Commission conversations. They slowed the rhythms of the meetings repeatedly, asking the Commissioners for postponements in order to properly consult elders, who may have included women. They understood their task not simply as testifying, but as what Johnny Mack, in a twenty-first century context, has called 'storied practice'.[24] In other words, that stories—or testimonies to Royal Commissions—must be told with respect for relationships and rituals. For their part, the Commissioners often granted these requests for delays, while always emphasising they were on a tight schedule. In addition to their challenges to the pacing of the legal ritual of the Commission, the Indigenous participants rejected the resource-rich story, especially in their repeated and explicit refusal of the concept of the 'Indian reserve'; a concept that made possible the resource-rich nation.

II. The Story of a Resource-Rich Nation

Borrowing from Charles Taylor, I argue that a 'social imaginary' of resource plenitude is at the core of the dominant Canadian cosmology of land and has

[21] See also: T Asad, *Genealogies of Religion: Discipline and Reasons of Power in Christianity and Islam* (Baltimore, Johns Hopkins University Press, 1993); D Chidester, *Empire of Religion: Imperialism and Comparative Religion* (Chicago, University of Chicago Press, 2014).

[22] M Engelke, 'Angels in Swindon: Public Religion and Ambient Faith in England' (2012) 39 *American Ethnologist* 155.

[23] See also: W Sullivan, 'Comparing Religions, Legally' (2006) 63 *Washington and Lee Law Review* 913; BL Berger, 'The Cultural Limits of Legal Tolerance' in C Bender and PE Klassen (eds) *After Pluralism: Reimagining Religious Engagement* (New York, Columbia University Press, 2010); BL Berger, 'Belonging to Law: Religious Difference, Secularism, and the Conditions of Civic Inclusion' (2015) 24(1) *Social & Legal Studies* 47.

[24] J Mack, 'Hoquotist: Reorienting through Storied Practice' in H Lessard, R Johnson, and J Webber (eds) *Storied Communities: Narratives of Contact and Arrival in Constituting Political Community* (Vancouver, UBC Press, 2011).

profoundly shaped Canadian claims to sovereignty. For Taylor, a social imaginary is a 'common understanding that makes possible common practices and a widely shared sense of legitimacy'.[25] Taylor argues that social imaginaries are built out of widely shared stories, images, and legends. Pinpointing what is 'common' about how people in Canada understand the legitimacy of the nation-state is a challenging and ongoing task in such a vast and diverse land. In 1969, however, philosopher George Grant, writing as an 'English-speaking Canadian', tried to specify how Christianity, industrialisation, and colonial conquest shaped his people's attempts to imagine their relation to the land on which they lived:

> That conquering relation to place has left its mark within us. When we go to the Rockies, we may have a sense that gods are there. But if so they cannot manifest themselves to us as ours. They are the gods of another race, and we cannot know them because of what we are and what we did. There can be nothing immemorial for us except the landscape as object.[26]

Though I too am an English-speaking Canadian, Grant's insistence that Indigenous people (who remained largely unmentioned in his account) were a 'race' apart is not a perspective that I share. However, his insight that a history of conquest in the name of both Christianity and capitalism has profoundly shaped the conditions of memory and social imagination in Canada is both apt and, for its time, prescient.

For an example of the founding myth of resource plenitude, consider a 1929 book entitled *The Mineral Resources of Canada*, written by Elwood Moore, a Professor of Economic Geology at the University of Toronto. A handsome book with 13 elegant maps depicting where mineral deposits lay across the country, it was the first volume in a series entitled the Canadian Citizen's Library, edited by another University of Toronto professor, Prof RM MacIver. The series had the goal of educating the Canadian citizen about the 'economic and social life of Canada'. MacIver was a political economist and sociologist, thought by some to be an 'ultra-socialist' supporter of labour unions, who would eventually become the Chancellor of the New School of Social Research in New York City—not only self-declared capitalists told the resource-rich story.[27]

MacIver noted that he hoped the Canadian Citizen's Library would 'meet the needs of Canadian citizens who seek to grasp the realities of the Canadian scene and to base their faith upon understanding'. This faith in the nation was premised on mapping the 'young country's' natural resources, while denying that this new land had a long history. Setting up an old world and new world contrast, MacIver argued that in Canada, 'Her people have brought with them the memories and traditions of their motherlands, often the dearer because of physical separation.

[25] C Taylor, *Modern Social Imaginaries* (Raleigh, Duke University Press, 2004), 23.

[26] GP Grant, *Technology and Empire: Perspectives on North America* (Toronto, House of Anansi, 1969) 17. I am grateful to Richard Moon for pointing me to this passage in Grant.

[27] ML Friedland, *The University of Toronto: A History* (Toronto, University of Toronto Press, 2013).

But their new environment contained for them no legacy from the past, and in it they were compelled to apply themselves afresh to the building up of a distinct civilization'.[28] MacIver's narrative of a history-less land ignored the long presence of Indigenous peoples in the territory now called Canada, and is a story still echoed today.[29]

This narrative of a new country as a blank slate is a story told repeatedly in maps of mineral exploration and settlement that urged new immigrants and Canadians living in more populous areas to venture into 'uninhabited' resource-rich territory. The land, however, was not unsettled. The colonial government knew this well from its extended treaty negotiations with Indigenous nations throughout the country. But the cosmology of land that insisted on seeing natural resources everywhere required a wilful ignorance of the long history of Indigenous settlement. This refusal to recognise Indigenous sovereignty was conditioned by both capitalist and Christian cosmologies of land.[30]

Some readers may pause here, wondering what 'secular' laws regulating the industry of resource extraction, with its rational, economic bottom lines, have to do with religious warrants. Historian of law and empire Lauren Benton points to an answer. Considering what she calls 'multijurisdictional legal orders' at a global comparative scale, Benton argues that European imperial expansion brought together imperial and indigenous 'legal regimes' in such a way that they developed shared—albeit conflicting—understandings of 'legal power'.[31] Benton notes that imperial and indigenous actors did not necessarily agree about the authority that undergirded this legal power, sometimes precisely because of the fuzzy lines between the religious and the secular: 'We perceive this clearly in territories of colonial and imperial expansion, where culturally and religiously different peoples employed legal strategies that exploited (and further complicated) unresolved jurisdictional tensions, particularly those between secular and religious authorities'.[32] In the Canadian case, John Borrows has most convincingly demonstrated the historical and ongoing effects—and even possibilities—of the jurisdictional tensions arising from this blending of legal, religious, and ritual practice.[33]

As Canadian and Indigenous ways of exercising public authority increasingly came into contact and conflict in northwest coast, the two sides were differently able to recognise and adapt to the claims of the other. Partly out of necessity in the face of colonial violence and dispossession, nations such as the Nisga'a, Gitxsan, and

[28] MacIver in ES Moore, *Canada's Mineral Resources* (Toronto, Irwin & Gordon, 1929), vii.

[29] See former Canadian Prime Minister Stephen Harper's comment that Canada is a land with 'much geography but very little history' in Canadian Press, 'Stephen Harper, Benjamin Netanyahu Sign Agreements', www.cbc.ca/1.2504635.

[30] See especially: King, *The Inconvenient Indian* (n 15).

[31] LA Benton, *Law and Colonial Cultures: Legal Regimes in World History, 1400–1900* (New York, Cambridge University Press, 2002), 5.

[32] ibid, 6.

[33] J Borrows, *Recovering Canada: The Resurgence of Indigenous Law* (Toronto, University of Toronto Press, 2002).

Tsimshian took seriously the 'public' aspect of the public exercise of authority in the Canadian nation. They engaged vigorously with both the ritual and legal modes of Canadian authority, well aware that the Dominion of Canada, ostensibly a secular, democratic order, based itself on both divine and monarchical power. One such mode of engagement was through their participation in petitions and Royal Commissions, such as the McKenna-McBride Royal Commission, in a province with hardly any negotiated treaties.[34]

III. The Legal Ritual of the McKenna-McBride Commission

The McKenna-McBride Commission is a fascinating—and troubling—example of a ritual of multi-jurisdictional tension. The idea that Canada was a young country with no history was not unique to the authors of *The Mineral Resources of Canada*—it was a story that the nation told to itself often, despite the long history of Indigenous peoples telling the colonial government otherwise. The testimonies of the McKenna-McBride Commission demonstrate this very clearly; they are historical documents remarkable for their clear presentation of the land claims of Indigenous peoples, in their own words, albeit through interpreters, both Indigenous and settler, male and female, and through the recording of stenographers.[35] In reading the testimonies of the Tsimshian and Nisga'a of the Nass Agency, it is clear that the Indigenous witnesses and Commissioners (who were all men) did not share common understandings of what land was for, and how it belonged to people. At the same time, we see that both groups oriented their roles and comments through cosmologies in which land was claimed through such concepts as the 'Crown', the 'Indian', the 'white man', the 'reserve', and 'God'.

Emerging out of a long-standing conflict between the Canadian and British Columbian governments over their respective authority over Indigenous land title, the joint federal-provincial McKenna-McBride Royal Commission sought to 'adjust' reserve lands, cutting them off if they were not 'efficiently' used.[36] Richard McBride, the Premier of British Columbia, was particularly hopeful that the Commission would 'solve' the problem of ongoing resistance by Indigenous peoples to surrendering their land so that it could be opened to white

[34] See especially: Harvey, 'Story People' (n 14); Foster and Berger, 'From Humble Prayers to Legal Demands' (n 3).

[35] See especially: Harris, *Making Native Space* (n 5). One such interpreter was Odille Morison. See ML Atkinson, 'The "Accomplished" Odille Quintal Morison: Tsimshian Cultural Intermediary of Metlakatla, British Columbia', in S Carter and PA McCormack (eds), *Recollecting: Lives of Aboriginal Women of the Canadian Northwest and Borderlands* (Edmonton, Athabasca University Press, 2011).

[36] The popular name reflected the role of Richard McBride, the Premier of British Columbia, in instigating the committee, and James McKenna, the federal government's main representative on the Commission.

settlement, agriculture, mining, and logging.[37] Putting his hopes in a process of travelling conversations between Commissioners and Indigenous peoples across the province, McBride's solution was one of achievement through deflection: again and again, the conversations show the Commissioners refusing to answer the Indigenous participants' questions about their title to the territory of British Columbia.

Resource extraction was one of the recurring sources of tension in the Commission's meetings. Commissioners wanted to know if the 'Indians' were making good use of their 'resources' on their reserves, while Indigenous witnesses consistently questioned why the Commission wanted such information, testified that white settlement was threatening their own resource practices, and rejected the very concept of reserves altogether. In the end, the McKenna-McBride Royal Commission did not recommend enough cut-offs to satisfy either the federal or provincial governments, and each government ratified a revised version only in 1924.[38]

The exercise of public authority in legal rituals undergirds the legitimacy of cosmologies of land, which in turn legitimate claims to territory. This is the case for both Indigenous and Canadian claims to land. In the Canadian case, from the very act of founding the Dominion of Canada and celebrating it on Dominion Day to the offering of 'Crown land' as grants to settlers, the authority to make such claims was displayed in both public rituals and legal texts. For Indigenous nations of the northwest coast, claims to territory were publicly authorised through feasting, totem poles, and the bestowing of names. In both cases, exercising public authority required religious warrants of varying levels of explicitness. For a Commissioner, a commonplace term such as the Crown was a reference, however obscure, to a monarch who reigned with the sanction and protection of God. For a Nisga'a or Tsimshian, the common refrain of inhabiting the land 'from time immemorial' grounded their claims in cosmic time.[39]

In Great Britain and Canada, Royal Commissions have been a particular legal ritual by which contentious issues, such as poor laws, education, child labour laws or Indigenous land claims have been addressed in the context of conversations that are at once ritualised and 'rationalised' through bureaucratic means.[40] As Adam Ashforth phrased it: 'Public "sittings" by Commissions of Inquiry can be considered as a form of symbolic ritual, akin to the holding of Court but in a modern rationalised form, wherein the subjects of State power speak, and are

[37] See also: PE Roy, 'McBride of McKenna-McBride: Premier Richard McBride and the Indian Question in British Columbia', (2012) 172 *BC Studies*.

[38] Harris, *Making Native Space* (n 5), 217.

[39] For another example of the religious warrants for resource extraction, consider Darren Dochuk's study of Christianity and the oil industry in the United States: 'Such was the providential view of petroleum that fused Christianity and capitalism into an indomitable union'. D Dochuk, 'Blessed by Oil, Cursed with Crude: God and Black Gold in the American Southwest' (2012) 99 *Journal of American History* 51, 55.

[40] See also: K Flanagan, 'Commissions of Inquiry as Ritual: Bourdieu, the Marquis and the Endowed Schools of Ireland, 1854–58' (2011) 19 *Irish Studies Review* 281.

heard'.[41] As with many other Commissions, the McKenna-McBride Commission was a ritual meant to effect the rationalisation of resources—to sort out through investigation of a 'singular question', namely 'the Land Question', how to better allocate land in British Columbia to further white settlement, mining, and agriculture.[42]

IV. A Common God

Again and again, the Tsimshian and Nisga'a witnesses at the Commission reiterated that their people had occupied the land 'from time immemorial' and that, in the words of Nisga'a witness SL Allan of Kincolith in 1915: 'we know that God put us here in the first place the same as he placed the white people on their land'.[43] Like many of the testimonies, Allan's was an eloquent appeal and an engaging story, laden with detail about the surrounding lands and the ways in which Nisga'a cultivation of the land had been ignored:

> I also want to speak about a place up the river here, probably about six miles up the mouth of the Naas known as Cratsville, which is not a reserve. We used to cultivate this piece of ground up there and you will see if you go up yourself from one end of this place to the other it is thick with crab-apples but now it has been taken up by the Government and given to the white people. Of course we don't blame the government because they did not know that we owned this place for an orchard, and the people that used to go there and gather these apples they are still alive and right at the back of this flat there is a valley opening up to the mountain from which we used to get marten, mink and goat, and if the white man come and live on this place they won't give us a passage there to go to our hunting-grounds; that also belongs to the Nishga people and I will thank you very much if you will try and settle this thing for us.[44]

Later on in the meeting, Allan spoke again, this time prefacing his comments with a direct acknowledgement of how the Commission's power was rooted both in God and King:

> I thank God because from him we get a source of all strength and wisdom and I also thank the Royal Commission for coming to see us as they also get their power from God. The people of the Nishga tribe all heartily thank the Royal Commission because they can

[41] Ashforth, 'Reckoning Schemes of Legitimation' (n 4) 12.

[42] On 'singularity' see Flanagan, 'Commissions of Inquiry as Ritual' (n 40) 283; Ashforth, 'Reckoning Schemes of Legitimation' (n 4) 7.

[43] All citations from the McKenna-McBride Commission are from the 'Testimonies' section of the Union of British Columbia Indian Chiefs (UBCIC) website, 'Our Homes are Bleeding: Digital Collection' www.ubcic.bc.ca/Resources/final_report.htm. Allan in 'Meeting at Kincolith', 'Our Homes Are Bleeding' (n 43), 54. The interpreter for the Kincolith meeting was J Maxwell Collison, the son of longtime Anglican missionary at Kincolith, William Collison, and a Dominion Fisheries Overseer. See R Palmer, 'Meziadin River Fish Ladders' (2003) 36 *British Columbia Historical News* 18.

[44] Allan in 'Meeting at Kincolith' 56.

> see that the Royal Commission has the power of our King and that is why they are called the Royal Commission.[45]

In one fell swoop, Allan made explicit the religious and the royal warrants for the Commissioners' power, and called them to acknowledge both.

JJ Harvey, also speaking at the Kincolith meeting, began his testimony with a similar refrain that carefully acknowledged the intertwined power of God and King, without giving up Nisga'a claims to Aboriginal title and to their own practices of resource extraction:

> Under the power of God and under the flag of our King we know that no man should be poor or badly off, so I thank you gentlemen for giving me your kind attention for a few minutes. From time immemorial as long as the Nishga people have been living they were never really hard up for food or anything that was necessary to keep them alive, and even today they are pretty well off although they are not as well off to our way of thinking as they were then. The grievance that I put before you today is that we are not allowed to cut a tree down on the outside of this bit of ground for wood. And so I ask it to be free from now on for us to cut wood on our land.[46]

Harvey, like Allan, acknowledged that the Nisga'a hunted animals and felled trees—they extracted resources—and argued that they did so with the sanction of a God that was both Nisga'a and Christian, in such a way that the King would endorse.[47]

Already in the years before the Commission, Nisga'a writers had been astute observers of how the state used Christianity to undergird its territorial authority. In a 1911 letter to the editor of the Prince Rupert *Empire*, Nisga'a chief (and Anglican church member) Andrew Mercer pointed to the biblical grounding of Canadian legal ritual, as symbolised by the swearing of oaths on the Bible and as found in the Ten Commandments:

> If the surveyor and those that have staked pieces of land up in the Naas valley wish to come again, let them go to Ottawa first and make the government settle our land. And if our land is settle, then let the surveyor and those that have their stake come again, for we do not want to stop them. But we want a full settlement. Also we want to right of what is lawful. Same thing as you want to do right, as you all perceive it from the Holy Bible. Whenever the J.P. or a judge were in court they used Bible for to do right. We also see and read in it, in the Holy Bible, that 'Cursed is he that removeth his neighbor's land mark,' and that you break one of the Ten Commandments, 'Thou shall not covet,' for you have knock us down and take our possession.[48]

To dispute the legitimacy of the very concept of reserves and to challenge the legality of white settlement, Indigenous witnesses drew comparisons between

[45] ibid 64.

[46] Harvey in 'Meeting at Kincolith' 56.

[47] See also: CR Menzies and CF Butler, 'The Indigenous Foundation of the Resource Economy of BC's North Coast' (2008) 2 *Labour/Le Travail* 131.

[48] A Mercer, 'Indians' View of Land Question' *The Evening Empire*, January 11, 1911.

the divine sanction underlying Aboriginal sovereignty and that undergirding Canadian colonialism. Central to Indigenous approaches to legal rituals of sovereignty, from the nineteenth-century and onward, has been their insistence on dealing with the Crown or representatives of the Crown, whether the Privy Council or the Governor-General; this is also an insistence that the divine warrants of Canadian power be recognised.

The Commissioners' response to Indigenous testimony was consistent. They repeatedly claimed that they had no power to sort out questions of Aboriginal title, and that there were legal proceedings to which the Indians had recourse in sorting out such questions. Knowing that the question of Aboriginal title was unsettled, the Commissioners wilfully ignored these 'primordial' issues, hoping to jump ahead to sort out the boundaries of reserves. The Royal Commissioners sought to diminish their own cosmologically grounded power, in order to exercise it.

The Commissioners, like the Indigenous participants, also turned to evidence from resources, asking often about fisheries, hunting practices, and whether Indian communities actually still supported themselves from such processes of resource extraction. Take, for example, one illuminating interchange between Commissioner Shaw and Tsimshian witness Moses Johnson of Port Simpson:

> Q. Do you know how many full-grown men belong to the tribe, say over 18 years of age married and single?
>
> A. I wish to know why you are asking these questions?
>
> Mr. Commissioner Shaw: Well there are a good many reasons—in the first place we want to find out how many people you have; how many families in order that we may be able to see whether the lands you have now are enough for your own use—to find out how many children you have of school age and if you have schools adequate for their use and a great many other questions?
>
> A. I fail to see what connection these questions have in regard to the Indian Reserve question.
>
> Q. Do you object to answer that question?
>
> A. I wish to know what respect this question has on the Indian Reserve question.
>
> Q. I explained that to you—do you object to answer my question, if so I will go to something else.
>
> A. I cannot answer that question.
>
> Q. Do all your people live here on this reserve?
>
> A. They lived here from time immemorial before such a thing as a reserve was thought of—all the different tribes lived here.
>
> Q. What I want to know is this, this is what is known as Port Simpson No 1 is it not?
>
> A. We don't know of any number at all being attached to it. We have a name for it which was known in the old days and before any reserves were laid out; these reserves were

> made and forced upon us unknowingly; we never asked for them but we were forced to take them.[49]

In what was clearly a battle of wits, Johnson refused to answer Shaw's questions, as a way of marking his profound disagreement with the underlying terms of the Commission itself. Where the Commissioners sought 'hard numbers' of populations and resource extraction practices in order to redraw the boundaries of the reserves, the Nisga'a and Tsimshian witnesses refused to participate in this practice of colonial accounting, aware of its drastic consequences for their sovereignty and communities.[50]

For their part, the Commissioners used their own version of a cosmology of land to back up their repeated refrains that they were powerless to effect the change demanded by the Nisga'a and Tsimshian. Central to this cosmology was a commitment to the binding power of land title given to settlers. While they could redraw reserve lines, they could not just 'take away' land from 'white people'. As Commissioner Macdowall put it to the Nisga'a of Lakkalzap:

> I think, however, you must be acting under a misapprehension when you think we can give land already in the possession of white people—we cannot do that; we can only give land such as is owned by the Provincial Government. We are always ready and happy to explain anything regarding this Commission and its powers; we want the Indians to learn the truth about it because we consider that it would be doing you and the other Indians an injury if we led them to believe that we had greater powers than we possess and therefore we want them to know the truth about the powers we possess.[51]

When confronted by Nisga'a Richard Woods with the statement that politicians in Ottawa had definitely said that they could return to the Nisga'a land that was in the possession of white men, or pay them recompense for this land, Commissioner Macdowall responded with disbelief: 'You mean that Mr Scott told you that this Royal Commission would have power to take land away from white people and give it to the Indians?'[52] This dispute over the power of the Commission to dispossess white people of their land demonstrates how the Canadian cosmology of land was rooted in racist norms of landholding, themselves undergirded by the Christian doctrine of discovery.[53]

Insisting that they only had the power to grant the Indians 'Crown land' (or land putatively owned by the monarch), the Commissioners repeatedly counselled the Nisga'a and Tsimshian that they should understand white settlers as their neighbours, their employers, and their fellow countrymen (the entire Commission was largely a conversation among men). To do otherwise, Commissioner Carmichael declared, was both folly and irresponsibility:

[49] Johnson in 'Meeting at Port Simpson', 'Our Homes are Bleeding' (n 43) 38.

[50] D Neu and C Graham, 'The Birth of a Nation: Accounting and Canada's First Nations, 1860–1900' (2006) 31 *Accounting, Organizations and Society* 47; D Neu, '"Presents" for the "Indians": Land, Colonialism and Accounting in Canada' (2000) 25 *Accounting, Organizations and Society* 163.

[51] Macdowall in 'Meeting at Lachkaltsap', 'Our Homes are Bleeding' (n 43) 95.

[52] ibid 96.

[53] Miller, 'American Indians, the Doctrine of Discovery, and Manifest Destiny' (n 9).

> You people thoroughly realize do you that this will probably be the last opportunity of a Commission coming through to deal with you Indians in the way that we have been trying to deal with you; as long as that is so, I have nothing more to say but I think for the younger men and the future of the Indians it is an awful pity to see you throw away the opportunities that we are honestly trying to place before you.[54]

To refuse the terms of the McKenna-McBride Royal Commission, Carmichael argued, was to squander the 'future of the Indians'. Fully convinced that a cosmology of land rooted in Aboriginal title had been superseded by one of Crown lands and white settlement, the Commissioner participated in a wider cultural narrative that understood Indians as lazy, and culturally incapable of cultivating their land, exploiting their resources, and organising their communities in way that made rational, economic sense.[55] The Crown carried with it not only echoes of divine right, but also a seemingly common-sense practice of monarchical land tenure and resource extraction.

V. Archives of Legal Ritual

Commissioner Carmichael was eventually proven wrong in his insistence that the Nisga'a were 'throwing away' their future. The persistent refusal of the Nisga'a to accept the term 'reserve', and their simultaneous pursuit of Canadian legal mechanisms to argue for their sovereignty, eventually led to the establishment of the Nisga'a Nation in 2000.[56] Though not without their critics among other Indigenous nations, the Nisga'a were able to exercise their public authority through moving among and between various cosmologies of land—staunchly reiterating the refrain of 'time immemorial' while making use of what John Borrows has called 'Canada's Indigenous Constitution'.[57]

Were they alive today, the Commissioners might be surprised by the continued usefulness of the McKenna-McBride documents as archives for an 'Indian Land Question' that has still not been 'solved'. In the wake of the federal government's revision of the Indian Act in 1926, outlawing fundraising and the hiring of lawyers to pursue land claims, the Allied Tribes of British Columbia was no longer a formal organisation. But its successor, the Union of British Columbia Indian Chiefs, formed in 1969, has now digitised the testimonies, maps, and final report of the Commission, as well as the 1919 'Statement of the Allied Tribes of

[54] Carmichael in 'Meeting at Port Simpson', 'Our Homes are Bleeding' (n 43) 37.

[55] See especially: JS Lutz, *Makúk: A New History of Aboriginal-White Relations* (Vancouver, UBC Press, 2008).

[56] See especially: 'Nisga'a Final Agreement | Nisga'a Lisims Government', www.nisgaalisims.ca/nisgaa-final-agreement; H Foster, H Raven, and J Webber (eds) *Let Right Be Done: Aboriginal Title, the Calder Case, and the Future of Indigenous Rights* (Vancouver, UBC Press, 2007).

[57] J Borrows, *Canada's Indigenous Constitution* (Toronto, University of Toronto Press, 2010).

British Columbia' in response to the report. The 1919 statement, though it notes allies among Protestant organisations and names the Governor-General as its first audience, no longer makes its claims by drawing on Christian language or a common God or King. The UBCIC has preserved and made accessible the testimonies and related documents of the Royal Commission in part to enable Indigenous nations to pursue land claims. This includes applications to reverse the cut-offs of the McKenna-McBride Commission.[58]

Despite these legal accomplishments and others, the story of the resource-rich nation continues to remake the land—both Indigenous and Canadian.[59] These days, mining companies have a 'duty to consult' First Nations as they pursue resource extraction projects, and Indigenous nations can make use of the right to 'religious freedom' to call for protection of their 'sacred sites' in the face of mining or logging.[60] As Sari Graben has shown, however, the 'cost-benefit analysis' that companies and courts use to assess the significance of a 'sacred site' for Indigenous peoples is often a blunt instrument, not much more nuanced than the hard numbers questions of the Royal Commissioners.[61] Religious freedom has also proven to be an ambiguous tool.[62] The God-talk of Indigenous witnesses at the McKenna-McBride Commission calls us to reconsider even today what is labelled as 'sacred' or 'religious' in the adjudication of the meaning of land. Such reconsideration shows that Nisga'a, Tsimshian, and Canadians alike all worked with cosmologies of land, and still do. Indigenous peoples have long sought to defend their ancestral homelands with recourse to Creator-oriented cosmologies; so too, I argue, has the Canadian state claimed land and resources with recourse to divine power. The question, then, becomes: if God is deemed the keeper of the land, how should human beings share it?

[58] Union of British Columbia Indian Chiefs, 'Our Homes Are Bleeding' (n 43); Union of British Columbia Indian Chiefs, 'Stolen Lands, Broken Promises,' *Stolen Lands, Broken Promises Researching the Indian Land Question in British Columbia*, 2nd edn (2004) www.ubcic.bc.ca/Resources/rilq.htm#axzz3auCw4HqC.

[59] R Daly, *Our Box Was Full: An Ethnography for the Delgamuukw Plaintiffs* (Vancouver, UBC Press, 2004).

[60] See especially: J Promislow and L Sossin, 'In Search of Aboriginal Administrative Law' in C Flood and L Sossin (eds) *Administrative Law in Context*, 2nd edn (Toronto, Emond Montgomery, 2012); S Lawrence and P Macklem, 'From Consultation to Reconciliation: Aboriginal Rights and the Crown's Duty to Consult' (2000) 79 *Canadian Bar Review* 252.

[61] S Graben, 'Resourceful Impacts: Harm and Valuation of the Sacred' (2014) 64 *University of Toronto Law Journal* 64.

[62] MD McNally, 'Native American Religious Freedom Beyond the First Amendment' in Bender and Klassen, *After Pluralism* (n 23).

6

In/Visible Religion in Public Institutions: Canadian Muslim Public Servants

AMÉLIE BARRAS, JENNIFER A SELBY AND LORI G BEAMAN

> I never call it 'the holiday party'. People call it the 'holiday party' because they want to accommodate everybody but I'm like, you know what? It's a Christmas party. We live in a predominantly Christian society. It's a Christmas party.
>
> Nour, 30 years old, high school teacher

I. Introduction

As Nour explains, the workplaces of Canadian public servants are not neutral, and are permeated by a number of values that are worth examining. The lack of neutrality evident for our participants in the 'holiday party' reflects broader ambiguities in the Canadian state's understanding of secularism.[1] Canada does not have a constitutional separation of church and state. Still, official expressions of contemporary Canadian institutions demarcate boundaries that determine religiosity's visibility and invisibility, and delineate 'public' and 'private' spheres. These differentiations are subject to debate, but state institutions generally uphold these categories to ensure neutrality. Our aim in this chapter is to consider how these boundaries appear in the working lives of Canadian public

[1] We approach secularism as an inherently ambiguous discourse that shifts with time and context and is intrinsically related to contemporary understandings of religion, namely its Christian articulations. It is precisely this malleability that renders it such an expeditious tool of governmentality. See, for instance: J Jakobsen and A Pellegrini (eds), *Secularisms* (Durham, Duke University Press, 2008); WF Sullivan, *The Impossibility of Religious Freedom* (Princeton, Princeton University Press, 2005); T Asad, *Formations of the Secular: Christianity, Islam, Modernity* (Redwood, Stanford University Press, 2003); S Reimer-Kirkham et al, 'Sacred Spaces in Public Places: Religious and Spiritual Plurality in Healthcare' (2011) 19 *Nursing Inquiry* 202; ES Hurd, 'International Politics after Secularism' (2012) 38 *Review of International Studies* 943.

servants who self-identify as Muslim and live in Montreal, Quebec, and St. John's, Newfoundland and Labrador (NL).[2]

The narratives of our interlocutors expose the presumptions and power dynamics laden in these delineations of 'neutrality'. In some cases, neutrality affects the structure of institutions (eg, the configuration of space or objects in rooms), but more commonly, it intends to ensure even-handedness through the notion that public institutions should be either religiously neutral or inclusive of all religions in their dispersal of services. These directives may be applied to the bodies of employees, and in particular to their dress, but also to the way in which state services are delivered; the impartial language, tone, and gesture of delivery. We aim to chart where these distinctions between visible/invisible and public/private are marked in practice and under what circumstances boundary trespassing is flagged. While it is commonly understood that mainstream Christianity has been successfully privatised and that Christians respect these demarcations in Canadian government spaces, the visibility of Islam is often identified as challenging the secular narrative of this balance, itself imagined as being stable, fixed, and timeless. These delimitations are also deeply shaped by ethnocentric and orientalist influences.[3] Drawing on 23 semi-directed interviews with Muslim public servants in Montreal and St. John's, this chapter argues that Canadian public institutions are not neutral.

In mapping these boundaries, we take a social constructivist approach to religion, and understand the private/public boundaries as constantly produced, policed, enacted, and transgressed.[4] The narratives of Canadian Muslim public

[2] Data for this chapter stems from almost 90 qualitative interviews conducted in two Canadian cities from 2011–13. We sought to consider the negotiation of religious difference in non-remarkable situations. We gratefully acknowledge funding from the Religion and Diversity Project, the Social Sciences and Humanities Research Council and the Swiss National Science Foundation, as well as research assistance from Caitlin Downie, Jennifer Williams, and editorial assistance from Marianne Abou-Hamad. Lori G Beaman would also like to acknowledge the ongoing financial support of her research through her Canada Research Chair in the Contextualization of Religion in a Diverse Canada.

[3] T Asad, *Genealogies of Religion: Discipline and Reasons of Power in Christianity and Islam* (Baltimore, Johns Hopkins University Press, 1993) 28; S Razack, *Race, Space, and the Law: Unmapping a White Settler Society* (Toronto, Between the Lines, 2002); K Knott, *The Location of Religion: A Spatial Analysis* (London, Equinox, 2005) 41.

[4] K Knott, 'Theoretical and Methodological Resources for Breaking Open the Secular and Exploring the Boundary Between Religion and Non-Religion' (2010) 2 *Historia Religionum* 115, 122. See also JZ Smith, *Map is Not Territory: Studies in the History of Religions* (Leiden, Brill, 1978); JZ Smith, *To Take Place: Toward Theory in Ritual* (Chicago, University of Chicago Press, 1987); N Smith, *Uneven Development: Nature, Capital and the Production of Space* (Oxford, Blackwell, 1984); BD Metcalf, 'Introduction: Sacred Worlds, Sanctioned Practice, New Communities' in BD Metcalf (ed), *Making Muslim Space in North America and Europe* (Berkeley, University of California Press, 1996); JA Beckford, *Social Theory and Religion* (Cambridge, Cambridge University Press, 2003); K Knott, 'From Locality to Location and Back Again: A Spatial Journey of the Study of Religion' (2009) 39 *Religion* 154; D Massey, 'Politics and Space/Time' in K Michael and P Steve (eds), *Place and the Politics of Identity* (New York, Routledge, 1993) 155. Martin Stringer reminds us that Knott's approach is informed by the work of Lefebvre, where: 'All space, in Lefebvre's view, is socially constructed in that we cannot think about space without taking into account the way in which social relations determine the space and social interactions describe or understand the space': see M Stringer, *Discourses on Religious Diversity: Explorations in an Urban Ecology* (Farnham, Ashgate, 2013) 38.

servants show how the 'imagined' locations of religions—namely the invisibility of Christianity and hypervisibility of Islam—index public/private limitations. As we will see, conflicts and controversies arise when non-mainstream Christian traditions transgress these confines.

We begin by briefly contextualising these cities. One element that slightly alters the experiences of interlocutors in Montreal is the 2013-proposed Charter of Secularism that sought to prohibit public servants from wearing 'visible' religious symbols.[5] The first section then turns to our participants' discussions of their annual 'holiday' party to consider how, despite efforts by these institutions to render this dimension invisible, the event's tone and structure remains Christian.[6] The second section documents how, in contrast to these so-called invisible Christian dimensions, our participants' non-Christian Muslim identities are rendered *hypervisible* in their work environments.

We employ a broad definition of the category of 'public servant' to include federally and provincially employed physicians, university employees, and postal workers, among others.[7] This definition allows us to capture a greater number

[5] The Parti Québécois was at the head of a minority government in Quebec from September 2012 to April 2014. During the last year of its mandate, it introduced a controversial legal project (the Charter of Secularism), which aimed to reinforce the 'secular' character of public institutions. The two central features of this Charter were that it sought to provide a framework for reasonable accommodation and to prohibit public servants from wearing visible public symbols. See Bill 60, Charter affirming the values of State secularism and religious neutrality and of equality between women and men, and providing a framework for accommodation requests, 1st Sess, 40th Leg, Quebec, 2013. Although Bill 60 is the most constraining document to date, it was preceded by Bill 94, tabled by the Liberal Party in 2010, which sought to prohibit public service providers and public service receivers from wearing full-face veils. See Bill 94, An Act to establish guidelines governing accommodation requests within the Administration and certain institutions, 1st Sess, 39th Leg, Quebec, 2010.

[6] The spatiality of Muslim prayer in Canadian public hospital buildings gives us another window into the normative and non-neutral orientations of secularism. A number of scholars have noted how Christianity remains implicitly pervasive in the physical infrastructures of many publicly funded and run hospitals in North America and Europe. See S Gilliat-Ray, 'From "Chapel" to "Prayer Room": The Production, Use, and Politics of Sacred Space in Public Institutions' (2005) 6 *Culture and Religion* 287, 304; Reimer-Kirkham et al, 'Sacred Spaces in Public Places' (n 1); W Cadge and M Daglian, 'Blessings, Strength, and Guidance: Prayer Frames in a Hospital Prayer Book' (2008) 36 *Poetics* 358; P Collins et al, *NHS Hospital 'Chaplaincies' in a Multi-faith Society: The Spatial Dimension of Religion and Spirituality in Hospital* (Durham, Durham University, 2007). Across Canada, hospitals were typically originally operated by Christian religious organisations. No longer run by religious orders (since 1954 in NL and 1970 in Quebec), some hospitals like St Claire's in St. John's and Hôtel Dieu in Montreal maintain their saintly names and physical reminders, like crosses on the exterior and interior of buildings. Prayer space accorded to patients and employees in these buildings falls to chapels, usually part of the hospitals' original structures. In one telling narrative, Aydin, 29, notes that the General Hospital where he works as a resident has a prayer room that is organised as a Christian space with 'benches and stuff' and where Christian images and iconography remain. He uses it on occasion to pray, but the configuration is not well suited for his needs. He did not know it had been renamed a 'multi-faith chapel,' until he showed it to Amélie, who noticed an official sign designating it as such. Before that point, Aydin had assumed that it was officially a Christian chapel because of how it was spatially organised.

[7] During the Quebecois debates around the Charter of Secularism in 2013, individuals working on contract for the state or working for private companies hired on a specific contract by the state were considered by some to be part of the 'public servant' category, and thus required to abide by the Charter (ie, to not wear 'visible' religious symbols). Other governments have interpreted this boundary

of participants from our sample and reflects the broader effects of racialisation and religionisation in Canada, which impact the accessibility of high-level public positions for Muslim Canadians.[8] Our sample did not include any government employees who might be characterised as holding high-ranking positions of state power. Indeed, even though they are among the highest educated of religious groups in Canada, few of Canada's estimated 1.054 million[9] Muslims hold full-time positions of political authority. The participants described in what follows were generally well travelled, had worked in a number of Canadian provinces (including British Columbia, Ontario, and Nova Scotia) and had post-secondary educations.

II. Muslims in Montreal and St. John's

The socio-political circumstances of Muslim minorities in Montreal and St. John's differ in our data, primarily owing to heightened concern among provincially based employees in Montreal about the 2013-proposed Charter of Secularism. Statistical data confirm that the experiences of Muslims in Quebec differ from their co-religionists in other parts of Canada. Ten per cent of the Montreal participants expressed concern regarding employment opportunities[10] and discrimination at work. Indeed, a noteworthy difference was that the Montreal participants said that they thought their religious freedoms were better protected in federal agencies than in provincial ones, which in their view were affected by the complexities of provincial identity and language politics.[11]

differently. In France, for instance, mothers who wish to accompany their children on public school outings have in some recent cases been considered as 'temporary' public servants, and been asked to remove their 'visible' religious 'symbols' (ie, their headscarves). In Turkey, MPs and lawyers who entered courtrooms were required, until recently, to remove their headscarves. These differences illustrate how the category of public servant shifts.

[8] According to 2001 Statistics Canada data, Muslims in Canada have the highest unemployment rate by religious group. On average they experience two months of unemployment every year and make $20,000 less than non-Muslim Canadians: cited in A Kazemipur, *The Muslim Question in Canada: A Story of Segmented Integration* (Vancouver, University of British Columbia Press, 2014) 121. 2007 PEW data examining poverty rates in six countries (the US, France, Germany, Spain, Britain and Canada) found the largest gap between Muslim and non-Muslim poverty rates to be in Canada: cited in Kazemipur, *The Muslim Question in Canada* 123.

[9] Statistics Canada, 'Immigration and Ethnocultural Diversity in Canada', Catalogue no 99-010-X (2011) www12.statcan.gc.ca/nhs-enm/2011/as-sa/99-010-x/99-010-x2011001-eng.cfm.

[10] Studies show how many university-educated Muslims in Quebec have had difficulty obtaining gainful employment, often due to the non-recognition of their foreign credentials. See S Arnopoulos-McLeod, 'Highly Qualified Muslim Immigrants Face Employment Discrimination', *Montreal Gazette*, 3 February 2014. See also V Namazi, 'Les trajectoires de l'intégration professionnelle des immigrants iraniens travaillant comme chauffeurs de taxi à Montréal' (PhD thesis, Université de Montréal, 2011).

[11] Provincially based public servants in our St. John's sample were not faced with the same proposed legislation but were nevertheless impacted by the Quebecois Charter's surrounding discourse.

There are also differences in the immigration histories, percentages of visible minorities, and socio-political make-ups of these two cities. In contrast to Montreal's 20.3 per cent, only approximately 3 per cent of St John's population constitute visible minorities.[12] Nonetheless, we have been struck by the overwhelming similarities in the public service work-related narratives of Muslims in Montreal and St John's and therefore do not separate or offer comparative analysis in this chapter. The predominantly Catholic population of Quebec,[13] and the largely Protestant population of NL,[14] result in a Christian normativity that permeates the work conditions of many of the public servants we interviewed in both places. This observation echoes what Lori G Beaman[15] and others[16] have argued with respect to how Christian hegemony is embedded in Canada's social institutions, shaping not only the ways that religion is imagined, but also, following Foucault,[17] how governmentalised expressions of shared values are enforced.

III. The (In)visibility of Christianity

A. 'Holiday Parties'

Even if it is typically a one-off annual event, the ubiquitous annual winter holiday gathering known as the office 'Christmas party' demonstrates the blurred boundaries of religious neutrality. We did not specifically ask about this event in our interview schedule, so the fact that most participants raised this one-evening

[12] Statistics Canada, 'Immigration and Ethnocultural Diversity in Canada' (n 9).

[13] The most common religious affiliation in Montreal is Roman Catholic (63.2%), followed by Muslim (5.9%) and Jewish (2.2%). Statistics Canada, 'NHS Focus on Geography Series—Montréal', Catalogue no 99-010-X2011005 (2011) www12.statcan.gc.ca/nhs-enm/2011/as-sa/fogs-spg/Pages/FOG.cfm?lang=E&level=3&GeoCode=462.

[14] By comparison with the rest of Canada, NL residents report to be more religiously practising (only 2% of Newfoundlanders claim to have 'no religion' compared to a 2001 Statistics Canada national average of 16%) and more Christian (the same data claim that 95% of the province's residents are Roman Catholic, United Church, Anglican, Pentecostal, or Salvation Army members). See AH Akbari et al, *Socioeconomic and Demographic Profiles of Immigrants in Newfoundland and Labrador* (Halifax, Atlantic Metropolis Centre, 2007); ST Cadigan, *Newfoundland and Labrador: A History* (Toronto, University of Toronto Press, 2009); R Tremblay and A Bittner, 'Newfoundland and Labrador: Creating Change in the 21st Century' in J Biles et al (eds), *Integration and Inclusion of Newcomers and Minorities Across Canada* (Montreal, McGill-Queen's University Press, 2011).

[15] LG Beaman, 'A Cross-National Comparison of Approaches to Religious Diversity: Canada, France and the United States' in LG Beaman and P Beyer (eds), *Religion and Diversity in Canada* (Leiden, Brill, 2008).

[16] BL Berger, 'The Cultural Limits of Legal Tolerance' in C Bender and PE Klassen (eds), *After Pluralism: Reimagining Religious Engagement* (New York, Columbia University Press, 2010); PE Klassen, 'Fantasies of Sovereignty: Civic Secularism in Canada' (2015) 3 *Critical Research on Religion* 41.

[17] M Foucault, *Power/Knowledge: Selected Interviews and Other Writings, 1972–1977*, ed C Gordon (New York, Pantheon Books, 1980) 95; M Foucault, *Politics, Philosophy, Culture: Interviews and Other Writings, 1977–1984*, ed LD Kritzman (New York, Routledge, 1988). See also P Bourdieu and L Wacquant, *An Invitation to Reflexive Sociology* (Chicago, University of Chicago Press, 1992).

job-related party is noteworthy.[18] In December 'the holidays' are omnipresent, with decorations and music, the commercialisation of the public sphere, and statutory holidays. Significantly, none of our participants—including those working for non-governmental private companies who are excluded from this sample—expressed offence or a desire to cancel Christmas-timed gatherings, or to rename them as 'holiday gatherings'. Rather, it is the lack of acknowledgement of blurred boundaries and the related silent privileging of Christianity that are experienced as problematic.

A number of government employees described the incongruity of the increasingly pervasive 'holiday party' moniker. One participant, Dalia, 31, who works in a Quebecois provincially run day care centre, pointedly states:

> Quebec is Catholic. We [Muslims] know that, and we're ok with that. And it's annoying when they say, 'Oh it's the Muslims that wanna take it [Christmas] off'. We don't wanna take anything off! Or the, that they banned Christmas songs in school. It's not our fault, they wanna ban them. We don't! I grew up learning 'Joyeux Noel' and all the songs; I still remember them when they come on the radio.

Dalia remembers these carols nostalgically and is in favour of keeping the 'Christmas' title of the party. Others are more bothered by the lack of acknowledgement of its Christian association. Ifra, 42, has pushed her university colleagues to recognise the Christian-ness of Christmas decorations and rituals in her supposedly secular workplace: 'I don't do it in a way that's saying, you know, "Thou shall not celebrate Christmas", but, but I do, I do remind people'.

Like Dalia, Nour, 30, who works as a secondary school teacher in Montreal, remembers the Christmas songs she sang as a child. She has been involved in organising her school's Christmas staff party, and describes how the most recent 'holiday party' was held at a Pakistani-run restaurant:

> For the past few years—this is the second year—I am one of the organizers of the Christmas party because um last year they had no, at the last minute their venue cancelled. There's a very popular restaurant in West Island who's owned by one of my family friends who I call uncle, we're that close. And so I stepped in and I said, 'I think I can get you guys a good deal'. And so people went and they loved it. And so it's a little bit ironic that they're having a Christmas party at a, at a Pakistani restaurant owned by a Muslim. But in that restaurant there's a Christmas tree because they're a client. They're accommodating to their clientele.

Even if Nour organises the party at a restaurant 'owned by a Muslim', the event clearly remains Christian for her: 'It's a Christmas party. We live in a predominately Christian society; it's a Christmas party'. In other words, although the

[18] That it was not part of our interview schedule may be reflective of our positionalities as non-Muslim Caucasian and Christian-identified women researchers. That is, it is perhaps partly due to our own privileged experiences of the 'holidays'.

party is imagined as religiously neutral, neither it, nor Canada more generally, are experienced by her in this way.[19]

Only one of our public servant informants formally critiqued the Christian normativity of 'the holidays'. Sara, 40, who works as a university-based postdoctoral researcher, is a mother of three and a convert to Islam who emigrated to Canada in the late 1990s from Eastern Europe. She describes how she has responded to this Christianising time of year on campus:

> The distance learning department um every, every year around Christmas time they used to send a postcard like wishing 'happy holidays'. Many Canadians they think that when they switch from 'merry Christmas' to 'happy holidays' they embrace all cultures and everything. So I replied to them. I sent them an email. I replied to them that I really appreciate that, you know, they send me this nice postcard, but my religious holidays passed like several months ago. And if they really want to be like accommodating, you know, and it's kind of easy to find in the calendar when, you know, Sikhs have holidays and when Hindus have holidays, and when Muslims have holidays. And then they can, just like they don't need to send postcards to people. They can just post you know on the university website that um happy holidays to all our Sikh students you know or to all our Muslim students, or to all our Muslim employees.

Sara sought to make evident the underlying Christian-ness laden in the university's annual message. She acknowledges the thoughtfulness of the distance-learning department, but then tackles the paradox of their gesture. She sees Christmas first and foremost as a 'religious holiday'—a dimension that does not vanish by 'switch[ing] from "Merry Christmas" to "happy holidays"'. By comparing Christmas with Sikh, Hindu, and Muslim holidays, she highlights how the timing of the message has an explicit Christian dimension. Her unease with attempts to replace 'Christmas' by 'holiday' might represent an (unsuccessful) attempt to 'evacuate' its Christian dimensions to create a 'cultural' and 'commercial' holiday. She suggests either a broadening to include other religious holiday reminders, or eliminating the institutionally sponsored mail-out altogether. For her, 'the holidays' are not a part of Canadian or university cultures. Sara did not receive a reply to her email.

We found that one's religious beliefs and relative position of authority impact one's experience of the 'holiday party'. More permanent and authoritative senior positions in the government job structure afforded the possibility of influencing work environments so that, even if the timing remains unchanged, the festivities better accommodate diversity.[20] For instance, while some senior employees in executive positions like Tobias, 71, choose to facilitate the traditional trappings of

[19] To be clear, we are not arguing that Christmas parties themselves are imbued with Christianity. Rather, our participants experience these parties as Christian.

[20] Scholars have highlighted how the notion of 'authority' is unstable and fragmented and 'fundamentally the result of continual negotiation': see, eg, F Peter and E Arigita, 'Introduction: Authorizing Islam in Europe' (2006) 96 *The Muslim World* 537, 538.

the party, others like Sabrina, 27, use their positions to shift the terms of the typical social gathering.

Tobias, 71, who recently retired from a more than 30-year executive position within the provincial government, discusses organising what he sees as the 'traditional trappings' of the party, even if he himself does not participate. Tobias explains that while he does not feel pressure to facilitate the drinking of alcohol in the workplace for acceptance or promotion, he does not want to be perceived as 'uptight' or unapproachable by his staff. He also seems amused by the situation. Alcohol may not be theologically linked to the birth of Christ but it remains present in many office Christmas parties: 'my staff, at the end of the day around Christmas time they'd have a drink'. Tobias has translated this common practice within his understanding of the Christmas traditions of his staff. He does not purchase or drink alcohol himself but is willing to facilitate a celebratory ambiance for employees for one afternoon before the office would close.

Not all participants are comfortable with facilitating an annual party with alcohol. Sabrina, 27, an outspoken and gregarious co-director of a provincial-government-funded centre for Aboriginal people, does not question the Christmas party. Instead she explains how she laboured to organise an appropriate gathering that mitigated her discomfort with alcohol, but also ensured that her employees felt the annual party was celebrated. By organising a family-friendly laser-tag event she believes that she came up with an arrangement that offered everyone a relaxing and rewarding moment:

> Nobody needs to go and get loaded drunk at a staff party. It's better for us to go out and play laser-tag for two hours and have pizza. And then people can bring spouses and their kids and it's more, it's fun! Who wants to look at just the people that they work with all day long? I don't like half of them [laughs]. And I'm, not that I don't like them, but I wouldn't choose to spend time with them. You know? So. If I'm drunk, I mean, who knows what I'll [laughs]. Can you imagine what I might say? So. I've been really lucky [to be able to organise it].

Sabrina appreciates that her position allows her to choose the location and terms of the annual party, and welcomes the end results.[21] Tobias and Sabrina's approach to the holiday party acknowledged the tangible presence of Christianity in the workplace calendar, but also showed that some of the party's elements could be adjusted to ensure that it was more open to others. Generally, appropriate food and drink were of greater concern than the visible Christian dimensions of the annual celebrations within so-called secular public institutions.

In sum, despite attempts to imagine public service offices as neutral, they remain imbued with religious references and practices. They are, indeed, experienced by our participants as reflecting the Christian character of the Canadian

[21] Notably, Sabrina does not seem to be perturbed by the perception of the potential violent undertones of the laser-tag activity.

public sphere. While positions of authority enable some of our participants to be involved in the organisation of the festivities,[22] most did not have a problem with the Christian-ness of these gatherings. What was identified as more problematic was its superficial rebranding as a 'holiday party' in the auspices of religious plurality and inclusivity, without changing the timing or details of the activities. Most notably, rather than being experienced as a transgression, the ongoing presence of Christianity is almost invariably worked-out and lived as a dimension that is constitutive of the Canadian public realm and, for these public servants, constitutive of their everyday work lives.

IV. Hypervisible Islam

A. Hypervisibility and the Collapsing of Identity

While on the one hand many of our Muslim participants' workplace experiences are marked by attempts (successful or otherwise) to respond to 'invisible' Christianity, on the other hand their Muslim-ness has often been rendered hypervisible in their work environments. Plainly stated, our Muslim participants' religiosity was *the* foregrounded part of their identities in their interactions at work, whether this was desired or not.[23] More theoretically, this constriction of identity reflects a trend toward a singular focus on religious identity in scholarship and public discourse. Indeed, in recent years, after being long omitted from consideration, religion has become a primary lens. Muslims in particular are reduced to religion, and the complexity of their identities is discounted.[24] While their non-Muslim colleagues did not necessarily see the religious lives of Muslim civil servants as problematic, the religious identities of Muslims were frequently the object of scrutiny, discussion, and negotiation. With this broader trend in mind, we turn now to consider the ways in which our participants' minority status, and in particular their ethnicity, race, or religion, are subsumed into a singular focus on Muslim-ness. We chart how self-described Muslim public servants in

[22] This alternate authority resonates with Gilliat-Ray's observation on prayer rooms, where she points out that: 'had the decision-making about these details [on the organisation of prayer rooms been left] in the hands of Hindus, Sikhs, or perhaps Muslims, it is probable that there would have been no table. There may have only been a couple of chairs for the elderly/infirm, and there may have been indicators of separate areas for males or females': see Gilliat-Ray, 'From "Chapel" to "Prayer Room"' (n 6) 304.

[23] The irony of our own study fore-fronting Muslim-ness in these participants' lives is not lost on us.

[24] On this point see, eg, D Kumar, *Islamophobia and the Politics of Empire* (New York, Haymarket Press, 2012); T Asad, *Formations of the Secular* (Stanford, Stanford University Press, 2003); NM Dessing et al (eds), *Everyday Lived Islam in Europe* (Farnham, Ashgate, 2013). While this focus on religious identity seems to affect Muslims most acutely, it is not only about Islam in that the will to make religion *the* main prism permeates public policy more broadly. See WF Sullivan, *A Ministry of Presence: Chaplaincy, Spiritual Care, and the Law* (Chicago, University of Chicago Press, 2014).

our sample expressed both acceptance and frustration with this reality. Here as well, an individual's position and status within the workplace play a significant role in determining the extent to which this identity collapse takes place: those in executive positions are able to avoid these categorisations more than those in less authoritative positions.

Hijab-wearing women experience this collapse most acutely. Just as other studies have underscored the hypervisibility of this garment in the Western public sphere,[25] the female public servants in our sample who wore hijabs characterised this garment as the most significant barrier to gaining meaningful employment and status in their workplaces. Vincent Geisser has aptly described the post-9/11 period in the West as being characterised by 'hijabophobia', or the irrational rejection of the hijab.[26] This sentiment has been well-charted in social scientific literature, which shows how non-Christian religious symbols are perceived as superseding all other personal philosophical positions.[27] Our interlocutors similarly noted this stigma. Ouria, who began wearing her hijab at 22, describes it as 'exhausting', because she is constantly called to explain it, in and outside of her workplace: 'It's enough [*y'a plus de goût*]. It's like, ok then, can we move onto something else?' A female family physician stopped wearing hers at her practice. She says she loses too much time explaining the significance of the garment to curious patients. Another woman, Ifra, wears Pakistani-style dress to work on occasion but does not cover her hair. She notes: 'Oh my God, that's work [wearing hijab] in this culture. It's a lot of work'.

Nour, 30, similarly feels that her hijab frames external perception of her politics and beliefs in her workplace. She says that she senses that she was hired as a hijabi public high school teacher in Montreal because the school was Anglophone, which made it more accommodating of her visible religiosity.[28] While her hijab may not have impeded her hiring, Nour describes how students, their parents, and her colleagues hold preconceived notions about her beliefs and politics based on the garment:

> I have to teach students about contraception. I have to teach them about safe sex. I don't believe in sex before marriage, but I don't let my beliefs, I don't tell the kids 'oh you have

[25] eg, JW Scott, *The Politics of the Veil* (Princeton, Princeton University Press, 2007); JA Selby, *Questioning French Secularism* (New York, Palgrave Macmillan, 2012); A Barras, *Refashioning Secularisms in France and Turkey* (London, Routledge, 2014); N Jeldtoft, 'The Hypervisibility of Islam' in NM Dessing et al (eds), *Everyday Lived Islam in Europe* (Farnham, Ashgate, 2013).

[26] V Geisser, 'Islamophobia: A French Specificity in Europe?' (2010) 8 *Human Architecture: Journal of the Sociology of Self Knowledge* 39, 43.

[27] eg, S Mahmood, *Politics of Piety: The Islamic Revival and the Feminist Subject* (Princeton, University of Princeton Press, 2005); N Fadil, 'Managing Affects and Sensibilities: The Case of Not-Handshaking and not Fasting' (2009) 17 *Social Anthropology* 439; S Silvestri, 'Faith Intersections and Muslim Women in the European Microcosm: Notes Towards the Study of Non-Organized Islam' (2011) 34 *Ethnic and Racial Studies* 1230.

[28] A significant number of participants in the Montreal data made a distinction between Anglophone and Francophone environments, with the notion that the former was more respectful of their identities, including their religious freedom. This distinction recalls Kazemipur's point regarding the impact of language politics for Muslims in Quebec: see Kazemipur (n 8) 113.

> to be celibate'. I don't do that. So I have never ever let that come in my, so if someone were to say to me just because I choose to cover my head I'm, because that's what the implication is. You know you're, you have to be secular. But why can't you teach in a secular setting and then have your own personal beliefs?

Nour resents the assumption that she will not teach her students about safe sex in a sexual education class because of her religious beliefs; she follows the school's curriculum even if she herself does not condone premarital sex or homosexuality. The way in which her religious dress is interpreted by some parents and staff—or at least in Nour's perception—is as a rejection of shared Canadian sexual norms.[29]

Some hijabi participants described how they are excluded from public service job opportunities in ways that were not always overt. Shama, 32, of Iraqi origin, discusses her internship experiences with the Quebec justice system and in the legal department of a Quebec municipality. Now employed as a lawyer in a private law firm in Montreal, she is conscious of the perception of her hijab by potential colleagues and clients. For Shama, the veil is not negotiable; other elements of her beliefs and practices—like praying during the workday or shaking hands with non-relatives of the opposite sex—are less pressing. The latter, she explains, might prove problematic in working with clients, so she prefers not to push on this point. She therefore negotiates these other practices on a case-by-case basis.

As far as she knows, she was the first hijabi 'in the hallways of the courthouse'. Shama explains that her overall experience as an intern with the justice system was positive. In fact, she was surprised at how well she was received: 'I'm really lucky. I was assigned to one of the most open judges!' Her veil appeared to pose a greater challenge when she interned with the legal department of a Quebec municipality, in particular for those working in the administrative office:

> You know, my internship supervisor: perfect. No problem. It was really the others, the others, the secretaries and all of them. They all lived in the, in the area … Those weren't the best six months of my life.

Shama's supervisor told her she was an exceptional intern and so she wonders why her employment was not extended when the position she filled was subsequently advertised. She speculates that she was hired by the legal department on a temporary internship basis, thereby allowing the department to satisfy a desire to showcase religious diversity and to comply superficially with equity policies, without actually hiring her permanently. Like some participants in our sample,

[29] This scenario mirrors broader controversies regarding gender equality, especially how Quebecois articulations of secularity have begun to dovetail with stricter and more gendered French Republican values on secularism in public institutions. On this see, eg: D Koussens, 'Le port de signes religieux dans les écoles québécoises et françaises: Accommodements (dé)raisonnables ou interdiction (dé)raisonnée?' (2008) 11 *Globe: revue internationale d'études québécoises* 115; D Koussens, 'Neutrality of the State and Regulation of Religious Symbols in Schools in Québec and France' (2009) 56 *Social Compass* 202; JA Selby, 'Un/veiling Women: Secularism and Sexuality in Full-face Veil Prohibitions in France and Québec' (2014) 43 *Studies in Religion* 439.

Shama attributes this negative experience of low-level and insecure employment to the particularities of her homogenous and 'racist' work environment.

This hypervisibility of Muslim-ness affects not just women who wear headscarves. Akeem, 29, depicts his work conditions when he began a laboratory-based research position in a university science department:

> [Before] I came to do my Masters I contacted a supervisor and told them I was coming and everything. And then um before I came here—I learned this after coming here—my supervisor, he thought, like, he knew that I was coming from the Middle East, so he just assumed that I'm a Muslim. And then he went around … telling people that 'oh, I have a Muslim student coming' and he suggested, uh like I don't know if he did actually or if he said in front of people, that he's going to suggest to the administration to provide a prayer room for me. And then people [in the lab] start being mad and then saying like 'why?' And he's like, 'cuz we know he's a Muslim and they need a room to pray'. And people are saying like 'we're Catholic or we're Christians, no one asked us if we wanted a room. This is discrimination against us'. And there was a big controversy about it. So when I came here and then uh the first day my supervisor asked me he's like … and I said 'oh, oh, I'm not, I'm not Muslim'. And he's like 'but you're from the Middle East' … then when I went to work and then I started to know people it's like 'oh, you are the student everyone's talking about' … They saw it like a discrimination against them. Like, 'How come no one asked us?'

This seemingly good-hearted gesture by a non-Muslim faculty member was most likely sought to facilitate Akeem's integration in his new work environment. Yet, Akeem is non-practising and takes care to avoid being identified as a practising Muslim.[30] Indeed, conscious of his outsider foreigner status, Akeem has not sought any accommodations—religious or otherwise—that would separate him from his labmates. He wants the focus to be on his knowledge of science. His supervisor's gesture caused him considerable personal discomfort. He says it initially alienated him from his non-Muslim labmates, who made a number of comments about how no one had ever asked them, as Christians, if they needed prayer space, and suggested: 'this is discrimination against us'. Even after the error was corrected, the so-called humour in his workplace zeroed-in on his purported religiosity and Otherness, with his labmates 'jokingly' nicknaming him 'Osama', adding to his alienation. Another respondent might have challenged his colleagues' association of Osama bin Laden with Muslim-ness, but Akeem wanted to be perceived as 'ok' by his peers, which presumably meant as 'not a radical'. This incident and others made Akeem hyper-aware of how 'they will always associate me with Islam because I'm from the Middle-East'. The point being that no matter what he did, he could not escape this linkage, manifested first in the unrequested accommodation and later in the Islamophobic name-calling masquerading as humour.

[30] Akeem was reluctant to be interviewed for this research project, as he believed his experiences would not be representative of a five-pillar conception of the traditions of Islam. He identifies as Muslim and has actively avoided the mosque since moving to Canada five years ago.

B. Hypervisibility as Authoritative

Not all our participants experienced this collapse of identity as problematic. Some felt it gave them more credibility and leverage in their jobs. Thirty-year-old head-scarved Dalia, for instance, attributes part of her good reputation as an early childhood educator in a publicly-run day care centre to the fact that parents know that she is a Muslim and think her religiosity helps her to better educate and discipline their children:

> [The parents] they said that because I'm Muslim there are certain things that I will do, you know, I will be more picky about. Like, before going to eat we wash our hands, after eating we wash our hands, after going to the bathroom we wash our hands. Because there are many teachers, you know, who don't do that, they don't care … They saw that I was taking care of their child.

Other participants, especially those in more established positions, embraced the possibility of becoming spokespeople or ad-hoc theologians for 'acceptable' Muslim religiosity in their workspaces. These Muslim public servants willingly 'out' themselves in ways that make their religious identities predominant. Hassan, 29, has taken an unofficial role as religious mediator at a Crown corporation. Working in a human resources department where questions of dispensation and accommodation are raised quite often, Hassan has met with imams outside work hours to determine what might be an Islamically appropriate response to particular workplace employee issues. When asked about the implications of his employer's request that he evaluate the validity of another employee's religious request, Hassan explains that this role emerged slowly: his colleagues know that he is a Sunni Muslim, as he frequently discusses his beliefs at lunchtime. In one case, he expressed his opinion on whether a mail delivery person had the right to refuse delivery on a Friday because of *jumu'ah* prayer. A question that arose was whether the prayer practice was similar to the Christian Sunday congregational prayer, and so would require the individual to be absent for the entire day. After seeking advice and referencing his own understanding of appropriate practice, Hassan determined that no, the employee should not have the right to an entire day, because such participation called for a one-hour absence, which could be compensated by moving the timing of the mail deliverer's lunch break.

In a different case, Hassan determined that Eid celebrations warranted a few days off, relying on existing institutional policies concerning personal leave days. He framed this request as comparable to Christmas, and noted that the department has an equity policy and that one could alternatively have recourse to the Charter:

> I told my boss that Eid can fall on this day or that day. So if it is this day, well in this case I won't be in the office. And if it is this day, well, I told her, it is always more or less two days, ok? … I have personal days, and she said, 'No, no. Take the time that you need with your family … It's like our Christmas'. It's like, you know, my [boss] is really open … and they know [the managers] that we can lodge human rights complaints.

Hassan's position as a human resources officer, combined with his willingness to make theologically based decisions, establish him as a '*porte-parole* of religion'. Because of his 'visible' religious identity, willingness to dispense knowledge about Islam, and his connections in the Muslim community, he considers himself to be authorised to speak about religious matters, and is at the same time authorised in the eyes of his colleagues to arbitrate these matters. In performing this role he may also participate in collapsing the multitudinous expressions of Islam into a narrow version of its traditions.

As occurred in the case of the 'holiday' parties, participants who held senior positions were often singled-out as resource persons on Islam, by both Muslims and non-Muslims, even if they sought to keep their religious lives private. Raja, a medical doctor in her fifties, discusses how one of her Muslim residents asked for her advice on where he could pray. She took care to make clear that he should not pray at work openly in the resident room as she felt to do so was 'highly highly inappropriate'. Rather, he should pray in the hospital chapel to keep his religiosity separate from his work colleagues. Hijab-wearing Raja is thus given a certain authority by her student regarding religious and workplace propriety. Even if, in contrast to Hassan, she does not seek this role, she nevertheless delimits the boundaries of 'acceptable' Islam, demarcating private from public spaces. Thus, our interlocutors' positions of authority in their public institutions play a central role in explaining why they are identified and authorised as spatial arbiters of appropriate practice.

Whether participants like Nour, Akeem, or Raja express deep concerns and unease with respect to this constriction of their identities, or whether they choose to embrace it like Dalia and Hassan, they all act as representatives of a collapsed normative 'Islam' in their workplace. For all of these public servants, their Muslim identities are lived as overdetermined, hypervisible, and a source of negotiation and discussion at work. This hypervisibility also affirms the secular tendency to attribute visibility to Islam but not to Christianity.[31] It further 'Others' Islam and reaffirms visible Muslim practice as 'transgressive' or at least as 'special', in contrast to the beliefs and practices of majority-Christian workers that remain invisible. Many of our participants questioned this 'special' role in our interviews, especially when they experienced it as affecting their equal access to public institutions (eg, hiring process, access to permanent position, discrimination, and so on).

V. Conclusion

Our participants' descriptions of the (in)visibility of Christianity and Islam in public service institutions highlights the ambiguity of neutrality in public

[31] Asad, *Formations of the Secular* (n 24); Sullivan, *The Impossibility of Religious Freedom* (Princeton, Princeton University Press, 2005).

institutions and the way it is experienced and negotiated by religious minorities. These experiences tell us something about the current casting of secularism in Canadian public institutions and the need to acknowledge the asymmetry in the visibility and invisibility of different religious traditions.

In the first place, the experiences of our respondents highlight how Christianity, cloaked under a rhetoric of impartiality, continues to structure time, space and social relations, and how this normativity permeates the work lives of public servants. As a common cultural practice, the 'holiday party' illustrates these organising practices. At the same time participants' narratives speak to the role played by authority in the production of these practices. Recall Sabrina who explained that, because she is a manager in her organisation, she was able to propose a family-oriented, alcohol-free, laser-tag party, replacing the annual adult-only licensed evening event. Or Nour, who became one of the organisers of her school's Christmas party, and held it at her uncle's Pakistani restaurant, a restaurant that displays a Christmas tree because 'they're accommodating to their clientele'. Thus, employment status influences these employees' ability to shape more diverse work environments and to be intimately involved in 'the production of meaning, concepts and consciousness of space'.[32]

In the second place, the narratives of our participants are an invitation to re-examine the delimitation of space in terms of where religion and non-religion (or to be more precise, non-mainstream minority religions) are positioned. Our participants point to continuous, but flawed organisation around a public/non-religious and private/religious dichotomy, with the holiday party moniker being an example of this boundary-blurring. So too are workplace policies that seek to ensure religious diversity that force public servants to trespass areligious norms and invisibility through discourses of 'request', with which not all of our participants were comfortable engaging. In other words, to have access to desired food, prayer spaces, or times, for example, public servants must make a request, whether formally or informally. Wana, 20, takes days off for Eid holidays because she makes a formal request with her supervisor, but Raja, who is visibly Muslim with her hijab, prefers not to be singled out through the same request. Ironically, this prevalent paradigm of request in government offices requires employees to frame their religiosity as something 'public', thereby contributing to their hyper-visibility and continuing to render invisible the privileges afforded to majorities within the workplace.[33]

[32] Smith, *Uneven Development* (n 4) 77.

[33] See A Barras, 'Exploring the Intricacies and dissonances of religious governance: The case of Quebec and the discourse of request' (2016) 4(1) *Critical Research on Religion* for more on this discourse of request.

A final and related point is that the narratives of our public servant interlocutors encourage us to revisit what is meant by impartiality of public services and how 'neutrality' is articulated, a question that arose in the debate about Quebec's 2013 Charter of Secularism. Our interlocutors' descriptions of how Muslim identity is experienced as hypervisible, as a transgression, as often being *the* prism that defines them as public servants, not only questions the notion of impartiality at its core, but calls for reflection on how these constant 'Othering' processes produce a certain kind of space. Policing and (re)producing such inequitable public/private boundaries affirms non-neutral values.[34] Nour, for one, is not fooled. For her, 'We live in a predominantly Christian society'.

[34] See K Knott, 'Inside, Outside and the Space In-Between: Territories and Boundaries in the Study of Religion' (2008) 44 *Temenos* 83, 94.

7

The Prayer Case Saga in Canada: An 'Expert Insider' Perspective on Praying in the Political and Public Arenas

SOLANGE LEFEBVRE

God still has a place in the public life of Canada, although a variable one, depending on one's point of view. The Constitution mentions God in its preamble, in mottos, prayers, and sermons. Judges can notably conclude a swearing-in by stating, 'So help me God'. More specifically, Christian symbolism is quite present in Quebec, appearing in the fleur-de-lys, in architecture, and in the symbols within the National Assembly of Quebec. The crucifix above the speaker's chair has received its share of attention, but in the 'Red Room' of that same building there also sits a throne with an inscription, '*Dieu et mon droit*' (God and my right), from an evidently British tradition.

Quebec, with its Roman Catholic majority, has been going through a systematic secularisation process over the last 15 years. But the province also has something in common with the rest of Canada, namely prayers in municipal assemblies. Quebec also maintains the crucifix on the walls of many public buildings, giving rise to the most consistently debated issue at the National Assembly. Recently, religious expressions, the prayer, and religious symbols have been questioned, notably by engaged groups of atheists in political deliberations.

I have only once attended a municipal assembly, in a multicultural and multi-religious area of Montreal, where I noted a crucifix on the wall. The mayor, with his hands clasped in front of him, invited us to maintain a moment of silence before commencing the deliberations. All present stood up, assuming meditative poses. Many cities and towns across Canada, whether in response to complaints or not, have decided to replace the prayer with a moment of silence. Some of them alternate between different prayers, as in Edmonton.[1] As an anthropologist,

[1] www.cbc.ca/news/canada/edmonton/prayer-at-city-council-what-is-faith-s-place-in-local-government-1.3050820.

I am both sensitive to and intrigued by the attachment people have to traditional expressions, notably in the political sphere.

In Quebec, the prayer case followed a legal path full of twists and turns that started when a complaint was submitted to the Human Rights Tribunal by an atheist, Alain Simoneau. That initial complaint was favourably received by the tribunal in 2011 but overturned by the Quebec Court of Appeal in 2013. The initial decision called for the termination of all prayers during Saguenay municipal assemblies, a result that was ultimately reaffirmed by the Supreme Court of Canada in 2015. This chapter retraces and analyses this legal saga.[2]

After the Supreme Court ruled in favour of Simoneau, and asked Saguenay to cease the prayers, the expressions of attachment offered by some mayors were portrayed in two distinct manners by the media. The first is well illustrated by the mayor of Calgary, Naheed Nenhsi, a practising Muslim. After the ruling, the city stopped its public prayer, but the mayor said he was doing so to apply the law, not because he agreed with the Supreme Court's decision:

> Naheed Nenhsi says he liked the idea of opening council with a prayer for two reasons. Meetings can get 'petty and silly,' and sometimes taking a moment can ground the participants. But he also believes there is a difference between religious neutrality, and secularism: 'To me religious neutrality which the government must adhere to,' explains the Mayor, 'doesn't mean being secular. It means inviting people to the conversation, to bring all of themselves to the conversation, including their faith'. He says a lot of people get caught up on the idea of the 'separation of church and state,' but he believes that in Canada it's possible to create a society that recognizes multiple faiths, without excluding anyone.[3]

A second manner in which this attachment is expressed combines Mayor Nenshi's sense of the benefits of recognising religion publicly with an element of 'us versus them' reasoning. Prayer is presented as the affirmation of the faith and traditions of the local and national community, especially in Quebec. We find this logic in several of Jean Tremblay's statements, the mayor of Saguenay who led the legal battle:

> At some point, yes, you have to bend on some occasions, but you also have to stand up for yourself. You have to be able to say no, not this time, especially when it comes to touching us, the Quebecois, in such a profound manner, when it comes to crumbling like this.[4]

Part of the Canadian political establishment seems undeniably attached to certain religious traditions. In the case of the prayer, while elected officials appeared

[2] The rest of the chapter refers to these decisions: *Simoneau v Tremblay* [2011] QCTDP 1; *Saguenay (Ville de) v Mouvement laïque québécois* [2013] QCCA 936; *Mouvement laïque québécois v Saguenay (City)* [2015] SCC 16.

[3] CBC Radio, 180 with Jim Brown, May 3, 2015, www.cbc.ca/radio/the180/animal-testing-gender-wage-gap-ecomodernist-manifesto-1.3052639/public-prayers-a-mayor-s-response-1.3052891.

[4] 'Jean Tremblay va se soumettre à la décision de la Cour suprême', *Ici Radio-Canada.ca*, 16 April 2015, http://ici.radio-canada.ca/regions/saguenay-lac/2015/04/16/002-jean-tremblay-reaction-priere-cour-supreme.shtml. Note that all foreign language texts included in this chapter have been translated by the author.

divided on the issue, representatives from hundreds of cities, towns and villages expressed the wish to preserve it, in addition to—for some—maintaining the crucifix in public buildings.

The courts deliberated on the question of whether the prayer has a discriminatory effect on members of the public present at municipal council meetings, who are either not Christian, or do not believe in a superior being. More broadly, they deliberated on the question of state neutrality. This chapter reflects on these fundamental matters in the context of the Saguenay case in comparison with the lesser-known Ontarian cases (1999, 2004) and the city of Laval case (2006).[5] In so doing, it also exposes the most controversial sub-question at stake, in particular, regarding the demonstration of discrimination through reliance on an anthropological theory of ritual that resided at the centre of the expert's contributions.

I. The Ontario Courts

There are two important existing rulings on the recitation of prayers in Ontarian municipal assemblies. The first, by the Court of Appeal for Ontario (1999), required municipalities to cease the recitation of the 'Lord's Prayer' at the beginning of public assemblies and suggested that a more inclusive prayer would perhaps be less intrusive, notably the one recited at the House of Commons. The second, by the Ontario Superior Court (2004), allowed the recitation of a prayer modified along the guidelines provided by the Court of Appeal. Saguenay will likely modify its prayer to conform to this model.

In 1999, the decision of the Court of Appeal for Ontario stated that the prayer (then the Lord's Prayer) pronounced during the city council of Penetanguishene was unacceptable, and that to read passages from the Bible imposed 'Christian observances on non-Christians and religious observances on non-believers'.[6]

In Renfrew County, in 2000, a prayer—inspired by the one recited at the House of Commons—was adopted as a replacement for the Lord's Prayer in the hope of being more inclusive. Nevertheless, an expert in religious studies, Antonia R Gualtieri, argued that the prayer was exclusionary and should not be permitted because it offers a theistic framework and because 'any activity which claimed to be non-sectarian in the sense of encompassing all religions (ie symbolically mediated world-and-value-views) in a pluralist society would have to accommodate the Humanist phenomenon'.[7]

[5] *Freitag v Penetanguishene (Town)* [1999] CanLII 3786 (ON CA); *Allen v Renfrew (Corp of the County)* [2004] CanLII 13978 (ON SC). *Commission des droits de la personne et des droits de la jeunesse v Laval (Ville de)* [2006] QCTDP 17.

[6] *Freitag v Penetanguishene* (n 5) para 21.

[7] *Allen v Renfrew* (n 5), para 13.

The *Allen v Renfrew* case of 2004 presented the issue of prayer as follows:

> The Renfrew County Council commences its monthly meetings with a prayer. This practice has been followed as long as anyone can remember and likely since the Council was established in 1861. The prayer recited was the Lord's Prayer until November 2000 when a new non-secular prayer was adopted in its place. The applicant Robert Allen is a resident of Renfrew County who does not believe in God or in participation in prayers. He seeks a declaration that the respondent Council's practice of opening meetings with a prayer is a violation of his Charter right to freedom of conscience and religion, together with an injunction restraining this practice and damages for mental distress.

In spite of the objection of Gualtieri, the court deemed the prayer acceptable. In the following, Judge Hackland of the Superior Court explained the moral and religious meaning of the prayer:

> On my reading of this prayer it can be characterized as an effort to impose a moral tone on the proceedings and to promote certain values, in particular good governance. The prayer identifies the gifts of 'freedom, opportunity, and peace' that we enjoy in Canada and asks for 'wisdom, knowledge, and understanding' to preserve the blessings of this country. In my opinion there is no specifically theological message in this, Christian or otherwise. However, the prayer does begin with phrase 'All mighty God, we give thanks for the great blessings which have been bestowed on Canada and its citizens' and the prayer clearly reflects the belief that God is the source of these blessings and that the requested wisdom, knowledge, and understanding derives from God. In this limited respect there is a religious message.[8]

But the judge continued along the following lines to make an argument in favour of the prayer:

> In a pluralistic society religious, moral or cultural values put forward in a public governmental context cannot always be expected to meet with universal acceptance. This is to be contrasted with the use of a specifically Christian prayer, such as the Lord's Prayer or readings from the bible, when non-Christians are involved (ie as in *Freitag* and *Zylberberg*). In my view, it would be incongruous and contrary to the intent of the *Charter* to hold that the practice of offering a prayer to God per se, is a violation of the religious freedom of non-believers. This conclusion derives considerable support from the fact that the preamble to the *Charter* itself specifically refers to the supremacy of God.[9]

In sharp contrast, in Quebec, the Human Rights Tribunals ruled more clearly in favour of banning all prayers, referring to the Ontarian Court of Appeal's decision in *Freitag*.[10] In 2011, Quebec's Court of Appeal overturned the decision of the Human Rights Tribunal and determined that the prayer, along with a few religious symbols, could persist. It analysed the Ontario courts' decisions in detail and sided with the arguments set out in *Renfrew*.[11] The Supreme Court recognised

[8] ibid, para 18.

[9] ibid, para 19.

[10] *Commission des droits de la personne et des droits de la jeunesse v Laval (Ville de)* (n 5), paras 127, 146, 191. *Saguenay (Ville de) v Mouvement laïque québécois* (n 2), paras 252, 286, 287.

[11] *Saguenay (Ville de) v Mouvement laïque québécois* (n 2), paras 89–95.

the relevance of the Ontario tribunals, but chose to analyse the Quebec case differently, in its specific context.

II. The Quebec Cases

A lawyer for the city of Laval contacted me during the winter of 2006. The city's lawyers had been tasked with responding to an expert's report that had been submitted a few weeks earlier, before the end of the hearings. I was asked to comment on whether the recitation of the prayer could be considered a public ritual, one that might be strongly exclusive of non-believers. Laval lost its case before the Human Rights Tribunal and did not pursue an appeal. The tribunal had recommended the cessation of the prayer, since it was deemed discriminatory against atheists.[12] A similar case was heard in Saguenay, for which I was again summoned as an expert, together with Gilles Bibeau, a renowned academic and anthropologist. While Saguenay lost the initial case, they would ultimately win before the Court of Appeal. As previously stated, the Supreme Court heard the case on 14 October 2014 and rendered a final decision in favour of the plaintiff in April 2015.

In both cases, during the first proceedings, when the plea was heard before the Human Rights Tribunal, the onus was on the plaintiff to demonstrate the extent of the discrimination. The issue of state neutrality was not a central question to be addressed within the limitations of the Human Rights Tribunal's jurisdiction. It therefore refused to investigate the presence of religious symbols in the municipal buildings of Saguenay. In the specific context of the human rights process, the main questions were as follows. Does prayer have a discriminatory effect against those present who do not believe in a superior being? And, if indeed it is even possible, how can one demonstrate the strength of this discriminatory effect?

A. The Contested Prayers

What were the prayers, and what were the contexts in which they were recited? In Laval, the bylaws concerning the internal management of the Municipal Council specified:

> Art 11: As of the time scheduled for the meeting and as soon as there is quorum, the chairperson of the meeting should go to the place reserved for him in the board room, 'from where, seated at all times, he directs the debates'.

[12] P Bosset, 'Pratiques et symboles religieux. Quelles sont les responsabilités des institutions?' Conference text (Quebec, Commission des droits de la personne et des droits de la jeunesse, 2000), www.cdpdj.qc.ca/Publications/pratiques_symboles.pdf.

> Art 12: All persons present in the board room are to get up and stand, and the chairperson can then recite a prayer: 'Dear Lord, we beseech you to grant us the grace and wisdom required to conduct our meeting and the proper administration of our city. Amen'.

No religious symbols were present in the boardroom for Laval's municipal assemblies. The chairperson made the sign of the cross, and sometimes other members of the board did so as well—but this gesture was not required by the bylaws. The prayer itself was not listed on the agenda.

In Saguenay, following the initial complaint, the opening prayer was modified in 2008 to conform to the prayer that was upheld in the earlier decision by the Ontario court and recited in the closed sessions of Canada's House of Commons:

> Almighty God, we thank You for the great blessings that You have given to Saguenay and its citizens, including freedom, opportunities for development and peace. Guide us in our deliberations as a member of the council and help us to be well aware of our duties and responsibilities. Grant us wisdom, knowledge, and understanding that will enable us to preserve the benefits enjoyed by our city so that everyone can benefit and make wise decisions. Amen.[13]

In addition to this prayer and the sign of the cross made by the acting mayor (without requiring the attendees to stand), a crucifix hangs in the room and a small statue of the Sacred Heart rests in another boardroom—symbols described in detail in the 2011 case.[14]

Taking into account the 2015 Supreme Court decision, it is important to recall certain details. In 2008, following the filing of the complaint by Simoneau, the city amended its regulations so that the prayer would be more likely to survive judicial scrutiny. The city invoked the unanimous will of the councillors to justify the continuation of the 'tradition' of the recitation of the prayer. A two-minute period was allotted between the recitation and the beginning of the meeting so that people who did not wish to attend could enter after the prayer. In addition, it opted for the inclusion of the new prayer, as previously cited. All these modifications had been recommended by the city's lawyers, in order to clarify that the prayer is essentially for the 'mayor and councillors', and not necessarily the public.

The Supreme Court, however, agreed with the tribunal, and held that interposing a two-minute wait did not negate the discriminatory effect.[15] Moreover, the Court argued that the recent fusion of several cities into Saguenay contradicted the claim

[13] 'Since 1877, Parliament has commenced its proceedings with a prayer read by the Speaker before the doors of the House were opened to the public'. See Canada, Parliament, House of Commons, Table Research Branch, Précis of Procedure, 5th edn (Ottawa, Canada Communication Group, 1996) 19. In 1994, the sectarian prayer which had historically been used was replaced with a non-sectarian prayer, which is read in English and French before the doors are opened to the public. Except for the mention of Queen Elizabeth and the Governor General, the prayer at Renfrew County Council is the same': *Freitag* (n 5), para 45.

[14] *Simoneau v Tremblay* (n 2), para 14s.

[15] Inviting citizens to physically leave the chamber during the prayer highlights its exclusionary effect. *Mouvement laïque québécois v Saguenay* (n 2), para 101.

that the prayer represented a municipal tradition. Finally, it held that the claim by the city that the prayer was meant to advance the freedom of conscience and religion of the councillors, made it clear 'that the prayer was intended as support by the city for the religion professed by individual councillors'.[16] In short, according to the Supreme Court, the changes proposed by the lawyers for Saguenay reinforced the discriminatory effect of the prayer, while undermining state neutrality.

Regarding the content of the prayers, the experts were also asked to address the following question: 'Up to what point is the prayer inclusive or exclusive of diverse beliefs?' Everyone agreed that the text of the prayer was 'ecumenical' in the Christian sense of the term, thus signifying that the prayer could be a common point of reference for diverse Christian denominations, confessions, or churches. In addition, the wording of the prayer could also be appropriate for the collective of monotheistic Abrahamic religions—Judaism, Christianity, and Islam. But the sign of the cross clearly gives a Christian meaning to the prayer, as do the religious symbols involved in *Saguenay*. It nonetheless remained unclear how constrained people felt to make the sign of the cross, even among the councillors, and even if the Mayor of Saguenay had purposefully performed the sign of the cross among them. In *Laval*, these gestures were more discreet and left up to the individuals involved.

But it would be here that the inclusiveness of a general prayer ends, since a supernatural entity or an interventionist god was evoked. Nevertheless, in my expertise, I explained that even the latter has to be placed into context, since some researchers show that 'believing in God' is understood in different ways. For many, God is not a person, but a hidden dimension of the cosmos, the self, or the social, even for some atheists.[17] Consequently, I explained that atheism is not always 'exclusivist,' namely an atheism infused with religious expressions. But some people or movements firmly adhere to atheism and are strongly opposed to any idea of a God or supernatural entity, notably people involved in diverse humanist associations who have expressed points of view opposed to the recitation of the municipal prayers. Even if this could make certain individuals feel uncomfortable, nevertheless, I could not accept the theory of ritual to explain this discomfort, in creating a space constructed to exclude 'non-believers'.

III. The Main Disputes

As mentioned above, I was involved as an expert when it became necessary to respond to another expert's report submitted before the end of the hearings.

[16] *Mouvement laïque québécois v Saguenay* (n 2), para 100.

[17] eg, R Lemieux and M Milot, *Les croyances des Québécois. Esquisses pour une approche empirique* (Quebec, Presses de l'Université Laval, 1992) 248. Some statistical records mention that a certain number of religious adherents understand themselves as atheists, their affiliation being more cultural than religious.

This expert, Daniel Bary, was hired by the Mouvement Laïque Québécois (MLQ), a secular association whose members had been quite involved in contesting the prayers in political settings. In both *Laval* and *Saguenay*, similar reports were submitted. In legal terms, the cities' respective defences stress the importance of responding to the following questions elaborated in *Freitag*:

> Does the governmental conduct by the Town infringe the Charter of freedom of conscience and religion and therefore violate s 2(a) of the Charter?
>
> (a) Does the purpose of the Town's practice violate s 2(a) of the Charter?
> (b) Does the effect of the Town's practice infringe the rights of the appellant under s 2(a) of the Charter?[18]

It is worth mentioning that the attitudes of the mayors were quite different. The mayor of Laval, Gilles Vaillancourt, was very discreet about the debated issues, as were all municipal personnel. The mayor of Saguenay, Jean Tremblay, on the contrary, made it a personal cause, making several dramatic statements in the media while professing his Catholic faith.

A. The Extent of Discrimination and the Theory of Ritual

During the *Laval* case, the plaintiff had difficulty in demonstrating discrimination as required by the Human Rights Tribunal. The MLQ expert's strategy was to define the prayer as a 'religious ritual', which would connote the idea of inside-outside group exclusion. In this way, the city council was presented as a group of believers, united by a ritual, standing against the plaintiff who felt excluded when remaining, for instance, seated during this interval. In the *Saguenay* case, the argument remained the same.

The concept of ritual has barely been mentioned in the Canadian legal landscape, its meaning and legal force uncertain. Pierre Bosset, who was then a researcher for *Commission québécoise des droits de la personne et de la jeunesse*, has stated: 'Subject to a comprehensive review of various municipal charters, no legislative disposition—except perhaps those providing the power to regulate the conduct of the municipal council debates—provides for the possibility of imposing a religious ritual or the wearing of a religious symbol'.[19] He frames the recitation of the prayer as a ritual that ought not be forced onto individuals, but refers to case law that makes no use of the concept, ie *Zylberberg*, which broaches the questions of the 'recitation' of a prayer, of 'opening and closing exercises', a practice, a religious activity.[20] As previously discussed, the Ontario decisions are in accordance, where we again find the concepts of practice and recitation.

[18] *Freitag v Penetanguishene* (n 5), para 14.
[19] Bosset, 'Pratiques et symboles religieux' (n 12), 10 (fn 38), 12.
[20] *Zylberberg v Sudbury Board of Education (Director)* [1988] 52 DLR.

The concept of ritual has rarely been employed by the Supreme Court, with a list of just over 40 usages. The religious usages are generally related to Aboriginal peoples, while one reference is found in the *Amselem* case pertaining to the Jewish ritual of the sukkah. All the others simply mention ritual within an enumeration of the diverse dimensions of religion.[21] The Bouchard-Taylor report mentions the ritual of government prayer, and recommends its cessation, no doubt inspired by the texts of the Human Rights Tribunal.[22]

But to return to the expertise, the MLQ's report described the prayer ritual as follows:

> In the case of a prayer recited collectively in front of an assembly, we are dealing with a ritual identity: despite the wording of the prayer, its role has less the function of involving spiritual entities, as would be the case for a formal religious ceremony, but more of defining the unity of thought and belonging among the individuals present. This identifying and social character of ritual (secular or religious) that links the individual to a group of belonging is another universal characteristic of ritual.

As stated in *Laval*, the report refers to different authors, but with partial or incomplete quotations—and in my view, the omissions were quite significant. In brief, I thought that the partial definition of a ritual could embrace many religious expressions, including those not usually designated as 'rituals', like basic prayers. The following quotation from my expert report includes these omissions, here given emphasis:

> Aggregates of real objects and symbolic means are implemented and ordered between them within the interior of the rite: *sanctified place (altar, tomb), defined time (end of Ramadan, office hours), object (censer, sacerdotal vestment, gong)*, gestures (sign of the cross, hands folded and head tilted), speech (prayer, singing, preaching), attitude (standing, genuflection, prostration). All of these elements are catalysts of imagination and action.[23]

A real ritual, as I tried to explain, includes all the elements mentioned, as an elaborated setting, and it can be effective enough to provoke an inside-outside, group exclusion effect. The MLQ expert suggested that the prayer, gesture and attitude alone formed a ritual. I expressed my reservations regarding that understanding of 'religious ritual' in the present context. In the fields of religion and anthropology, a 'religious ritual' indicates a deployment of gestures, words, symbols and actions that are much more developed than those involved in these prayer cases, worship services being a good example.[24]

[21] eg *Lax Kw'alaams Indian Band v Canada* (Attorney General) [2011] SCC 56, 2011 3 SCR 535; *R v Sparrow* [1990] 1 SCR 1075; R v Côté [1996] 3 SCR 139.

[22] G Bouchard and C Taylor, *Building the Future: A Time for Reconciliation* (Quebec City, Government of Quebec, 2008) 20.

[23] C Rivière, *Socio-anthropologie des religions* (Paris, Armand Colin, 1997) 81–84.

[24] See P Smith, 'Rite' in P Bonte and M Izard (ed), *Dictionnaire de l'ethnologie et de l'anthropologie* (Paris, Presses universitaires de France, 2000) 630–31.

Moreover, as I tried to explain, in the contemporary era, the individual is not merely subservient to the collective. Even a 'religious ritual' will not necessarily garner the adhesion of all present. This explains why, in Canada, some civic ceremonies can be introduced with Indigenous rituals (that assume a more strictly 'ritual' character, in fact, than in the case of prayer, respectively deploying evocations, songs, dances, clothing, gestures, symbols, etc), without individuals feeling constrained to adhere to the worldview and beliefs involved. According to contemporary sociology, religious content has lost much of its persuasive force, such that sociology tends to analyse religion in 'cultural' rather than 'confessional' terms.

The sociology of religion has reflected in detail on this phenomenon known as the 'individualisation' of religion, particularly in the West.[25] This means that individuals freely and individually interpret the meaning of religious expressions or rituals. Consequently, with respect to cases of discrimination on the grounds of belief, it seems difficult to demonstrate that an adult feels 'constrained' to adhere to a doctrine through the simple act of reciting a short prayer. The theory of ritual seems difficult to apply, to demonstrate discriminatory effect. The other expert cited in the *Saguenay* case, Gilles Bibeau, agreed.

IV. The Decisions

While this chapter has already addressed several aspects of the judgments, it is important to briefly recall the decisions of the courts with regard to the debated issues, especially the link between discrimination and the theory of ritual. Recall that we have referenced two decisions from the Ontario courts, two from the Quebec Human Rights Tribunal, one decision from the Quebec Court of Appeal, and a final decision from the Supreme Court.

A. The Extent of Discrimination and the Theory of Ritual

I will now address the question of the recitation of the prayer as a ritual that excludes atheists and causes them potential cognitive damage, the central allegation made by the experts and lawyer for the MLQ. In *Laval*, Judge Rivest referred to the concept of ritual about 18 times and made six references to 'rites'. The judge gave a detailed account of the debates between the experts, and rejected the concept of ritual:

> Even though the experts do not agree on whether or not it represents a 'rite' or a 'ritual', they all agree that it constitutes a text of a religious nature. The prayer recited by the

[25] See F Champion, 'Religion flottant, éclectisme et syncrétisme' in J Delumeau (ed), *Le fait religieux* (Paris, Fayard, 1993) 741–72.

City Council itself constitutes the exercise of a religious practice in a public session of the Municipal Council.[26]

In the context of *Saguenay*, Judge Pauzé, used the concept of ritual over 30 times and adopted the meaning proposed by the MLQ's expert. The judge not only cited and rejected my expertise, but also Gilles Bibeau's, who had maintained that the recitation of the prayer fails to qualify as ritual and, if it does, only a 'minimal' one.[27] The judge did not endorse this view and concluded that the type of practice observed in *Saguenay* 'has the effect of associating the recitation of the prayer to the religious ritual of a particular faith'[28] and that it represents a 'ritual identity … that confers a coercive character to the religious practice since we cannot escape it, except at the cost of physical or symbolic exclusion'.[29] On another important aspect with regard to the religious sense of the prayer, one that was never in doubt in the context of *Laval*, Judge Pauzé concluded:

> Regarding the prayer, the experts that have heard the defending parties are for their part employed to explain that it does not necessarily have a religious signification: it can, according to Ms. Lefebvre, belong to the current of religious individualization and, according to Mr. Bibeau, it could represent no more than a symbolic ritual deprived of religious significance.[30]

Judge Pauzé held, 'it would be … inappropriate to conclude that prayer and the symbols have no religious significance since the defendant himself unequivocally grants them such a character'.[31]

In their reasons, setting aside the decision of the tribunal, the three judges of the Court of Appeal endorsed both my own and Gilles Bibeau's expertise:

> The recited prayer is suitable for a great number of religions and is recited in a context that does not qualify as a ritual and even less as an identity ritual [and that] Choosing to stay outside while the prayer is being recited can certainly be considered an insignificant and negligible inconvenience and cannot in any case, always from an anthropological point of view, prejudice the cognitive functions of a person, as alleged by Mr. Baril.[32]

In commenting on my own and Bibeau's expertise, the Court of Appeal wrote:

> I agree with the opinion of these experts that the values expressed by this contested prayer are universal and that they do not identify one religion in particular. According to these experts, this prayer conforms to a modern theistic doctrine, open to certain non-invasive and reasonable religious particularisms.[33]

The Court of Appeal did not affirm the universality of the prayer, but rather that of the values that are mentioned, such as justice and wisdom. Even if it endorsed

[26] *Commission des droits de la personne et des droits de la jeunesse v Laval* (n 5), para 164.
[27] *Simoneau v Tremblay* (n 2), paras 169–70.
[28] ibid, para 239.
[29] ibid, para 251.
[30] ibid, para 229.
[31] ibid, para 234.
[32] *Saguenay (Ville de) v Mouvement laïque québécois* (n 2), para 87.
[33] ibid, para 88.

the city's opinion, the court passed some negative comments on the behaviour of the Mayor of Saguenay in a section entitled 'The Attitudes of the Mayor':

> the respondents have attempted to use the attitude of the mayor to define the actual impact, [this court refused to. The court nonetheless deems] the remarks and the behaviour of the mayor unacceptable … as it displays an absence of basic reserve on the part of someone who occupies the function of an elected official and participates in the governance of the city on a daily basis.[34]

The mayor had been quite visible in the Quebec media, affirming his Catholic faith vociferously.

The Supreme Court concluded, like the judges in the first case, that the prayer represents a ritual, which it described in detail. The Court used the concept only once, and explicitly contextualised it in the style adopted by the city of Saguenay:

> The recitation of the prayer involved a ritual that reveals its true nature. At the start of every public meeting of the municipal council, its members entered the chamber one at a time as their names were called. The mayor and councillors then stood for the recitation of the prayer. The mayor and several councillors made the sign of the cross while the mayor said, speaking into the microphone, [TRANSLATION:] '[i]n the name of the Father, the Son and the Holy Spirit'. He then recited the prayer, which ended with the same words, plus the word '[a]men'.[35]

The Court qualified the recitation of the prayer as ritual by evoking the elaborate gestures of the mayor and the councillors. It held that the recitation of the prayer by the mayor and the councillors 'had a religious purpose'[36] The influence of the mayor's public professions of faith on the Court's decision is apparent:

> I concede that the state's duty of neutrality does not require it to abstain from celebrating and preserving its religious heritage. But that cannot justify the state engaging in a discriminatory practice for religious purposes, which is what happened in the case of the City's prayer. The mayor's public declarations are revealing of the true function of the council's practice:
>
> [translation] I'm in this battle because I worship Christ.
>
> When I get to the hereafter, I'm going to be able to be a little proud. I'll be able to say to Him: 'I fought for You; I even went to trial for You'. There's no better argument. It's extraordinary.
>
> I'm in this fight because I worship Christ. I want to go to heaven and it is the most noble fight of my entire life.[37]

We will revisit this particular question in the conclusion.

[34] ibid, paras 147–53.
[35] *Mouvement laïque québécois v Saguenay* (n 2), para 102.
[36] ibid, para 114.
[37] ibid, para 116; *Simoneau v Tremblay* (n 2), para 88.

B. Final Judgments on State Neutrality and Prayer

The Court of Appeal advocated a 'benevolent neutrality' of the state.[38] It also relied on the decision of the European Court of Human Rights, in *l'Affaire Lautsi* in Italy.[39] The *Lautsi* decision, according to the Court of Appeal, showed that a state can be respectful of history and cultural traditions, while maintaining certain religious expressions. In short, against the odds, the Court of Appeal decided to reverse the first decision.

The Supreme Court ultimately came to the same result as the Human Rights Tribunals, but with important elaboration on the issue of state neutrality, since it falls within its jurisdiction. It declared that the government must embody a strong neutrality (to not have the appearance of taking part in a religion), and that the prayer recited in *Saguenay* was discriminatory. While the long and rich judgment deserves detailed treatment, I will only point out a few significant elements.

First, as previously suggested, the way Mayor Tremblay acted clearly had a great impact on the decision. In discussing the understanding of neutrality defended by the Court of Appeal, the Supreme Court's Judge Gascon wrote:

> I concede that the state's duty of neutrality does not require it to abstain from celebrating and preserving its religious heritage. But that cannot justify the state engaging in a discriminatory practice for religious purposes, which is what happened in the case of the City's prayer. The mayor's public declarations are revealing of the true function of the council's practice.[40]

In reference to this position, the Supreme Court discussed the Ontario judgments in detail, notably the *Renfrew* case: 'These cases are of no assistance to the respondents. Insofar as the practice authorized in *Renfrew* was one whose effect constituted an insubstantial impairment, that case can be distinguished from the case at bar'.[41] One might think that in so doing, the Supreme Court has left the door open to understanding some forms of prayer as non-discriminatory practices.

Second, the Supreme Court, by endorsing this point of the Court of Appeal, refused to examine the question of the presence of religious symbols and objects, the Human Rights Tribunal having chosen not to investigate these matters.[42] It also failed to address the frequent mentions of God in Canada, notably in the national anthem, as did the tribunal. The Supreme Court nonetheless discussed the mention of God in the preamble to the Constitution:

[38] *Saguenay (Ville de) v Mouvement laïque québécois* (n 2), para 76 cites J Woehrling, 'L'obligation d'accommodement raisonnable et l'adaptation de la société à la diversité religieuse' (1998) 43 *Revue de droit de McGill* 325, 371.

[39] Let us note that the *Lautsi* case advocated the maintenance of the crucifix on the walls of a public school in Italy, a context in which minors are concerned (*Lautsi v Italy* App no 30814/06 (ECtHR (GC), 18 March 2011)).

[40] *Mouvement laïque québécois v Saguenay* (n 2), para 116.

[41] ibid, para 140.

[42] ibid, para 10.

> The reference to the supremacy of God in the preamble to the *Canadian Charter* cannot lead to an interpretation of freedom of conscience and religion that authorizes the state to consciously profess a theistic faith. The preamble, including its reference to God, articulates the 'political theory' on which the *Charter*'s protections are based.[43]

V. Final Discussion

This analysis of the decisions and the story of my experience as an expert witness evokes a few important themes. First, in comparing the *Laval* case—which was comparatively ignored in the media, given that Laval did not appeal and that Mayor Vaillancourt was far more discreet than Mayor Tremblay—we can conclude that the way Tremblay handled the case had a significant impact on the final decision of the Supreme Court or, at least, the way it was framed.

I cannot help but question a certain contradiction in the way the Supreme Court insists on the 'religious meaning' of the prayer, but discards any religious meaning in the mention of God in the Constitution. On the one hand, a prayer to God is implicitly religious, but on the other hand, can the mention of God be but a matter of political thinking?

While affirming the importance of state neutrality, the Supreme Court also takes into account the extent of discrimination on a case-by-case basis, in its complex decision of nearly 100 pages. On the one hand, it affirms the necessity of state neutrality, but it also assesses the extent of discrimination of any prayer. In the context of *Saguenay*, the Court explains, discrimination is obvious. But, in referring to the Ontario cases, the Court also suggests that it could be otherwise inasmuch as it takes the depth or degree of discrimination into account. Could municipalities argue that their form of prayer has a minimal effect on individuals and, consequently, on state neutrality? Some have since decided to maintain prayers, arguing that their practices and intentions considerably differ from those of the Mayor of Saguenay. Could this long battle have led to the development of a nuanced judgment? State neutrality is affirmed, but should every prayer recited in a political context be subjected to a detailed examination to assess whether it is in fact discriminatory?

And how could this 'theory of ritual' play out in future analysis? If, from an anthropological standpoint, a few religious words and gestures are insufficient to form a ritual, it is interesting to see how the Supreme Court addressed

[43] ibid, para 147.

the question, in considering the *way* the prayer was recited, and the gestures and attitudes adopted by the Mayor of Saguenay and his entourage. But did we really require this theory of ritual to frame 'the feeling' of being excluded from a group? How can courts adequately address questions of discomfort and feelings of exclusion? If state neutrality is at stake, why do we need this 'discrimination test?' This chapter has tried to demonstrate how complex the legal discussion is when it comes to religious discrimination and its potential social and political reverberations.

8

Physicians' Rights to Conscientious Objection

BRUCE RYDER

Canadian law protects the rights of patients to equal access to medical services and to be treated with equal dignity.[1] At the same time, well-established principles of Canadian human rights law protect physicians from being forced to choose between engaging in professional practice and following the dictates of their sincerely held conscientious[2] beliefs.[3] Many Canadian medical associations have policies that recognise that a physician has a right to object to providing a patient with a treatment or procedure if it conflicts with the physician's conscientious beliefs.[4] However, these policies are inconsistent and confusing.[5]

[1] The rights of patients to equal access to health care are protected by the constitution and human rights statutes. S 15(1) of the *Charter of Rights and Freedoms* prohibits governments, entities exercising governmental functions (like professional regulatory bodies), and entities implementing governmental programmes (like the delivery of public health care services by hospitals), from adopting policies or following practices that have the effect of denying equal access to health care services or benefits on the basis of prohibited grounds of discrimination. Human rights statutes in Canada likewise prohibit private or public actors from discriminating in the provision of health care services.

[2] In this chapter, I will use the terms 'conscience' or 'conscientious' to refer to both religious belief systems and to non-theistic moral belief systems, as both are protected by human rights law.

[3] S 2(a) of the Charter prevents governments from enforcing laws or policies that have the purpose or effect of coercing individuals to abandon sincerely held religious or conscientious beliefs or practices, unless they can be justified by a compelling justification pursued by proportionate means pursuant to s 1 of the Charter. Similarly, statutory prohibitions on religious discrimination in all Canadian jurisdictions make it illegal for public and private employers to put in place barriers to equal access to employment on the basis of religion or conscience (either intentionally or in the effects of their policies), unless the employer can demonstrate that it is not possible to accommodate those beliefs or practices without undue hardship. Religious freedoms and religious equality rights are allied in advancing the right of religious persons to participate equally in Canadian society without abandoning the tenets of their faith. Governments, regulatory bodies and employers must accommodate individuals' freedom to hold and express religious or conscientious beliefs, to act in accordance with those beliefs, and to engage in practices grounded in those beliefs unless doing so would interfere with the rights of others or with compelling social interests. See Bruce Ryder, 'The Canadian Conception of Equal Religious Citizenship' in Richard Moon (ed), *Law and Religious Pluralism in Canada* (Vancouver, UBC Press, 2008).

[4] For an overview and analysis of these policies, see Jacquelyn Shaw and Jocelyn Downie, 'Welcome to the Wild, Wild North: Conscientious Objection Policies Governing Canada's Medical, Nursing, Pharmacy, and Dental Professions' (2014) 28 *Bioethics* 33–46.

[5] ibid, 34.

A clearer approach to the reconciliation of patients' and physicians' rights in the context of conscientious objection is needed.[6] To this end, a number of Canadian medical associations have recently revised or adopted policies that aim to establish principled frameworks for respecting both physicians' rights to conscientious objection and patients' rights to equal access to health care services.

In this chapter, I will discuss three recent policies that seek to accomplish this goal: the College of Physicians and Surgeons of Ontario's policy on 'Professional Obligations and Human Rights', adopted in 2008 and updated in March 2015;[7] the College of Physicians and Surgeons of Saskatchewan's policy on 'Conscientious Objection', adopted in September 2015;[8] and the Canadian Medical Association's draft of a 'Principles-Based Approach to Assisted Dying in Canada' (that includes recognition of physicians' right to conscientious objection), put forward for discussion in June 2015.[9] While there are important differences between them, and the CMA policy is only in the early stage of development, these recent policies share the goal of recognising and reconciling physicians' rights to conscientious objection and patients' rights of access to health care.

I. Contestation of Conscientious Rights

Despite the grounding of physicians' right to conscientious objection in statutory and constitutional rights, and a consensus among regulatory bodies on the existence of those rights, when the exercise of conscientious rights by physicians has emerged into public view in recent years, heated public controversies

[6] A number of recent contributions to the academic literature are an excellent source of guidance on the development of conscientious objection policies for health care providers. In particular, see Jocelyn Downie, Carolyn McLeod and Jacquelyn Shaw, 'Moving Forward with a Clear Conscience: A Model Conscientious Objection Policy for Canadian Colleges of Physicians and Surgeons' (2013) 21 *Health Law Review* 28–32. See also the resources and publications on the website of the Conscience Research Group, headed by Carolyn McLeod: http://conscience.carolynmcleod.com/; and the special issue of *Bioethics* edited by Carolyn McLeod and Jocelyn Downie devoted to the issue of conscientious refusals in health care: (2014) 28(1) *Bioethics*. A useful discussion of the US experience can be found in Mark R Wicclair, *Conscientious Objection in Health Care: An Ethical Analysis* (Cambridge, Cambridge University Press, 2011), esp ch 3 regarding the appropriate scope and limits of rights to conscientious objection. For a review and critical analysis of legal developments on employees' rights to conscientious objection in the UK, see Andrew Hambler, *Religious Expression in the Workplace and the Contested Role of Law* (London and New York, Routledge, 2015) 147–78.

[7] College of Physicians and Surgeons of Ontario, 'Professional Obligations and Human Rights' (March 2015) ('CPSO 2015 Policy'), www.cpso.on.ca/policies-publications/policy/professional-obligations-and-human-rights.

[8] College of Physicians and Surgeons of Saskatchewan, 'Conscientious Objection' (19 June 2015) ('CPSS 2015 Policy'), www.cps.sk.ca/Documents/Council/2015-6-19%20Conscientious%20Objection%20Policy%20AS%20APPROVED%20IN%20PRINCIPLE%20BY%20COUNCIL.pdf.

[9] Canadian Medical Association, 'Principles-Based Approach to Assisted Dying in Canada' (June 2015), www.cma.ca/Assets/assets-library/document/en/advocacy/EOL/care-at-the-end-of-life-cma-framework-june2015-e.pdf.

have ensued. Many have expressed hostility to the idea that physicians should be entitled to exercise their conscientious rights in the performance of their professional duties. These voices have insisted that physicians should be forced to choose between engaging in their profession and following the dictates of their conscience. The policies recently adopted by Canadian medical associations have rejected this perspective, and thus affirmed an equal and inclusive conception of professional practice.

The special significance the public reaction attaches to a physician's reliance on conscientious beliefs for restricting his or her practice is striking. Individual physicians of course do not have an obligation to provide all medical services; that obligation is borne by the public health care system as a whole, not by individual doctors. Limits on the services doctors provide that are related to their clinical competence are generally accepted. Yet, when a physician asserts a limit to medical services he or she is willing to provide based on conscientious beliefs, the public reaction can be fierce. The idea that physicians' conscientious beliefs should have any place in a system dedicated to the delivery of accessible, publicly funded health care services is hotly contested.

For example, in February 2014, in an outraged online post, an Ottawa woman revealed that she had been informed that the doctor on call at an Ottawa walk-in clinic did not prescribe 'artificial contraception' for religious reasons.[10] Similarly, in June 2014, the *Calgary Herald* reported with alarm that a Calgary doctor at a walk-in medical clinic refused to prescribe contraceptive pills.[11] The Calgary and Ottawa stories generated a great deal of media attention, even though the patients in question reported no difficulty obtaining birth control prescriptions at other nearby clinics. Public concern seemed to be focused not so much on the important question of whether access to medical services was compromised, or patients' dignity compromised, but on the very idea that religious or conscientious beliefs would play a role in the actions of members of a public profession. Indeed, in a poll that was conducted alongside the story on the *Calgary Herald*'s website, 74 per cent of respondents took the view that 'doctors should leave their beliefs at home'.[12]

The debate is an illustration of Lori Beaman's observation that

> we are in the midst of a struggle that imagines the presence of religion in Canada in a number of ways. One of these imaginaries is in some measure linked to the imaginary of a multicultural Canada that includes a multiplicity of religious voices, symbols, and

[10] Kate D, 'It Happened to Me: I Asked for Birth Control and Got a Form Letter Saying "No"', 4 February 2014, www.xojane.com/it-happened-to-me/it-happened-to-me-my-doctor-refused-to-refill-my-birth-control. The story generated a great deal of subsequent media attention. See, eg, Elizabeth Payne, 'Some Ottawa doctors refuse to prescribe birth control pills', Ottawa Citizen, 31 January 2014, http://ottawacitizen.com/news/local-news/some-ottawa-doctors-refuse-to-prescribe-birth-control-pills.

[11] Manisha Krishnan, '*Calgary doctor refuses to prescribe birth control over moral beliefs*', Calgary Herald, 27 June 2014, www.calgaryherald.com/health/Calgary+doctor+refuses+prescribe+birth+control+over+moral+beliefs/9978442/story.html.

[12] ibid.

> practices with as fluid a boundary as possible between the public and the private. A second model is a rigid separation between the public and the private, with religion relegated to the private sphere, a 'true' laïcité similar to that of France.[13]

A problem with the latter imaginary—that conscientious believers do not have a right to act in accordance with their beliefs in the public sphere—is that many people sincerely believe that they are bound to comply with their beliefs in all spheres of their lives. Their conscientious convictions do not possess a split public/private character. Rather, they are comprehensive worldviews to which they are always bound to adhere. Thus, forcing them to act contrary to their beliefs, whether in the public or private realm, can have profoundly fracturing impacts on their personal integrity.

A related problem is that if we adopt policies that force believers to act contrary to their conscientious beliefs when they enter the public sphere, we are putting pressure on them to choose between adherence to their beliefs and full participation in Canadian life. As Chief Justice McLachlin has noted, '[r]eligion is an integral aspect of people's lives; and cannot be left at the boardroom door'.[14] If we require doctors to park their beliefs at home, and they sincerely believe that compliance with their beliefs is mandatory in all spheres of their lives, the result is their exclusion from participation in the medical profession, a very serious form of discrimination on the basis of conscience.

II. Potential Harms Caused by Conscientious Objection

Even if we accept that Canadian human rights law extends protection of conscientious rights to the public sphere, we might still argue that claims to accommodation of conscientious objection fall outside the scope of protected rights because their exercise involves significant risk of harm to others. Conscientious objection is different from other forms of conscientious accommodation that have no appreciable impact on the rights of others. For example, when courts have affirmed the rights of a Sikh police officer to wear a turban,[15] or of a vegetarian prisoner to accommodation of his dietary needs,[16] or of a Sikh student to wear a kirpan in public school,[17] or of an Orthodox Jew to build a sukkah

[13] Lori G Beaman, 'Between the Public and the Private: Governing Religious Expression' in Solange Lefebvre and Lori G Beaman (eds), *Religion in the Public Sphere: Canadian Case Studies* 44 (Toronto, University of Toronto Press, 2014) 49.

[14] *Chamberlain v Surrey School District No 36* 2002 SCC 86, [2002] 4 SCR 710, para 19.

[15] *Grant v Canada* [1995] 1 FC 158 (TD).

[16] *Maurice v Canada* 2002 FCT 69.

[17] *Multani v Commission scolaire Marguerite-Bourgeoys* [2006] 1 SCR 6.

on his condominium balcony,[18] they also found that protection of the claimants' conscientious rights did not have any significant impacts on the rights of others.

This is not always the case with conscientious objection claims. Douglas NeJaime and Reva Siegel have noted that these 'complicity-based conscience claims' have distinct features:

> The claim concerns the third party's conduct—for example, her use of contraception—but, crucially, it also concerns the claimant's relationship to the third party. Complicity claims are faith claims about how to live in community with others who do not share the claimant's beliefs, and whose lawful conduct the person of faith believes to be sinful. Because these claims are explicitly oriented toward third parties, they present special concerns about third-party harm.[19]

'Complicity-based' is a useful way of characterising conscientious objection claims because the claimant's goal is to obtain protection from having to participate in activities involving others. Conscientious objectors have no right to prevent others from engaging in lawful activities. But they do have a right to be protected from forced personal involvement in activities to which they object based on their sincerely held conscientious beliefs. To qualify for protection, the personal involvement they are seeking to avoid must be more than trivial or insubstantial. Cast too broadly, claimants could invoke conscientious rights to object to simply having to live or work in environments shaped by norms to which they object. Indeed, confusion about the limits of conscientious rights may be one of the reasons their invocation can provoke such a hostile public response. The focus of conscientious rights should be on the protection of individuals from being coerced to *participate*, in a non-trivial manner, in activities to which they sincerely object on religious or moral grounds.

As NeJaime and Siegel argue, the fact that claimants make complicity-based claims to avoid participation in activities involving others does not make them any less worthy of prima facie merit as rights claims than other claims to accommodation of sincerely held conscientious beliefs. But it does mean that they have 'distinctive potential to impose material and dignitary harm'[20] on others, and thus the exercise of rights to conscientious objection must be attentive to, and limited by, the necessity of respecting the rights of others. But the potential for harm to others should not lead us to deny the validity of conscientious objection rights altogether; the conversation should be about reasonable limits on the rights, not on their very existence.

Two types of harm can result from the exercise of rights to conscientious objection. When physicians or other service providers seek exemption from a law or legal obligation, they risk depriving others of equal and timely access

[18] *Syndicat Northcrest v Amselem* [2004] 2 SCR 551.

[19] Douglas NeJaime and Reva B Siegel, 'Conscience Wars: Complicity-Based Conscience Claims in Religion and Politics' (2015) 124 *Yale Law Journal* 2516, 2519.

[20] ibid, 2527.

to the service. This harm can be particularly acute in the health care context, given the importance of the services at stake to patients' lives and health. The potential deprivation of equal and timely access to services is what NeJaime and Siegel mean by 'material harm'. Even when no material harm results, because the patient accessed services in a timely fashion from another service provider with minor inconvenience, the exercise of rights to conscientious objection can cause dignitary harm to those denied or refused service by a particular service-provider. The message conveyed by the refusal can be demeaning and stigmatising. Conscientious objectors may not intend to convey anything other than a message about their own sincerely held personal beliefs, but persons denied service may experience refusals of service as a condemnation of their choices and identities in a profound way.

As NeJaime and Siegel emphasise, the material and dignitary harm that may be caused by the exercise of rights to conscientious objection can be magnified when the objection is based on norms that have served to sustain social subordination on the basis of gender and sexuality.[21] Indeed, conscientious objectors have frequently refused to provide services related to abortion, contraception, or the rights of same-sex couples, thus raising concerns that conscientious objection is a new way of perpetuating deeply rooted relations of social subordination. A woman whose physician objects to providing her with access to abortion or contraceptive services, or a same-sex couple denied access to a marriage licence by a state official, may be outraged by the apparent reassertion of limits on hard-won rights.

The harms posed by the exercise of rights to conscientious objection may be exacerbated when a further dimension of power exists in the relationship in which the objection is raised, as is the case with physicians and their patients. Patients are often in vulnerable positions when they seek medical services, and physicians are trusted authority figures with a great deal of power flowing from their status, knowledge and expertise.

Since conscientious beliefs frequently embody norms that have served as a basis for pervasive and persistent patterns of social subordination, and may be invoked in a power relationship and in a manner that puts at risk rights recently attained after long struggle, the need for the respectful and nuanced reconciliation of a highly combustible situation of competing rights is evident. It is not surprising, then, that the public debates on physicians' conscientious rights have been emotionally charged and highly polarised, especially on the issues of access to abortion, contraception, same-sex civil marriage, and, most recently, medical assistance in dying. But the fact that we are on combustible social and legal terrain should not blind us to the validity of the full range of human rights claims at issue, and the ways in which the rights of all can be fully respected.

[21] ibid, 2574–78.

III. Protecting Both Patients' and Physicians' Rights

In his contribution to this volume discussing the conscientious rights of marriage commissioners, Richard Moon notes that courts and tribunals in Saskatchewan did not ask whether the government had fulfilled its duty to accommodate the conscientious objections of marriage commissioners who objected to performing same-sex civil marriages.[22] The government was not called upon to demonstrate, as it should have been according to human rights principles, why a 'single-entry point' system could not be an effective way of preserving equal access to civil marriage and avoiding dignitary harm resulting from the communication of refusals of service while simultaneously accommodating marriage commissioners' conscientious objections 'behind the scenes'.[23] By failing to do so, the Saskatchewan courts and tribunals failed to maximise the fulfilment of the full range of human rights at issue, thus creating a hierarchy that failed to accord equal respect to rights to conscientious objection.[24]

Similarly, public debates in Canada about rights to conscientious objection in the medical context have been characterised by insufficient attention to the nuanced ways in which the rights of patients to dignified and timely access to medical services, and the rights of physicians not to be compelled to act contrary to their religious or conscientious beliefs, can both be protected.

The Supreme Court of Canada in a series of decisions,[25] and the Ontario Human Rights Commission in its *Policy on Competing Human Rights*,[26] have recognised the importance of seeking creative ways to accommodate competing rights to avoid or minimise conflict between them. A number of general principles articulated by the Court and the Commission are helpful in guiding the development of laws and policies, including the following ideas: no rights are absolute; there is no hierarchy of rights; the full context, facts and human rights values at stake must be considered; the core of a right is more protected than its periphery; and laws and policies should aim to respect the importance of both sets of rights as much as possible. If it is possible to protect rights to conscientious objection without compromising equal access to services or the dignity of those seeking services, and without imposing any other forms of undue hardship, then these human rights principles require that the law give effect to conscientious claims.

[22] See Ch 9 p 183.

[23] ibid.

[24] Ryder (n 3) 101.

[25] eg, *R v NS* [2012] 3 SCR 726; *Dagenais v Canadian Broadcasting Corp* [1994] 3 SCR 835; *R v Mentuck* [2001] 3 SCR 442.

[26] Ontario Human Rights Commission, *Policy on Competing Human Rights* (2012), www.ohrc.on.ca/en/policy-competing-human-rights. For discussion and analysis of the policy, see Shaheen Azmi, Lorne Foster and Lesley Jacobs (eds), *Balancing Competing Human Rights Claims in a Diverse Society* (Toronto, Irwin Law, 2012).

IV. College of Physicians and Surgeons of Ontario 2015 Policy

At the same time as the issue of conscientious refusal by physicians was receiving increased media attention in 2014, the CPSO launched a review of its 2008 policy on 'Physicians and the Ontario Human Rights Code'.[27] Whether, and in what circumstances, physicians have a right to object on conscientious grounds to the provision of medical services were questions at the heart of the review. Ongoing debates about the CPSO policy, and similar debates about the conscientious objection policies of the College of Physicians and Surgeons (CPSS) and the Canadian Medical Association (CMA) discussed below, provide an illuminating window into the highly contested nature of religious and conscientious rights in the public sphere.

When it launched the review of its human rights policy, the CPSO announced that it was 'inviting feedback from all stakeholders, including members of the medical profession, the public, health system organisations and other health professionals on the current policy'.[28] The CPSO received dozens of written briefs and 1,800 contributions to an online discussion forum that was open from June to August 2014.[29] The submissions and comments regarding the policy revealed a diversity of strongly held views, some emphasising the importance of protecting physicians' conscientious rights, others insisting that individual conscientious views should play no role in the actions taken by members of a public profession.

While in some ways the 2008 CPSO policy under review was laudable in incorporating basic human rights principles, in other ways it ignored them. Neither the structure nor the language of the policy gave equal respect to patients' and physicians' rights. Indeed, the policy used the language of rights only to describe patients' rights. The rights of physicians were not mentioned—only[30] their obligations to not violate patients' rights. Yet, the CPSO and its policies must also comply with the prohibitions on discrimination on the basis of creed and religion in the Ontario Human Rights Code and section 15 of the Charter, as well as the protection of freedom of conscience and religion in section 2(a) of the Charter. This bundle of statutory and constitutional rights prevent the CPSO from imposing barriers to equal participation in the profession or employment on the

[27] College of Physicians and Surgeons of Ontario, 'Physicians and the Ontario Human Rights Code', December 2008.

[28] http://policyconsult.cpso.on.ca/?page_id=3403.

[29] http://policyconsult.cpso.on.ca/?page_id=3405.

[30] The policy did note that '[p]ersonal beliefs and values and cultural and religious practices are central to the lives of physicians and their patients' (CPSO (n 27) 3), but did not connect this acknowledgement to the protection of doctors' religious and conscientious rights by the Code and the Charter.

basis of religion or conscience. Similarly, section 2(a) of the Charter prevents the CPSO from imposing coercive pressure—directly or indirectly, in the purposes or the effects of its policies—on its members to act contrary to their conscientious or religious beliefs. As a result, the CPSO is under an obligation to accommodate doctors' religious and conscientious beliefs as much as possible without compromising the rights of patients. The obligation of accommodation extends 'to the point of undue hardship' in the statutory jurisprudence. In the Charter context, the CPSO's obligations pursuant to the reasonable limits provision in section 1 include the adoption of policies that accomplish important objectives—like assuring patients' timely and equal access to medical services—in a manner that minimally impairs Charter rights or freedoms. The CPSO is under an obligation to not force doctors to choose between practising their chosen profession and living in accordance with their consciences if it can do so without compromising patients' rights or other compelling interests.

The 2008 CPSO policy began by reciting section 1 of the Human Rights Code: the right of every Ontario resident to receive equal treatment with respect to goods, services and facilities without discrimination on a list of prohibited grounds. 'This imposes', the policy affirmed, 'a duty on all those who provide services in Ontario—which includes physicians providing medical services—to provide those services free from discrimination'.[31] The 2008 policy should have added, but did not, that every member of the profession has a right to not be discriminated against on the basis of creed or religion, and to not be subject to coercive pressure to abandon religious or conscientious beliefs.

Instead of affirming and aiming to respect the equal importance of both physicians' conscientious rights and patients' rights to access medical services, the 2008 policy cast a pall of suspicion over the exercise of physicians' conscientious rights:

> If physicians have moral or religious beliefs which affect or may affect the provision of medical services, the College advises physicians to proceed cautiously with an understanding of the implications related to human rights.[32]

While physicians should of course exercise their conscientious rights in a manner that respects the rights of patients, the CPSO's policy should also affirm the conscientious rights of physicians and the CPSO's obligations to accommodate the exercise of those rights. In this regard, the Ontario Human Rights Commission's 2008 submission on the CPSO's draft policy was not helpful. It contributed to the deficiencies of the CPSO's 2008 policy by not mentioning physicians' rights to equal treatment without discrimination on the basis of creed, and indeed undermined the existence of those rights by stating that '[i]t is the Commission's position that doctors, as providers of services that are not religious

[31] CPSO (n 27) 2.
[32] ibid 3.

in nature, must essentially "check their personal views at the door" in providing medical care'.[33]

The Commission's 2014 submission to the CPSO's policy review[34] similarly failed to specify the source, nature and importance of physicians' conscientious rights. But the Commission's views have evolved to a more balanced position than it took in 2008, no doubt in large part a result of the important work the Commission has done in the development of its *Policy on Competing Human Rights*[35] and in its *Human Rights and Creed Research and Consultation Report*.[36] The Commission's 2014 submission, unlike its 2008 submission, spoke of both physicians' '*rights* and obligations'. Notably, the Commission in its 2014 submission dropped the position it took in 2008 that physicians' must 'check their personal views at the door' when providing medical care. The Commission's 2014 submission usefully urged the CPSO to '[r]ephrase competing rights principles in regard to the OHRC's *Policy on Competing Rights* and emphasise the aim to respect the importance of both sets of rights'.[37] Moreover, the Commission's 2014 submission acknowledged, unlike its 2008 submission, that 'organizations such as hospitals, clinics and professional associations also have a duty to accommodate physicians, not just patients; and that the duty to accommodate covers creed and other grounds'.[38] The medical profession as a whole, together with those responsible for health care policy and service delivery, have obligations to ensure that patients have equal access to medical services *and* that the conscientious rights of providers are respected.

The CPSO's 2015 Policy has taken important steps forward in recognising the competing rights at issue. Like the 2008 Policy, it begins with an affirmation of physicians' obligation to avoid discrimination in the provision of services.[39] Unlike the 2008 Policy, the 2015 Policy recognises that physicians have a right, protected by section 2(a) of the Charter, 'to limit the health services they provide for reasons of conscience or religion'.[40] The 2015 Policy fails to mention that prohibitions on discrimination in both the Charter and the Code also require that physicians' conscientious beliefs be accommodated. Otherwise, the right to participate equally in the medical profession and in employment is put at risk

[33] Submission of the Ontario Human Rights Commission to the College of Physicians and Surgeons of Ontario Regarding the draft policy, 'Physicians and the Ontario Human Rights Code' (2008), www.ohrc.on.ca/en/submission-ontario-human-rights-commission-college-physicians-and-surgeons-ontario-regarding-draft-0.

[34] OHRC submission regarding College of Physicians and Surgeons policy review: Physicians and the Ontario Human Rights Code (1 August 2014), www.ohrc.on.ca/en/ohrc-submission-regarding-college-physicians-and-surgeons-policy-review-physicians-and-ontario-human.

[35] Ontario Human Rights Commission (n 26).

[36] Ontario Human Rights Commission, *Human Rights and Creed Research and Consultation Report* (2013), www.ohrc.on.ca/en/human-rights-and-creed-research-and-consultation-report.

[37] OHRC submission (n 34).

[38] ibid.

[39] CPSO 2015 Policy (n 7) 2.

[40] ibid, 4.

for physicians with conscientious objections to providing particular services. It is important to recognise that we are dealing not just with the task of reconciling doctors' religious freedom with patients' equality rights; we are also dealing with the task of reconciling the equality rights of both doctors and patients.

Another deficiency of the CPSO's 2008 Policy was its failure to provide clear guidance to physicians about the scope and limits of their rights of conscientious refusal. Indeed, the 2008 Policy stated that

> The law in this area is unclear, and as such, the College is unable to advise physicians how the Commission, Tribunal or Courts will decide cases where they must balance the rights of physicians with those of patients.[41]

It is true that delineating the scope and limits of the duty to accommodate physicians' conscientious rights involves a highly contextual balancing that will depend on a host of factors making it difficult to provide concrete advice in advance. The Commission's 2014 submission to the CPSO helpfully noted that the CPSO's and other institutions' duty to accommodate conscientious objection by physicians 'might be limited by undue hardship because of cost, health or safety, or when there is significant interference with the rights of others', including, of course, patients' right to timely and equal access to medical treatment or procedures.[42]

The 2008 CPSO Policy set out a number of 'College Expectations' relating to disclosure and dignified treatment of patients that reflect human rights principles regarding the balancing of competing rights.[43] These requirements are necessary to ensure that conscientious rights are exercised in a manner that does not compromise the rights of patients.[44] The 2015 CPSO Policy incorporates these 'expectations' outlined in the 2008 Policy and also takes a more confident and clearer line in advising physicians on the limits of their right to conscientious objection:

> While the *Charter* entitles physicians to limit the health services they provide for reasons of conscience or religion, this cannot impede, either directly or indirectly, access to these services for existing patients, or those seeking to become patients.[45]

To fulfil their obligations to patients, the 2015 Policy provides that physicians who limit their services for reasons of conscience must do so in a manner that respects patient dignity, ensures access to care, and protects patient safety. To respect patients' dignity, physicians must communicate their objection directly and with sensitivity to patients, without expressing any personal judgment about patients' beliefs or identities, and they must refrain from promoting their own personal beliefs when interacting with patients. To ensure access to care, physicians must

41 CPSO (n 27) 3.
42 OHRC submission (n 34).
43 CPSO (n 27) 4.
44 They are also found in Downie, McLeod and Shaw's model conscientious objection policy (n 6).
45 CPSO 2015 Policy (n 7) 4.

provide information about all available clinical options, and must not withhold information about the existence of any procedure or treatment because it conflicts with their conscience or religious beliefs. To protect patient safety, physicians must provide care in an emergency, where it is necessary to prevent imminent harm, even where providing that care conflicts with their conscientious or religious beliefs.[46] These principles seek to protect physicians' rights to conscientious objection so long as patients' access to health care services is not compromised. In the vast majority of cases, both physicians' and patients' rights can be respected if these principles are followed. In emergencies where a physician's conscientious objection cannot be accommodated without putting a patient at risk, a patient's right to life and security of the person must prevail.

The most controversial question in recent Canadian debates about conscientious objection policies has been whether a physician has a duty to refer patients to other physicians who are willing to provide medical services to which the physician has a moral or religious objection. This issue has long been a point of contention.[47] For advocates of a broad interpretation of rights to conscientious objection, to require physicians to refer patients is to make them complicit in treatments or procedures (such as abortion or assisted dying) to which they have fundamental moral or religious objections.[48] To others, referrals are necessary to ensure that patients' rights of timely access to medical services are not compromised. For example, Downie, McLeod and Shaw's model conscientious objection policy provides that:

> Physicians can decline to provide legally permissible and publicly funded health services if providing those services violates their freedom of conscience. However, in such situations, they must make a referral to another health care provider who is willing and able to accept the patient and provide the service.[49]

The 2008 CPSO policy did not require physicians to initiate referrals. Instead it provided that physicians must:

> Advise patients or individuals who wish to become patients that they can see another physician with whom they can discuss their situation and *in some circumstances help the patient or individual make arrangements to do so*.[50]

[46] ibid 5.

[47] See, eg, the debate that took place in the Canadian Medical Association Journal in 2006–07 between Sanda Rodgers and Jocelyn Downie (who took the position that physicians do have a duty to refer), and Jeff Blackmer, Executive Director, Office of Ethics of the Canadian Medical Association (who took the position that a physician does not have a duty to refer, only a duty to advise a patient that she may consult other physicians, and, if asked, 'should also indicate alternative sources where she might obtain a referral'). Sanda Rodgers and Jocelyn Downie, 'Abortion: Ensuring Access' (2006) 175(1) *Canadian Medical Association Journal* 9; Jeff Blackmer, 'Clarification of the CMA's Position Concerning Induced Abortion' (2007) 176(9) *Canadian Medical Association Journal* 1310.

[48] See, eg, Protection of Conscience Project, *Submission to the College of Physicians and Surgeons of Ontario* (20 February 2015), www.consciencelaws.org/publications/submissions/submissions-013-001-cpso.aspx.

[49] Downie, McLeod and Shaw (n 6) 31. See also Carolyn McLeod, 'Referral in the Wake of Conscientious Objection to Abortion' (2008) 23(4) *Hypatia* 30.

[50] CPSO (n 27) 4 (emphasis added).

The circumstances in which 'helping' the patient 'make arrangements' is required, and what the nature of those 'arrangements' should be, was not specified. In contrast, the 2015 CPSO policy takes an unequivocally hard line on the contested issue of referrals. It provides that:

> Where physicians are unwilling to provide certain elements of care for reasons of conscience or religion, an effective referral to another health-care provider must be provided to the patient. An effective referral means a referral made in good faith, to a non-objecting, available, and accessible physician, other health-care professional, or agency. The referral must be made in a timely manner to allow patients to access care. Patients must not be exposed to adverse clinical outcomes due to a delayed referral. Physicians must not impede access to care for existing patients, or those seeking to become patients.
>
> The College expects physicians to proactively maintain an effective referral plan for the frequently requested services they are unwilling to provide.[51]

This provision provoked a legal challenge launched in March 2015 by the Christian and Medical Dental Society of Canada, the Canadian Federation of Catholic Physicians' Societies and five physicians with conscientious objections to participating in a number of procedures or the prescribing of a number of drugs.[52] The claimants argue that the provision of the CPSO 2015 Policy requiring them to provide an 'effective referral' violates their rights protected by section 2(a) and section 15 of the Charter. Unless the CPSO can demonstrate that alternative means of ensuring access would not be as effective in protecting patients' rights, the claimants will have a strong argument that requiring physicians with conscientious objections to provide formal referrals is not a minimal impairment of their Charter rights. The claimants also object to the requirement in the CPSO 2015 Policy that physicians must provide drugs or perform procedures in emergencies, where necessary to prevent imminent harm, despite their conscientious objections to doing so. The CPSO will not have difficulty demonstrating that limiting the exercise of physicians' conscientious rights where necessary to protect patients against imminent threats to their lives or health is reasonable and justifiable pursuant to section 1 of the Charter.

V. College of Physicians and Surgeons of Saskatchewan 2015 Policy on Conscientious Objection

The CPSS also found itself embroiled in controversy surrounding the issue of referrals when it unveiled a draft policy on 'Conscientious Refusal' in January

[51] CPSO 2015 Policy (n 7) 5.

[52] *Christian Medical and Dental Society et al v College of Physicians and Surgeons of Ontario*, Ontario Superior Court of Justice, Court File No 15-63717. See Sean Murphy, 'Tunnel Vision at the College of Physicians', 13 April 2015, http://news.nationalpost.com/full-comment/sean-murphy-tunnel-vision-at-the-college-of-physicians.

2015.[53] Like the CPSO 2015 Policy, the CPSS draft policy provided that physicians 'have an obligation to provide health information, referrals and health services to their patients in a non-discriminatory fashion' and that 'physicians' freedom of conscience should be respected'.[54] This requires physicians to provide their patients with the health information required 'to make legally valid, informed choices about medical treatment … even if the provision of such information conflicts with the physician's deeply held and considered moral or religious beliefs'.[55] The draft CPSS policy showed greater respect for physicians' conscientious beliefs than the CPSO policy by providing that the obligation to inform patients 'may be met by delegating the informing process to another competent individual for whom the physician is responsible'.[56] This capacity to delegate the informing process is desirable because it limits physicians' involvement in providing information on clinical options to which they object without compromising patients' rights.[57]

In contrast, on the issue of referrals, the draft CPSS Policy, like the 2015 CPSO Policy, took an unequivocally hard line:

> Physicians can decline to provide legally permissible and publicly-funded health care services if providing those services violates their freedom of conscience. However, in such situations, they must make a timely referral to another health care provider who is willing and able to accept the patient and provide the service.[58]

This provision generated a storm of protest from the supporters of physicians' rights to conscientious objection.[59] Their arguments apparently carried more weight with the CPSS than they did with the CPSO. The CPSS revised its draft policy, changing its name from 'Conscientious Refusal' to 'Conscientious Objection', and replacing the requirement that physicians' provide referrals with a more nebulous requirement that they 'arrange access'. The College approved the revised policy in principle on 19 June 2015. After a period of public consultation over the summer of 2015, the CPSS adopted the revised policy on 19 September 2015.[60]

[53] College of Physicians and Surgeons of Saskatchewan, 'Policy—Conscientious Refusal' (January 2015), www.cps.sk.ca/Documents/Council/2015%201%2019%20Conscientious%20Objection%20policy%20approved%20in%20principle%20by%20Council.pdf.

[54] ibid, 1.

[55] ibid, 2.

[56] ibid, 3.

[57] Why delegation should be permitted only to persons 'for whom the physician is responsible' is not clear.

[58] CPSS Draft Policy (n 53) 3.

[59] See eg Justice Centre for Constitutional Freedoms, 'In Defence of Charter Freedoms: A legal analysis of the constitutionality of the "Policy—Conscientious Refusal"' (March 2015), www.jccf.ca/wp-content/uploads/2013/01/In-Defence-of-Charter-Freedoms-A-legal-analysis-of-the-constitutionality-of-the-Policy-Conscientious-Refusal.pdf. A number of other organisations, including the Catholic Civil Rights League, the Christian Medical and Dental Society and the Evangelical Fellowship of Canada, made written submissions to the CPSS in February and March 2015 urging it to remove the referral requirement from the draft policy.

[60] CPSS 2015 Policy (n 8).

In language inspired by the CPSO's 2015 Policy, the CPSS 2015 Policy begins by affirming that conscientious rights must be exercised in a manner that respects patients' dignity and safety, and facilitates access to care.[61] The CPSS 2015 Policy then goes on to provide physicians with significantly greater flexibility (compared to the January draft and the CPSO 2015 Policy) about how to go about meeting their informational and referral obligations. The CPSS 2015 Policy states that physicians are required to provide patients with full and balanced information, even if the provision of such information conflicts with the physician's conscientious beliefs. But the policy defines this obligation in a minimalist manner. First, it does not require physicians to provide information themselves. Rather, a physician's informational obligation 'may be met by arranging for the patient to obtain the full and balanced health information … from another source'.[62] The obligation is thus downgraded to arranging access to information, rather than providing it personally. Second, the arranged source of information does not have to be another physician or health care provider. While the College's expectation is that the other source will generally be another physician or health care provider, it is not necessary. The physician may direct patients to other sources of information so long as the physician has met his or her obligation to provide timely, effective access to full and balanced information.[63] Third, even limited in these ways, the 'arranging information' requirement can be evaded so long as a physician demonstrates why its fulfilment 'is not possible and what alternative methods to attempt to meet those obligations will be provided'.[64]

Similarly, the CPSS 2015 Policy replaces the referral requirement in the draft policy with a requirement that physicians exercising their rights to conscientious refusal 'make an arrangement that will allow the patient to obtain access to the health service if the patient chooses'.[65] As with the informational obligation, an objecting physician is not required to fulfil this obligation by arranging a meeting with another physician or health care provider, but the policy does not specify what alternatives would be acceptable.

The CPSS 2015 Policy offers broad protection to physicians' rights of conscientious objection by not requiring them to provide information personally on clinical options to which they object and not requiring them to make formal referrals to other physicians who are available to provide the health care service at issue. However, the degree of flexibility regarding these obligations set out in the final policy is strikingly broad, and may have the effect of compromising patients' timely access to full and balanced information and to health care services. The President of the Saskatchewan Medical Association was reported to

[61] ibid, 3.
[62] ibid, 4.
[63] ibid.
[64] ibid, 5.
[65] ibid, 4.

have said that doctors could fulfil the policy 'by directing patients to the Internet in order to self-refer to another doctor or to a phone number to find the information they need'.[66] This comment does not inspire confidence that the policy puts in place meaningful obligations that will ensure that patients obtain timely access to information and services.

While the CPSS 2015 Policy provides broad protection to conscientious rights by taking a minimalist position on objecting physicians' obligations to ensure patients receive information and referrals, potentially putting patients at risk, it takes a firm position on when physicians are required to provide care to which they object. As described above, the CPSO 2015 Policy requires physicians to provide care contrary to their conscientious beliefs in cases of 'emergency, where it is necessary to prevent imminent harm'.[67] The CPSS 2015 Policy contains a similar emergency provision that requires objecting physicians to provide care where necessary to prevent imminent harm and goes further, requiring objecting physicians to provide care whenever necessary to protect a patient's health or wellbeing:

> When it is not possible to arrange for another physician or health care provider to provide a necessary treatment without causing a delay that would jeopardize the patient's health or wellbeing, physicians must provide the necessary treatment even if providing that treatment conflicts with their conscience or religious beliefs.[68]

This useful clarification is a specific instance of the general principle that physicians' rights to conscientious objection cannot be exercised in a manner that puts at risk patients' rights to timely access to health care services, a principle that is not stated as clearly in the CPSO 2015 Policy.

VI. Medical Assistance in Dying

In addition to the heated public debates generated in 2014 and 2015 by the CPSO and CPSS deliberations on their conscientious objection policies, these issues have taken on an even higher profile and sense of urgency following the Supreme Court of Canada's ruling in February 2015 in *Carter v Canada*.[69] In that case, the Court found that the prohibition on assisted suicide in section 241(b) of the

[66] Jason Warwick and Jonathan Charlton, 'Feedback sought in proposal on assisted suicide', Saskatoon Star-Phoenix, 19 September 2015, online at: www.thestarphoenix.com/Feedback+sought+proposal+assisted+suicide/11375959/story.html.

[67] CPSO 2015 Policy (n 7) 5.

[68] CPSS 2015 Policy (n 8) 5.

[69] *Carter v Canada* [2015] 1 SCR 331, 2015 SCC 5.

Criminal Code constituted an overly broad, and therefore fundamentally unjust, deprivation of the rights to life, liberty and security of the person in section 7 of the Charter of Rights and Freedoms. The Court issued a declaration that section 241(b) is of no force or effect to the extent that it prohibits physician-assisted death for a competent adult person who clearly consents to the termination of life and has a grievous and irremediable medical condition that causes enduring and intolerable suffering.[70] The Court suspended the declaration of invalidity for 12 months to give Parliament an opportunity to enact legislation that complies with the Charter.[71] Unless the Court extends the period of temporary validity of section 241(b) beyond 6 February 2016, physician-assisted death will become legal on that date.

A number of interveners in *Carter* asked the Court to confirm that physicians and other health care providers have a right to conscientiously object to supporting or participating in physician-assisted dying when it becomes legal. The Court declined to comment on the issue, apart from noting that the reconciliation of physicians' conscientious rights and patients' rights is an issue that legislatures and medical associations will need to address:

> a physician's decision to participate in assisted dying is a matter of conscience and, in some cases, of religious belief ... In making this observation, we do not wish to pre-empt the legislative and regulatory response to this judgment. Rather, we underline that the *Charter* rights of patients and physicians will need to be reconciled.[72]

In June 2015, the Canadian Medical Association issued a draft policy setting out principles to guide the development of an approach to the regulation of medical aid in dying in the wake of the *Carter* ruling.[73] The draft recognised physicians' right to conscientious objection, but also suggested that objecting physicians would be obliged to provide patients with referrals:

> Physicians are not obligated to fulfill requests for medical aid in dying. There should be no discrimination against a physician for their refusal to participate in medical aid in dying. In order to reconcile physicians' conscientious objection with patient access to care, a system should be developed whereby referral occurs by the physician to a third party that will provide assistance and information to the patient.[74]

In June and July 2015, the CMA received submissions on the draft principles and conducted an online dialogue in which almost 600 members participated.

[70] ibid, para 147.

[71] ibid, para 128.

[72] ibid, para 132.

[73] Canadian Medical Association, *Principles-Based Approach to Assisted Dying in Canada* (June 2015), www.cma.ca/Assets/assets-library/document/en/advocacy/EOL/care-at-the-end-of-life-cma-framework-june2015-e.pdf.

[74] ibid, pp A2-8 to A2-9.

In August 2015, it issued a report on these consultations.[75] The report noted that:

> The issue of reconciling the right of a physician who chooses not to participate in assisted dying while ensuring access to this service for eligible patients was by far the most hotly debated issue in the online dialogue.

Many participants in the online dialogue posted statements on why they would object on conscientious grounds to supporting or participating in physician-assisted dying. Many of these conscientious objectors rejected the referral requirement set out in the draft principles on the ground that any referral would make them complicit in the act of assisted dying.

The federal government has not yet developed a legislative response to the *Carter* ruling. However, seven months before the Supreme Court of Canada released its ruling in *Carter*, the Quebec National Assembly became the first province in Canada to legally recognise physician-assisted dying. Bill 52, An Act respecting end-of-life care,[76] which comes into force in December 2015, sets out the circumstances in which patients may request, and physicians may provide, medical aid in dying. The Act recognises physicians' right to conscientiously object to administering medical aid in dying:

> A physician may refuse to administer medical aid in dying because of personal convictions, and a health professional may refuse to take part in administering it for the same reason.[77]

A physician who objects is not required to provide patients with referrals to physicians who do provide medical aid in dying. Instead, physicians are obliged, as soon as possible, to notify the executive director of the health institution or local health authority, and forward the patient's request form.[78] The executive director is then required 'to take the necessary steps to find, as soon as possible, another physician willing to deal with the request'.[79]

In light of the Supreme Court's comments in *Carter*, the legalisation of physician-assisted death in February 2016 will be accompanied by the protection of physicians' rights of conscientious objection. Quebec's approach to the protection of both patients' and physicians' rights provides a valuable model that should guide the development of policies and legislation in the rest of the country. Given the high number of physicians that will object on conscientious grounds to participating in the provision of assisted-death services, preserving equal access to

[75] Canadian Medical Association, *A Canadian Approach to Assisted Dying: CMA Member Dialogue—Summary Report* (August 2015) www.cma.ca/Assets/assets-library/document/en/advocacy/Canadian-Approach-Assisted-Dying-e.pdf.

[76] SQ 2014, c 2.

[77] ibid, s 50.

[78] ibid, ss 31, 50.

[79] ibid, s 31.

those services across the country will no doubt prove to be a formidable challenge, as it has been with the provision of abortion services. But that challenge needs to be met, not by putting pressure on physicians to abandon their conscientious beliefs, but by governments and health care authorities ensuring that enough willing physicians are available to meet patients' needs.

VII. Conclusion

From our review of recent Canadian debates on physicians' right to conscientious objection, we have seen that a consensus exists among medical associations that physicians have a right to object to providing health care services on conscientious grounds. Like all rights, however, the right to conscientious objection is not absolute; it must be exercised in a manner that does not compromise patients' rights to equal and timely access to health care services. This means a physician cannot object to providing a service if the delay that would result from doing so would jeopardise a patient's life or health. Where conscientious objection can be exercised without threatening a patient's life or health, the physician has obligations to exercise the right to conscientious objection in a manner that respects patients' dignity, and provides them with the health care information and referrals necessary to ensure that they receive timely access to care.

As we have seen, the thorniest issue, one that remains a subject of continuing disagreement and contestation, is the nature of physicians' obligations to provide patients with information and referrals. When a physician objects to providing services on conscientious grounds, patients must be provided promptly with full information on the range of clinical options available to them and they must have access to other health care providers who can provide accessible and timely care. But do physicians have an obligation to provide patients with information and referrals themselves, or can they delegate those obligations to others? The CPSO and CPSS have taken very different positions on these issues. The CPSO policy appears to require objecting physicians to provide information and referrals themselves. Since many physicians' conscientious beliefs do not see a moral distinction between providing a service and facilitating a patient's access to a service, why would we give them the right to refuse one but not the other? What matters is that patients receive the information they need in order to access services in a timely fashion. The quality and timeliness of the information patients receive matters, not its origin.

The flexibility exhibited in the CPSS policy on the origin of the required information is preferable to the CPSO policy's apparently rigid insistence that physicians have obligations to provide information and referrals personally. Yet the CPSS policy goes too far in not requiring physicians to ensure that patients receive full and balanced information from reliable professional sources, and it goes too far in leaving open the possibility that physicians could be relieved entirely of their obligations to provide information and referrals in some circumstances.

Downie, McLeod and Shaw's model conscientious objection policy provides that '[t]he obligation to inform patients may be met by delegating the informing process to another competent individual for whom the physician is responsible'.[80] It makes good sense to permit delegation to individuals with the requisite competence.[81] The protection afforded to physicians' consciences is thereby expanded at no cost to patients' rights. In the language of statutory human rights jurisprudence, no 'undue hardship' is created by permitting physicians to delegate the informing process. And in the language of section 1 of the Charter, it is not a minimal impairment of physicians' rights to require them to provide information on services to which they object on conscientious grounds when the alternative of delegating the informing process to another competent person is an equally effective way of ensuring patients' timely and equal access to health care services.

Similarly, physicians' conscientious rights could be advanced without any restriction of patients' rights by permitting the delegation of the referral process to another competent individual. Nor is a formal referral necessary so long as patients receive information necessary to enable them to access required care in a timely fashion. This position provides greater accommodation to physicians' conscientious rights than the CPSO policy (which appears to require a formal referral in all cases and does not appear to permit delegation of the referral process), but less than the CPSS policy (which permits physicians to take a range of steps to allow a patient to obtain access). Medical associations could facilitate referrals by maintaining a directory of physicians that provide services that are frequently the subject of conscientious refusals (like abortion or medical assistance in dying), and the directory could be made accessible to physicians and patients. Physicians could be required to provide patients with information about how to access this referral service. In this way, the thorny issue of referrals could be resolved by medical associations in a manner that best protects the equal importance of both patients' rights of access to medical services and physicians' rights of conscientious objection.[82]

In the heated public debates about the rights of physicians or other public actors to exercise rights to conscientious objection, it is common for participants to inflate some rights' claims and deny any legitimacy to others. This is evident in assertions that doctors should park their conscientious beliefs at home, or

[80] Downie, McLeod and Shaw (n 6) 31.

[81] Although it is not clear why it is necessary to restrict the permitted delegation to persons 'for whom the physician is responsible'.

[82] A similar proposal is made by Margaret Somerville in 'A modest proposal for respecting physicians' freedom of conscience', *National Post*, 23 January 2015, http://news.nationalpost.com/full-comment/margaret-somerville-a-modest-proposal-for-respecting-physicians-freedom-of-conscience.

alternatively, that patients' rights to equal and timely access to health care services are not threatened by the exercise of physicians' rights to conscientious objection. Both assertions fail to grapple with the full range of human rights at issue. As we have seen in our review of recent debates regarding policies developed by Canadian medical associations, it is possible to devise policies that give full effect in most situations to both physicians' conscientious rights and patients' rights to timely, equal and dignified access to health care services. The principles devised in these policies will provide helpful guidance on how to protect rights to conscientious objection without compromising the rights of others in other social contexts.

9

Conscientious Objections by Civil Servants: The Case of Marriage Commissioners and Same-Sex Civil Marriages

RICHARD MOON

I. Introduction: Private Religion and Public Duty

When the definition of civil marriage was changed to enable same-sex couples to marry, a number of civil marriage commissioners objected on religious grounds to performing such marriages.[1] While some provinces agreed to accommodate the commissioners' religious objections, and excuse them from performing same-sex marriage ceremonies, other provinces were unwilling to do so and instructed their commissioners to perform these marriages or face dismissal.

The question of whether a province can require marriage commissioners to perform same-sex marriages, over their religious objections, has been addressed by the courts (and tribunals) in Saskatchewan in a series of cases involving: (1) a claim by a marriage commissioner that the government directive to perform such marriages amounted to religious discrimination, contrary to the province's human rights code;[2] (2) a complaint by a same-sex couple, who argued that the denial of services by a marriage commissioner amounted to discrimination contrary to the human rights code;[3] (3) a reference (a request by the provincial government) to the Saskatchewan Court of Appeal for its opinion as to whether it would be constitutional for the government to permit marriage commissioners to refuse to perform same-sex marriages for religious reasons.[4]

[1] 'Marriage and Divorce' including the definition of marriage, falls within the jurisdiction of the Government of Canada, under the Constitution Act 1867, s 91(26). However, the 'Solemnization of Marriage' falls within provincial jurisdiction under s 92(12).

[2] *Nichols v Dept of Justice, Government of Saskatchewan* (25 October 2006, Sask HRT). The Saskatchewan Human Rights Code 1979.

[3] *Nichols v MJ and the Sask HRC* 2009 SKQB 299.

[4] *Re Marriage Commissioners Appointed Under The Marriage Act* 2011 SKCA 3.

In each of these cases the issue of whether an objecting marriage commissioner can be required to perform same-sex marriages is framed by the courts as a contest between religious freedom and sexual orientation equality that must be resolved through the balancing of these competing interests. And in each of these cases the court strikes the balance in favour of sexual orientation equality, determining that the equality rights of same-sex couples outweighs the religious freedom of marriage commissioners.

The courts point to several factors that in their view reduce the strength of the commissioner's religious freedom claim. The most significant of these is that the commissioner is not required to engage directly in a practice that is contrary to his/her beliefs, but is expected only to perform, in his/her official capacity, an act that extends legal recognition to a same-sex relationship. But even if it is possible to depreciate the commissioner's claim in this way, it is not obvious that the competing claim to non-discrimination is comparatively stronger. In each of these cases, the court accepts that when a same-sex couple is refused services by an objecting marriage commissioner, the couple will have little difficulty finding another commissioner to perform their civil marriage. The couple is not denied a public service but is simply inconvenienced when they are directed to another commissioner.[5]

Despite what they say, the courts in these cases do not balance or trade-off religious freedom and sexual orientation equality, but instead give complete priority to the latter. A refusal by a marriage commissioner to perform a same-sex civil marriage ceremony is viewed by the courts as the cause of harm or injury to the couple (an act of discrimination), and not simply as a competing claim.

I will argue that there is no balancing in these cases because there is no freedom of religion interest to be balanced against the right to sexual orientation equality. The marriage commissioner's freedom of religion lacks substance not, or not simply, because the commissioner is a public official, or because the interference with his/her religious beliefs is indirect or partial. Rather, the religious objection of the marriage commissioner falls outside the scope of freedom of religion under section 2(a) of the Canadian Charter of Rights and Freedoms (the Charter), because it involves a belief about how others in the community should behave and be treated. A marriage commissioner has no claim to be exempted from the duties of his or her position on the basis of such a belief.

The protection of religious freedom, and more particularly the requirement that the state remain neutral in matters of religion, depends on a distinction between the religious and the political—between the sphere of personal or communal religious life and the sphere of political or civic life. Views and actions that relate to civic concerns—to the rights and interests of community members or to public welfare—even if rooted in a religious belief system, must be subject to the give and

[5] Moreover there is no suggestion in any of these decisions that the province should accommodate the religious practices of marriage commissioners by restructuring the civil marriage system in a way that avoids or minimises the conflict between religious freedom and sexual orientation equality.

take of political decision-making. In contrast, the religious or spiritual life of the individual or church community is viewed as a personal or internal matter that should be both excluded and insulated from politics. The role of courts in these cases is not to strike a balance between competing religious and civic interests, but rather to draw the line between the spheres of religious and political life.

In deciding whether the objection of the marriage commissioners should be viewed as an expression of personal conscience, or instead as a political judgment (a position that concerns the rights and interests of others in the community), the courts must take account of several factors. The most significant of these is whether the act that the commissioners object to performing is closely tied to the immoral behaviour they oppose—whether they can be seen as actively participating in the 'immoral' behaviour. The commissioners, in these cases, present their objection to performing same-sex civil marriages as a personal or private position that should be insulated from state action. Yet their religious beliefs relate to the actions and status of others in the community. The objecting commissioners believe that same-sex relationships should not be permitted. They think that the law is wrong to recognise these relationships. Their claim to exemption amounts to a rejection of the law (a law one may presume they opposed in political debate) and its recognition of the equal worth of same-sex relationships.

The objecting commissioners are free to live their personal lives in accordance with their views about sin and virtue. They are also free to associate with those who share their views. But when they enter the public sphere, their interactions with others should be subject to public norms. If the state has decided that sexual orientation discrimination should be prohibited (that gays and lesbians should be treated as full members of the community), those who hold a different view (and believe that gays and lesbians are sinners) should not be exempted from their public obligation to treat gays and lesbians in a non-discriminatory manner when providing goods and services or when acting in an official capacity. A public official, such as a marriage commissioner, should not be excused from performing his or her duties simply because she or he disapproves of the conduct of others and the law's acceptance or affirmation of that conduct.

A province may choose to accommodate the religious objections of marriage commissioners, as several provinces have done, provided it establishes a system that does not have a discriminatory impact on same-sex couples. The province, though, does not have an obligation under the Charter to accommodate the moral beliefs of a civil servant, when those beliefs relate to the rights and interests of others—and are better understood as a political position rather than as an expression of personal conscience.[6]

[6] For a different view see Bruce Ryder, 'The Canadian Conception of Equal Religious. Citizenship', in Richard Moon (ed), *Law and Religious Pluralism in Canada* (Vancouver, UBC Press, 2008) 101: 'Governments have obligations to affirm both religious rights and equal access to civil marriage ... [which] can be met by taking steps, to the point of undue hardship, to accommodate religious beliefs and to ensure that a sufficient number of public officials are willing an available to perfom civil marriage ceremonies for same-sex couples'.

II. Same-Sex Marriage: Politics and Rights

In recent years, Canadian courts have been asked to decide a number of cases in which religious individuals or groups have sought to be exempted from laws that prohibit sexual orientation discrimination. The courts have been asked to decide whether a human rights code ban on discrimination in the provision of services to the public was breached when the owner of a printing business refused to print letterheads for a gay organisation,[7] or when a B&B refused to rent a room to a same-sex couple.[8] The courts have also been asked whether the ban on discrimination is breached when a Christian group that operates (government-funded) assisted living facilities for mentally disabled adults prohibits its employees from entering into same-sex relationships,[9] or when a publicly funded Catholic school prevents a gay couple from attending the school's prom.[10]

The claim in these cases to exemption from anti-discrimination laws signals a shift in the public role of religious opposition to homosexuality. The religious claim that homosexuality is immoral or wrongful was until recently a political position in debates about the legal recognition of same-sex relationships. This position, though, was rejected by legislatures and courts, which decided first that same-sex relationships should be protected as a matter of liberty, and later that they should be respected or recognised as a matter of equality. In the religious exemption cases, those who consider homosexuality to be sinful, or immoral, now assert the right to be exempted from the application of ordinary law (most often anti-discrimination law). Religious opposition to homosexuality has become the basis for a personal or group rights claim. The exemption claim is a rearguard or defensive action. The claimants are not 'directly' challenging the legal recognition of same-sex marriages; nevertheless, they are 'personally' opposing the law's recognition of such relationships. The public debate about same-sex marriage did not go as they wanted, and so now they are seeking to opt out of the legal ban on sexual orientation discrimination or to personally reject the legal recognition of same-sex relationships. Individuals, who consider homosexuality to be sinful, are asking to be excused from performing any action that in their view supports or condones same-sex relationships. Religious groups that are opposed to same-sex relationships are seeking to run their (internal) affairs in accordance with their own norms—which may include a ban on same-sex relationships.

In the *Same-Sex Marriage Reference*, religious opponents of homosexuality sought unsuccessfully to transform the political argument against the recognition of same-sex marriage into a rights claim.[11] The federal government, in that case, asked the

[7] *Brockie v Ontario (HRC)* [2002] OJ no 2375.
[8] *Eadie v Riverbend B&B* (nn 2) 2012 BCHRT 247.
[9] *Ontario (HRC) v Christian Horizons* 2010 ONSC 2105.
[10] *Hall (Litigation Guardian of) v Powers* [2002] OJ No 1803.
[11] *Reference re Same-Sex Marriage* 2004 SCC 79.

Supreme Court of Canada for its opinion on a few issues, one of which was whether the redefinition of marriage to include same-sex relationships was consistent with the Charter. A number of religious groups argued that the recognition of same-sex marriages would breach religious freedom under the Charter of Rights, because it would undermine the value and meaning of marriage for religious individuals and communities. State recognition of same-sex marriage, it was claimed, would interfere with their religious beliefs and practices and therefore with their *Charter* rights.

The Court's answer to this was that the state's act of enlarging the definition of civil marriage to include same-sex marriage did not interfere with anyone's religious beliefs or practices: 'The mere recognition of the equality rights of one group cannot, in itself, constitute a violation of the rights of another'.[12] Religious organisations could continue to perform marriages in accordance with their spiritual beliefs—which in some, but not all, cases included a belief that marriage is open only to opposite-sex couples. The consequence of the change was simply that some individuals must now live in a society that permits others to engage in an activity that they regard as immoral—or that supports a moral view inconsistent with their own. The individual's ability to practice his or her faith (his/her religious freedom) is not restricted merely because public policy is at odds with his or her beliefs. The individual does not have the 'right' to live in a society that accepts his or her moral positions.

Even if the redefinition of civil marriage does not force anyone to engage in or refrain from any form of (religious) practice, it involves a public rejection of the deeply held religious beliefs of some members of the community. For the religious adherent, the sinfulness of homosexuality is not just an abstract idea, with no relevance to community life. The state's commitment to sexual-orientation equality, even though framed in secular or civic terms, must be understood as a rejection of the belief that homosexuality is wrongful. While the state may avoid passing direct judgment on the truth of a particular religious belief (as religious truth), it cannot avoid doing so indirectly, when determining public policy. When the legislature decides that a particular activity should be either supported or restricted, it does not frame its judgment in terms of what God has or has not commanded. But unless we hold on to some artificial distinction between public and religious morality, the legislature's judgment must be seen as a repudiation of a religious belief that is held by some in the community.

It is more difficult, though, to dismiss the religious freedom claim, when an individual is required to do more than simply live in a society that rejects his/her moral views. The civil marriage commissioners in Saskatchewan (and elsewhere) are being required, as part of their duties, to take action that they believe supports or condones the immoral behaviour of others. The question in this and other cases

[12] ibid, para 45.

is what kind or degree of involvement, or association, with same-sex relationships (when required by the state) should be viewed as interfering with the individual's religious beliefs or practices.

III. Religious Values in the Political Process

It is sometimes said that religiously based positions (and more particularly positions based on scripture) should not play a role in public debate and decision-making, because state law must be based on reasons that are accessible to all members of the community. Because religious beliefs rest on faith or familial and cultural socialisation rather than reasoned judgment, they cannot provide a publicly acceptable basis for law-making. To base state action on religious beliefs would be to impose the beliefs of some on others or to unfairly favour the religious beliefs of some over those of others. Political actors, then, must base their actions on non-religious values or must be able to defend their actions on non-religious grounds, even if their deeper motives are religious in character. That, at least, is the familiar argument.

However, in *Chamberlain v Surrey School District No 36*, the Supreme Court of Canada held that elected officials could draw on their religious values when making political decisions.[13] According to McLachlin CJ, 'Religion is an integral aspect of people's lives, and cannot be left at the boardroom door'.[14] The Canadian courts recognise that 'values' cannot be excluded from political decision-making simply because they are part of a religious belief system. But, at the same time, they accept that the state should not support particular religious practices. The distinction the courts seem to rely on, if only implicitly, is between, on the one hand, the elements of a religious belief system (religious 'values') that address civic issues, and are concerned with individual rights or public welfare, and on the other, religious 'practices' or beliefs—those elements of a belief system that address spiritual or other-worldly matters. While religious 'practices' should not be supported by the state and should instead be viewed as personal (or internal to a group), religiously grounded 'values' should not be excluded from politics and should instead be debated on their merits—on their conception of human good or public welfare. Where the line between the 'civic' and 'personal' or communal elements of a religious belief system (between value and practice) is drawn by the courts will reflect their views about the nature of human welfare, and the proper scope of political action, but perhaps also their assumptions about the appropriate forms of religious worship.[15]

[13] *Chamberlain v Surrey School District No 36* 2002 SCC 86. See also *Mouvement laique v Saguenay (City)* 2015 SCC 16.

[14] *Chamberlain* (n 13), para 19.

[15] For a discussion see Richard Moon, *Freedom of Conscience and Religion* (Toronto, Irwin, 2014) 52–65.

The claim that a religious belief or value may play a role in political decision-making when there is a parallel secular argument (when the same or a similar argument can be stated in non-religious terms) points to this distinction between religious practices or beliefs and civic views or actions. When a religious value or position (such as the eradication of poverty) has a secular analogue, it will be seen as addressing a public concern—as addressing public welfare or civil rights. When there is no parallel secular argument we are more likely to see the religious position as simply a matter of honouring God's will or adhering to the divine or supernatural order—in other words, as a religious 'practice' or belief (eg a ban on eating pork). Whether we regard religiously grounded opposition to same-sex relationships as addressing an issue of civic welfare (and part of public debate) or as simply a matter of honouring God or respecting the divine will (and excluded from political decision-making) will depend on whether this opposition can be comprehended within other normative systems—as addressing public or individual welfare.

In Canada the religious argument against same-sex relationships was not ruled out a priori (as a religious practice or belief which the state was not permitted to support or prefer) but was, instead, addressed directly by public decision-makers. The religious view ('value') that same-sex relationships are immoral or unnatural (and should not be given legal recognition) was eventually rejected by political and judicial decision-makers, who responded with legal measures banning sexual-orientation discrimination and affirming the equal value of same-sex relationships.[16] As a consequence, the performance of same-sex marriage ceremonies became part of the ordinary duties of civil marriage commissioners.

In some provinces, such as Ontario, commissioners were told that if they had religious objections to performing same-sex marriages, they would be excused from doing so.[17] However, in other provinces, such as Saskatchewan, commissioners were told that they must perform such marriages or resign their position. A group of commissioners in Saskatchewan, who considered same-sex relationships to be sinful, argued that the requirement that they perform same-sex marriages interfered with their religious freedom, and that they should be exempted from this requirement. The religious belief that same-sex relationships are immoral—a belief that played a role in the public debate about the

[16] In the early part of the new millennium, constitutional challenges were brought in several provinces against the common law definition of marriage, which restricted civil marriage to opposite-sex couples—'the union between a man and a woman'. In each of these cases, the court ruled that the exclusion of same-sex relationships from the legal definition of marriage amounted to discrimination on the grounds of sexual orientation contrary to s 15 of the Charter, and that this breach was not justified under s 1, the Charter's limitations provision. See, eg: *Halpern v Canada (Attorney General)* [2003] OJ No 2268 (ONCA); *Barbeau v British Columbia (Attorney General)* 2003 BCCA 251. In 2006 the federal government formally amended the definition of marriage to conform to these court judgments — Civil Marriage Act 2005.

[17] The Ontario 'single entry point' system is described below.

legal recognition of same-sex marriages but was rejected in the democratic and legal processes—now served as the basis for a rights' claim by objecting marriage commissioners—a claim to be exempted from their public duty to perform same-sex marriages. In other words, a religious 'value' that was treated as political—as something that might influence public policy—but was rejected by policy-makers, was converted into a personal 'practice' or belief (a matter of personal religious conscience) that lay outside politics—that should be protected or insulated from political judgment. The belief that homosexuality is sinful or immoral was now said to justify the exemption of religious objectors from the application of the law—and more particularly in this case, the exemption of civil marriage commissioners from the performance of their public duties.

IV. The Saskatchewan Trilogy

On three occasions the courts (and human rights tribunals) in Saskatchewan have considered whether marriage commissioners should be excused from performing same-sex marriages, when they have religious objections to such relationships. The issue has arisen in a slightly different way in each of the cases. Nevertheless, the result in each case is the same: that the right of same-sex couples to be free from discrimination outweighs the religious freedom of marriage commissioners to be excused from performing same-sex marriages.[18]

The Saskatchewan Marriage Act provides that a civil commissioner may be appointed to serve the members of a particular cultural/ethnic group.[19] However, most commissioners are appointed to serve the general community. A couple that wishes to be married in a civil ceremony must approach an individual commissioner to request his/her services. In a number of other provinces a different system operates. Ontario, for example, operates a 'single entry point' system, in which a couple wishing to be married in a civil ceremony applies for the

[18] Exemption claims have also been made by marriage commissioners in Manitoba and Newfoundland. In both provinces the human rights commission rejected the marriage commissioner's discrimination claims and did not forward the claims to a tribunal for adjudication. The process in both provinces is ongoing. The issue has also arisen in the UK. In *Eweida and others v UK* [2013] ECHR 37 the claim of a registrar in the London Borough of Islington to be excused from conducting civil partnership ceremonies for same-sex couples was rejected by the European Court of Human Rights. In the domestic courts it was noted that the registrar was a public official who performed 'a purely secular task'. Even though the Borough operated a single entry point system, her request to opt out was disruptive to the 'rota' and caused offence to gay colleagues (ibid, para 29).

[19] The Marriage Act 1995, s 30. But if a commissioner can be appointed to perform marriages for the members of a particular religious/ethnic group, does this mean that she/he can decide that someone is not a proper Mennonite if they are gay and refuse to perform the ceremony? Presumably couples who marry in a civil ceremony rather than in a church do so because they are not religious or because the religion with which they identify will not marry them as a gay couple or an interfaith couple.

services of a marriage commissioner at a central office, which then assigns a commissioner to perform their ceremony.[20]

A. *Nichols v Dept of Justice* (Sask)

Orville Nichols had been a civil marriage commissioner in Saskatchewan for more than 20 years, when the definition of marriage was amended to include same-sex relationships. Following the change, the province's Department of Justice directed all commissioners to perform such marriages. Mr Nichols responded by bringing a human rights code complaint against the province, in which he argued that the requirement that he perform same-sex marriages amounted to religious discrimination. Mr Nichols considered it 'morally wrong to officiate the marriage of a same-sex couple' and argued that he should not be forced to solemnise same-sex marriages 'contrary to his religious beliefs'.[21] He 'acknowledge[d] the legality of same-sex marriages' but said that 'his Christian religious beliefs do not recognize marriage between a same-sex couple'.[22]

Mr Nichols' complaint was dismissed by the Human Rights Commission (HRC). This dismissal was upheld by the Human Rights Tribunal.[23] The HRC noted (and Mr Nichols at times seemed to acknowledge) that he was not being asked to preside over a religious marriage ceremony involving spiritual vows. He is a civil marriage commissioner, a public official whose job is to preside over a couple's entry into a legal relationship rather than a religious union. Mr Nichols' claim to be exempted from the performance of his public duties is based on his religious objections to same-sex relationships and to the state's affirmation of such relationships.[24] His claim amounts to this—that his freedom to practise his religion was compromised when he was 'required' as part of his job to participate in the state recognition of a relationship that he regarded as sinful or immoral.

According to the Saskatchewan Human Rights Tribunal, 'a balance needs to be struck between the freedom of religion and other competing rights'.[25] The Tribunal found that in this case the harm to sexual orientation equality outweighed the

[20] The systems vary between provinces. Manitoba, for example, operates systems similar to that in Saskatchewan. The system in Quebec is closer to that in Ontario.

[21] *Nichols v Sask* (n 2) para 6.

[22] *Nichols v Sask* (n 2) para 6. In a later case he testified that 'he did not have a problem with same-sex couples marrying'; nevertheless, he said that he could not perform the ceremony because Christianity (as he understood it) does not recognise such marriages (*Nichols v MJ* (n 3) para 10).

[23] *Nichols v Sask* (n 2). In its decision, at para 24, the Human Rights Commission noted that Mr Nichols regarded the civil marriage ceremony as quasi-religious and understood his 'vocation' to have a religious component to it. He thought this even though he 'opted for a general appointment rather than one that would limit him to providing services to a particular community' (para 28).

[24] In *Sask v MJ* (n 3) Mr Nichols is reported at para 10 as saying 'that the bible directs him to believe that God hates homosexuality'.

[25] *Nichols v Sask* (n 2) para 29.

interference with Mr Nichols' freedom of religion. Mr Nichols argued that his religious beliefs could be accommodated without any tangible impact on the ability of same-sex couples to access the services of a civil marriage commissioner, since there were other commissioners who would be prepared to perform same-sex marriages. However, the Tribunal, quoting from the decision of the HRC, stressed that:

> The purpose of the *Code* is not simply to ensure that vulnerable groups have access to equivalent services. It is also to ensure that their dignity as human beings is protected by providing access to all public services without discrimination. In this context, one denial of a public service on discriminatory grounds is too many, and could well be actionable.[26]

Despite the Tribunal's insistence that the issue must be resolved through balancing, its judgment does not seem to involve any comparison or weighing of the 'competing' interests of religious freedom and sexual orientation equality. The Tribunal appears to give complete priority to the same-sex couple's 'right to equality'. In the Tribunal's view, even if a same-sex couple could easily find another commissioner to perform their civil marriage, the initial refusal is objectionable and amounts to a significant breach of the right to equality. This is so even though the refusal is based on the commissioner's sincerely held religious belief—a belief that the court formally agrees falls within the protection of section 2(a). When the commissioner, in his official capacity, expresses his religious belief to a same-sex couple (and directs them elsewhere), he is considered to have caused them injury. According to the Tribunal, while Mr Nichols 'is free to practice his religion as he chooses, he cannot "infringe on the rights of others"'.[27] However, it appears that the rights of others (of a same-sex couple) are breached whenever a commissioner openly refuses, for religious reasons, to perform a same-sex marriage ceremony.

B. *Nichols v MJ*

Mr Nichols' human rights code complaint against the Saskatchewan government was still under review by the HRC when he was approached by a same-sex couple, who wished to engage his services. Mr Nichols declined to perform the couple's civil ceremony and instead directed them to another commissioner whom he thought would be willing to perform the ceremony. The couple brought a complaint against Mr Nichols under the Saskatchewan Human Rights Code, arguing that his refusal to perform the ceremony amounted to sexual orientation

[26] ibid para 27.

[27] *Nichols v Sask* (n 2) para 29. Mr Nichols testified that he had in the past refused to perform marriages in circumstances in which he suspected the marriage was one of convenience or there was a history of assault or abuse in the relationship. While there may be some question about whether he is competent to make such judgments—these at least count as public reasons for refusal.

discrimination. The Tribunal decided that Mr Nichols had breached the Code. This decision was upheld on review by the Court of Queen's Bench.[28]

The Court accepted that Mr Nichols sincerely believed, on religious grounds, that it would be wrong for him to perform such a ceremony. But it noted that a marriage commissioner is a government actor and therefore subject to the Charter of Rights. The Court held that Mr Nichols had a public duty to perform such marriages and could not withhold his services based on his 'personal views'. Importantly, his 'personal right to freedom of religion … is not enforceable against [the same-sex couple] … for it is not [the couple that] is interfering with his religious beliefs'.[29] According to the Court, any accommodation that Mr Nichols might be owed 'is not the responsibility of those who seek the services he is legally empowered to provide'.[30] His refusal to perform the ceremony in this case 'constitutes discrimination in the provision of a public service on the basis of sexual orientation'.[31] But if Mr Nichols had the right to practise his religion (and the state had some duty to accommodate his religious beliefs), then perhaps his refusal to perform a same-sex marriage for religious reasons could be viewed not as an act of state discrimination, but simply as the exercise of religious freedom—as an expression of personal conscience. If his personal decision not to perform the marriage had no practical impact on the couple (as long as they are able to find quickly someone else to perform the ceremony), then the 'competing' interests of equality (non-discrimination in the provision of government services) and religious freedom (respect for Mr Nichols' personal religious beliefs) did not appear to be in conflict.

C. *Reference re Saskatchewan Marriage Commissioners*

In *Re Marriage Commissioners Appointed Under The Marriage Act*, the Saskatchewan Court of Appeal was asked for its opinion on the constitutionality of a legislative proposal that would permit provincially appointed civil marriage commissioners to refuse on religious grounds to perform same-sex marriage ceremonies.[32] The Court found that this arrangement would violate the section 15 equality rights of gays and lesbians and could not be justified under section 1 of the Charter.

[28] *Nichols v MJ* (n 3).

[29] ibid, para 56.

[30] ibid, para 57.

[31] ibid, para 57.

[32] *Re Marriage Commissioners* (n 4). The proposed exemption provided that '[n]otwithstanding *The Saskatchewan Human Rights Code*, a marriage commissioner is not required to solemnize a marriage if to do so would be contrary to the marriage commissioner's religious beliefs'. A second version of the exemption put before the Court 'grandfathered' the current group of commissioners allowing them not to perform same-sex marriages, but did not extend this exemption to newly appointed commissioners.

Under the Saskatchewan civil marriage system, a couple wishing to be married in a civil ceremony must approach a commissioner in their general geographic area to request his or her services. As the majority of the Court noted, 'commissioners are the route—the only route—by which individuals who wish to be married by way of a non-religious ceremony may have their union solemnized'.[33] The Court observed that under the proposed law a same-sex couple, who approach a marriage commissioner, could be told by the commissioner that he/she is unable to perform the marriage because of the couple's sexual orientation. The Court thought that the harm from such a denial would be significant:

> It is not difficult for most people to imagine the personal hurt involved in a situation where an individual is told by a governmental office 'I won't help you because you are black (or Asian or First Nations) but someone else will' or 'I won't help you because you are Jewish (or Muslim or Budd[h]ist) but someone else will'. Being told 'I won't help you because you are gay/lesbian but someone else will' is no different.[34]

Moreover, said the Court, a significant number of commissioners might decide that they are unable to perform same-sex marriages, and the law provides no assurance that a 'minimum complement of commissioners will always be available to provide services to same-sex couples'.[35] The Court had no difficulty then concluding that the legislative proposal would have 'the effect of creating a negative distinction based on sexual orientation' and that given the 'historical marginalization and mistreatment of gay and lesbian individuals', the proposal would be discriminatory contrary to section 15 of the Charter.[36]

In its section 1 (limitations) analysis, the majority of the Court accepted that the protection of the commissioner's religious freedom represented a substantial and compelling purpose, sufficient to justify the restriction of a Charter right. However, they went on to find that the proposed restriction on the rights of gay and lesbian couples failed both the minimal impairment and proportionality components of the limitations test. There were other ways, said the majority, in which the state might protect the commissioners' religious freedom without impairing, to the same degree, the right to equality. The majority identified as a less restrictive measure 'a "single entry point" system under which a couple seeking the services of a marriage commissioner would proceed, not by directly contacting an individual commissioner, but by dealing with the Director of the Marriage Unit or some other central office'.[37] In a single entry point system, accommodation of the commissioner's religious beliefs would take place 'behind the scenes' and would not be apparent to the couple. The majority made no judgment about whether a single entry point system would restrict the section 15 equality rights of gay and lesbian couples, or if it did, whether it would be a reasonable limit on those rights.

[33] *Re Marriage Commissioners* (n 4) para 9.
[34] ibid, para 41.
[35] ibid, para 42.
[36] ibid, para 45.
[37] ibid, para 85.

It concluded only that such a system would be 'less restrictive' of their equality rights than the proposed law.

The majority also found that the 'freedom of religion interests' accommodated by the proposed law 'do not lie at the heart of section 2(a)', because they concern the ability of the commissioners 'to act on their beliefs in the world at large' and not their freedom 'to hold the religious beliefs they choose or to worship as they wish'.[38] Moreover, said the majority: 'Persons who voluntarily choose to assume an office, like that of marriage commissioner, cannot expect to directly shape the office's intersection with the public so as to make it conform with their personal religious or other beliefs'.[39]

The question referred to the Court was whether the government's particular plan to accommodate 'marriage commissioners' was constitutional. The Court decided that the plan would breach the equality rights of same-sex couples and could not be justified under section 1. The more general question of the state's obligation to accommodate the religious beliefs of marriage commissioners was not addressed by the Court. Nevertheless, the implication of the Court's judgment that a centralised (single point of entry) system would protect the religious freedom rights of the commissioners without significantly impairing the equality rights of same-sex couples (so that they are able to access marriage services in the same ways as opposite-sex couples) might be that the state has a duty to institute such a system.

In *Reference re Marriage Commissioners*, the concurring judgment of Smith J suggested that the requirement that marriage commissioners perform same-sex civil marriages might not interfere with their religious beliefs or practices. Smith J observed that, in the performance of their duties, marriage commissioners are not 'compelled to engage in the sexual activity' to which they object; rather, '[t]heir objection is that it is sinful for *others* to engage in such activity'.[40] Furthermore, said Smith J, it is not at all clear 'that officiating at a civil marriage ceremony carries any implication or connotation at all that the marriage commissioner who officiates necessarily *approves* of the particular union'.[41] According to Smith J, any 'interference with the right of marriage commissioners to act in accordance with their religious belief… is [at most] trivial or insubstantial, in that it is interference that does not threaten actual religious beliefs or conduct'.[42] In Smith J's view, then, the decision by a marriage commissioner not to perform a same-sex marriage (based on the commissioner's belief that it would be wrong to perform such a marriage) would fall outside the scope of section 2(a) protection, and so its 'restriction' would require no justification under section 1.

[38] ibid, para 93.

[39] ibid, para 97. However, as I will suggest below, this finding does not simply lessen the weight of the claim, but should instead be seen as removing the claim from the scope of Charter protection.

[40] *Re Marriage Commissioners* (n 4) para 148.

[41] ibid, para 142.

[42] ibid, para 148.

V. Accommodating Religious Beliefs

In each of the judgments described in the previous section, the issue is framed by the court as the just balance between religious freedom and sexual-orientation equality. And, in each of these cases, the balance is stuck by the court in favour of sexual orientation equality. The court points to several factors to account for the limited value of the religious freedom claim. First it notes that when a civil marriage commissioner performs a marriage ceremony, she/he does so as a public official (performing a public role) and not as a private citizen or a religious authority. Second, the 'restriction' in such a case is not a direct interference with the commissioner's religious practice. Nor is the commissioner compelled by the state to engage directly in a practice she/he views as sinful (as in the case of a 'conscientious objector' being conscripted into military service). The commissioner is simply required, as part of her or his public duties, to perform an act that extends legal recognition to a same-sex marriage. Moreover, as the Court in the *Same-Sex Marriage Reference* noted, the performance of a public function by a civil servant need not be regarded as personal support for the 'sinful' activity. Finally, the commissioner holds powers that others do not. The commissioner has chosen to perform a public role. If she/he does not wish to be associated with an activity she/he regards as sinful, then she/he can give up the power to perform marriages.

Yet none of these factors seem sufficient to account for the court's easy choice of sexual orientation equality over religious freedom in the balancing process under section 1. If the freedom of religion claim is weak, so too, it might be said, is the sexual-orientation equality claim. The court considers a marriage commissioner's refusal to perform a same-sex marriage to be a significant breach of the right to equality, even though the affected couple may be able to find another commissioner with little difficulty—in other words, even though the couple's access to a government service is not impeded in any real way. The court emphasises that the harm experienced by the couple is not the denial of a service but rather the knowledge that a particular commissioner—a public official—objects to serving them because he/she believes that their relationship is immoral or sinful.[43] The commissioner's religiously based refusal to perform a same-sex couple's civil marriage is viewed by the courts as the source of the harm, and not simply as a competing moral claim. It is seen not as the expression of personal religious belief, but instead as an act of discrimination by a public official.

Furthermore there is no serious consideration in any of these judgments as to whether the government has a duty to accommodate the religious objection of marriage commissioners by restructuring the system in a way that avoids or

[43] See also *Eweida* (n 17) in which two gay colleagues were offended by a marriage registrar's request to be excused on religious grounds from performing same-sex civil partnership ceremonies.

minimises the conflict between religious belief and sexual orientation equality. In the *Marriage Commissioners* reference, the Court pointed to the single point entry system as an alternative that would not interfere to the same extent with the equality rights of gay and lesbian couples. The Court, though, did not consider whether the province had an obligation to introduce such as system in order to accommodate the religious beliefs of the objecting marriage commissioners. In a 'single entry point' system, a marriage commissioner could (depending on the number of commissioners) be excused by the province from performing same-sex marriages without any (noticeable) impact on the services available to same-sex couples (indeed without these couples being aware that a particular commissioner has been 'accommodated') and so without experiencing state discrimination based on their sexual orientation. If the religious freedom of marriage commissioners can be protected in a way that does not result in discrimination against gay and lesbian couples (and does not have other costs)—in other words, if both rights can be protected—should the province not be required to adopt this other system?

Sexual orientation equality prevails in these cases not because the religious freedom claim has little substance or is outweighed in the particular circumstance by the competing equality claim. The religious freedom claim has no weight, because the marriage commissioner's opposition to same-sex marriage—to homosexuality—even though rooted in a religious belief system, involves a moral/political position that does not fall within the scope of section 2(a) protection. A belief (religious or otherwise) about the rights and interests of others—about how others ought to be treated in the public sphere—should be viewed as a political position, and not as a personal religious practice or belief, and as such it should not be excluded or insulated from political decision-making. The view that same-sex relationships should be restricted or discouraged in the community (whether based on the belief that they are sinful or unnatural) is a political position rather than simply an expression of personal conscience. It is a position that has shaped political action over the years, and should therefore be subject to politics—to the possibility of rejection by democratic decision-makers. This is why there is no actual 'balancing' of interests in these cases. This is why the act of turning the couple away is regarded as discriminatory. And this is why the commissioner's refusal is treated as a state act of discrimination, and not simply a personal (or collective) religious belief that should be accommodated in the absence of undue hardship to others.

The distinction between personal belief (or religious community belief or practice), which should sometimes be accommodated, and moral or political beliefs ('values') about the actions of others, which should be subject to the give and take of politics, may be blurred by the courts' reliance on a subjective test for determining the scope of protected religious practice.[44] A marriage commissioner

[44] See *Syndicat Northcrest v Amselem* 2004 SCC 47.

may believe that it is immoral for him/her to engage in action that supports or condones the immoral actions of others. The commissioner's belief about what others should not do gives rise to a second order belief about the morality of his/her own action—about how he/she should respond to the immorality of others.[45] Moreover, the commissioner may argue, with some justification, that it is not for the courts to decide that his/her sincere belief that he/she should not support the sinful actions of others lacks weight—that it is not something that matters deeply to him/her.

The subjective test for determining the scope of section 2(a) protection—which provides that a practice/belief will be protected, if the individual has a sincere belief in its spiritual significance—reflects the courts' understandable reluctance to determine the content or significance of an individual's or group's religious beliefs. But the issue in the marriage commissioner cases is not what the commissioner sincerely believes or what is the proper understanding of her/his religious belief system. The commissioner's objection is framed as a belief about his/her personal practices or actions, but is focused on the immorality of the actions of others. The commissioner is asking the state to 'accommodate' her/his beliefs about what others should and should not do. The action of performing a marriage (or providing market services) is not in itself wrongful under the objecting commissioner's belief system. The 'action' is objectionable to the commissioner only because in a particular case it is connected to, or condones, what he/she regards as immoral or sinful conduct on the part of others. The commissioner may sincerely belief that she/he should not support the immoral actions of others; nevertheless his/her belief must be treated by the state as a political position that is subject to political judgment.

The marriage commissioner's accommodation claim is very different from the more familiar accommodation claims by civil servants that relate to religious dress or holidays. In most civil service accommodation cases, an individual (or group of individuals), who is employed by the government, seeks an exemption from a job requirement that is inconsistent with her or his religious practice—an exemption, for example, from a police uniform requirement for a Sikh man who wears a turban, or from a Saturday work requirement for a Seventh-day Adventist. In such cases, the civil servant's request is to be exempted from a rule or standard that is based on dominant cultural practices and in some cases (such as holidays) practices that are religious or, at least, have a religious origin. There is no conflict in these cases between different understandings of public morality (concerning the rights and interests of community members), and so accommodation can often occur without any significant impact on state policy. Accommodation in such cases often involves only a minor adjustment to the way in which the state

[45] This could extend to acts that have a remote connection to the 'sinful' behaviour and so enable a general avoidance of laws banning sexual-orientation discrimination. What degree of involvement in, or connection with, an 'immoral' act counts as supporting or condoning the act? Should an individual who makes wedding cakes or leases hall space be exempted from the ban on discrimination in the provision of services? For a discussion of the confused case law on this issue see Moon (n 14) 109–18.

has chosen to advance a particular policy. The practice can be treated as personal to the individual—as a non-political matter. The state is expected to accommodate these practices, if it can do so without significant cost, even though the individual might be able to find other employment that does not interfere with his or her religious practice. The marriage commissioners, in contrast, are not asking the state to accommodate their religious 'practices'. They are asking instead that their moral opposition to the state's recognition of same-sex marriages be accommodated. They are asking to be exempted from the performance of a public duty that, in their view, associates them with the sinful actions of others.

It is this distinction between a civil servant's personal religious expression and the performance of his/her public role or duty that was elided in the proposed Quebec Charter of Values[46]—which treated the wearing of religious dress or symbols, such as a hijab or turban, by a civil servant as a state act—as a breach of the requirement that the state remain neutral in matters of religion. The objecting marriage commissioners are seeking to suppress this distinction, but to the opposite effect. They argue that they should be excused from performing the duties attached to their civic role, because they believe that same-sex marriage is immoral and should not be recognised by the state. The refusal to perform such marriages is, they claim, simply an expression of their personal conscience.

The results in the three Saskatchewan cases are explicable once we recognise that freedom of religion does not support the accommodation of religious views about the rights and freedoms of others. A civil servant has no claim to be excused from performing the tasks associated with her/his position, simply because he/she is morally opposed to government policy, or to basic public values concerning the treatment of others in the community.

VI. Conclusion: Some General Comments About Accommodation

The Canadian courts have said that section 2(a) is breached any time the state restricts a religious practice in a non-trivial way. According to the courts, the state must justify the restriction under section 1 and this is said to involve a balancing of competing interests, the individual's freedom to practise her/his religion weighed against the state's ability to advance what it understands to be the public good. Yet despite their formal commitment to 'reasonable accommodation' or 'proportionality', the courts have been unwilling to require the state to compromise its policy in any significant way.[47]

[46] Bill 60, 1st Sess, 40th Leg, Quebec, 2013.

[47] See Benjamin L Berger, 'The Cultural Limits of Legal Tolerance' (2008) 21 *Canadian Journal of Law and Jurisprudence*.

In the Canadian religious freedom decisions, the state's duty to accommodate religion depends on a practical, but unstable, division of religion into personal/communal and civic elements. At issue in the religious accommodation cases is the line between the political sphere (of civic belief and action) and the sphere of personal or communal religious belief and practice. Accommodation of religious worship practices or beliefs (including communal and personal forms of worship and practice, and the internal operations of a religious community) seems like an appropriate response, to prevent the exclusion or marginalisation of a minority group, or more positively to protect the bonds of a religious association or to respect a collective tradition that has sought to address fundamental questions about meaning and value. However, when religion addresses, or touches upon, civic matters or public morality, and more particularly when it involves beliefs about the rights and interests of community members, it should remain subject to the give and take of politics. Respecting a religious community or tradition requires that its political claims be viewed as a legitimate part of public debate—as claims that may be either adopted or rejected in the democratic process.

10

A Freedom of Religion-Based Argument for the Regulation of Religious Schools

DANIEL M WEINSTOCK

This chapter defends a position that may at first glance have the air of paradox. The argument I will be mounting is to the effect that there are reasons, *grounded in the right to religious freedom*, to regulate religious schooling. In a nutshell, I will hold that restricting religious freedom may be the only way to take parents' religious freedom seriously while at the same time respecting the child's right to an open future.

The argument will be deployed in five stages: first, I will argue that freedom of religion theorists do not take freedom of religion seriously when they exclude the parental right to take steps to enrol their children into their religion as part of the content of that right. Second, I argue that children possess a right, qualified by the parental right just described, to an open future. Specifically, I argue that the way in which to make these rights compossible is to hold that the right to an open future involves the right not to be raised in unacceptably asymmetrical ways, though it does not rule out the parent's right to raise children in acceptably asymmetrical ways. The third step of the argument consists in arguing that whether children are being raised in acceptably or unacceptably asymmetrical ways depends upon the way in which they are raised by the conjunct of school, civil society, and home. One cannot, that is, simply look at any one of these contexts to determine whether the child's qualified right to an open future is respected. The fourth step of the argument consists in arguing, contra Matthew Clayton, that it is both empirically implausible and normatively undesirable for the responsibility for children being raised in an acceptably rather than an unacceptably asymmetrical way to be laid fully at the feet of parents, and of the way they organise the home and their children's access to civil society organisations such as religious institutions. The final part of the argument consists in showing that schools are best equipped to fulfil this function. Thus, the only way to allow parents to exercise their freedom of religion without violating their children's rights is for schools not simply to be vehicles for the transmission of parental values and beliefs.

I. The Intergenerational Dimension of Freedom of Religion

What does the right to freedom of religion encompass? What range of behaviours and practices should it protect against state interference? A prominent view, expressed with characteristic clarity in the last work published by the late Ronald Dworkin, is to the effect that the right to religious freedom is a special case of a much broader right, that Dworkin labels the right to 'ethical independence'. The right in question would protect citizens against any government that would 'restrict freedom just because it assumes that one way for people to lead their lives … is intrinsically better than another'.[1] The crucial point Dworkin wishes to make in writing about ethical independence rather than religious freedom is that it encompasses much more than just 'godly' religions. That is, it encompasses much more than convictions that stem from what are usually thought to be religious sources. On Dworkin's view, there is no way to justify religious freedom without 'interpreting' that freedom (rather than, say, basing oneself on dictionary definitions or on conventional understandings of the phenomena at issue), that is without making plain what it is about religion that makes it worthy of protection by a right. 'We must reject any account of the nature or scope of religion that would make a distinct right to religious freedom silly or arbitrary'.[2] The only way to do that, Dworkin argues, is to interpret religious conviction as a species of particularly deeply held moral conviction. It should be afforded protection for the same reason that it protects people against having to act against their moral consciences: because to do so would be to offend against their self-respect.[3]

I believe that there is a better interpretation of the concept of freedom of religion, one that both accepts Dworkin's stricture to the effect that interpretation must reveal the point of granting religion the protection afforded by a right, and adds perspicuity to it by distinguishing it from a concept alongside which it often appears in constitutional texts, that of conscience.

There is a difference between the obligations that one feels bound by for moral reasons, and the ones that one feels committed to on religious grounds. The justification of moral obligation, to put the matter somewhat simplistically, is moral argument. This is not to say that moral argument is what causes people to have certain moral convictions, and to ascribe the importance that they do to these convictions because of argument. Rather, it is to say that if one were to ask someone why she felt that her moral convictions have the strength that they do in her life, such that to act against them would be incompatible with her self-respect and sense of moral integrity, we would expect something on the order of a moral

[1] Ronald Dworkin, *Religion Without God* (Cambridge, Harvard University Press, 2013) 130.
[2] ibid, 109.
[3] ibid, 114.

argument. Were that person to justify, for example, not being made to act against their ethical vegetarianism, we would find it odd were they to invoke a family tradition, or a sense of fidelity to the past. One would expect an argument grounded in the need to avoid useless suffering, or to manage the planet's resources responsibly, or the like.

Religious traditions are sources of moral argument. Religions are, among other things, ways of making sense and of rank-ordering the moral obligations that one has, independently of religious considerations. But they are also traditions. As traditions, they do more than simply telling us how we should govern ourselves morally. To invoke recent work by Samuel Scheffler, they also orient us in time, and allow us to make sense of our individual, temporally finite lives in terms of a longer narrative.[4] When asked about why they observe certain religious rituals, or cleave to religiously edicted dietary restrictions, for example, such that they would feel as compromised in being forced to act against them as would persons of moral conscience were they forced to act against their moral convictions, it would make sense for a religious believer to invoke tradition, to say, in effect, this is how we have always done things around here, or this is our way of linking ourselves to past generations.

If these considerations are at all plausible, then it is a mistake to claim, as Dworkin does, that the only thing of value that is protected by a right to freedom of religion can be assimilated to moral conviction. Now, Dworkin and other like-minded theorists might argue that it does not follow from the fact that something is of value, that it should be considered by the state as being of sufficient value to warrant protection by a right.

I think however that there are multiple grounds to make the case that religious conviction ought to be protected as stringently as moral conviction. First, religious obligation shares with obligation born of morality a connection to self-respect and integrity. One might feel just as compromised were one to be forced to act against one's moral convictions, as one would were one to act against a strongly held moral principle.

Second, and as has already been suggested, for many people, living within a religious tradition is central to their conception of themselves as agents. As Scheffler points out, it is for many people a way of giving meaning to their lives by situating it in a broader narrative. The relative brevity of our lives may make them seem meaningless, unless we can present them to ourselves as links in a longer chain. Relatedly, for many people who live according to the precepts of a religion, being an agent is just acting in the terms provided by a religious tradition, interpreting and reinterpreting its tenets and rituals in a variety of contexts. The ongoing debate among Western and Muslim feminists about the meaning of the Muslim veil is an example of the failure on the part of those who view religion as

[4] Samuel Scheffler, *Equality and Tradition: Questions of Value in Moral and Political Theory* (Oxford, Oxford University Press, 2012).

being akin to moral conviction to understand the centrality of certain rituals and practices to a believer's sense of agency.[5]

None of this is to say, of course, that the right to religious freedom so construed cannot be overridden. The rights of others obviously constitute such a limit. One cannot invoke any right in order to ride roughshod over the fundamental rights of other agents. But governments can have legislative purposes that in certain circumstances can also call for the proportionate and parsimonious limitation of a right, including the right to religious freedom. This right should not be given greater protection than other civil and political rights. But absent an argument, there is no reason to think that it should be afforded less.

If tradition, and the values associated with it, constitute the grounds of the right to religious freedom, it follows that many of the obligations that will be protected by the right will be intergenerational in nature. These will have to do with keeping faith with past generations, but also with raising future generations so as to ensure the perpetuation of the religious tradition in question. In other words, religious freedom on this construal involves not only the right to act according to one's religious convictions in ways that are self-regarding, but also to act toward one's children in a way that reflects those convictions. For a member of religion X, freedom of religion involves in part the right to raise her children *as* an X. Indeed, for many religious persons, to ascribe a right to religious freedom to them that did not involve the right to raise their children into a religion would be to miss the point of that freedom altogether.

What range of behavior *vis-à-vis* one's children should be protected by the right to freedom of religion? In a sense, the purpose of this paper is to answer precisely that question. My intention in this section has simply been to make plausible the claim that there exists a way of construing freedom of religion that makes it distinct from freedom of conscience (and thus irreducible to Dworkin's right to moral independence), and that grounds it in the value of tradition, and that this construal quite naturally incorporates the right to raise children as members of a religious tradition into the core of the right.

II. The Right to an Open Future: An Interpretation

As I mentioned above, all rights can be limited, and in particular they can be limited by the rights of others. An immediate response to the claim I have just made, to the effect that parents have a right to raise their children as members of a religion, would invoke what Joel Feinberg has famously called 'the child's right

[5] Drawing on comtemporary scholars of Islam such as Talal Asad and Saba Mahmood, I explore this idea in greater detail in my 'Le paradoxe du multiculturalisme libéral', in S Guérard de la Tour (ed), *Perspectives sur le multiculturalisme* (Paris, Hermann, 2013).

to an open future'.[6] There seems to be a prima facie incompatibility between the implication that I have just derived from the right to religious freedom to do with parental rights, and the right of the child not to have life options foreclosed by the manner in which they have been raised.

I want to suggest in this section that the conflict is more apparent than real.[7] We can begin with the common-sense observation that, in many ways, parenting necessarily involves orienting a child toward certain futures rather than others. Parents cannot avoid making choices on behalf of their children—to live in the city or in the country, to invest time and money in the development of one's child's musical or athletic abilities, to go on family holidays that emphasise cultural discovery or the love of the outdoors, and so on. Every choice one makes along these dimensions and countless others inclines children toward the development of certain aptitudes and the acquisition of certain predispositions rather than others.

If this is the case, then the right to an open future, if it is to be a plausible constraint on parental behavior, cannot mean that parents must prescind from any form of orientation of their children's future choices. To do so would be to prescind from parenting.

There is a variety of principles that parents might adopt in order to decide how to orient their children, given that a certain amount of orientation is an ineliminable part of parenting. They could when faced with the kind of choice that I briefly alluded to above select randomly, or, as Matthew Clayton has suggested they ought to do, adopt with respect to their children an Archimedean decision-making stance, deciding on their good from a perspective detached from their own convictions about what is right and wrong, worthy and worthless.[8] Or they could decide to give their own comprehensive conceptions of the good some weight in determining how to orient their child.

Is there a way of breaking the tie between these three ways in which parents engage in the inevitable process of orienting their child? I suggest that there is. As Brighouse and Swift have argued, the value of families (as opposed, say, to collectivised modes of child-rearing) lies in their affording both parents and children the opportunity to enjoy relations marked by intimacy. Intimacy is a complex concept to express in a single definition, but it certainly involves a degree of authenticity and self-disclosure. I cannot be intimate with another human being if I do not reveal myself to her according to my real motivations and ideals.[9]

[6] Joel Feinberg, 'The Child's Right to an Open Future', in W Aiken and H LaFollette (eds), *Whose Child ? Children's Rights, Parental Authority, and State Power* (Totowa, Rowman and Littlefield, 1980).

[7] The next few paragraphs summarise an argument that I make at greater length in my 'How do children limit their parents' right to religious freedom ?', in C Laborde (ed), *Religion in Liberal Political Philosophy* (Oxford, Oxford University Press, forthcoming).

[8] Matthew Clayton, *Justice and Legitimacy in Upbringing* (Oxford, Oxford University Press, 2006) ch 3.

[9] Harry Brighouse and Adam Swift, *Family Values. The Ethics of Parent-Child Relationships* (Princeton, Princeton University Press, 2014).

But that is precisely the fate that would befall families in which parents oriented their children on the basis of randomly generated options, or on the basis of options that would be revealed to be optimal from a third-person, detached perspective. Rather than engaging in the unavoidable task of orienting their children on the basis of values that they actually cherish, and practices that are actually meaningful to them, they would be introducing their children to practices in a manner that forced them to dissemble, by concealing from their children the conceptions of the good that confer meaning upon certain practices and activities. It would be difficult to cultivate the intimacy that is a good both for parents and for children when parents parent either randomly or objectively.

So parents cannot but orient their children, and it seems as if the value of familial intimacy depends upon their doing so in a way that comports with their conceptions of the good, rather than abstracting from them. How, then, is the child's right to an open future to be given meaningful content?

Parents violate their children's right to an open future not when they parent on the basis of their comprehensive conceptions of the good, but rather when they do so in a manner that fails to provide children with all-purpose tools with which to make other choices. Imagine that some pluralistic account of human flourishing, such as those proposed by James Griffin, or by Martha Nussbaum, is true.[10] According to such conceptions, there are a number of dimensions along which humans develop. It seems plausible that a child is made ready for a life of meaningful choices if, though his upbringing has emphasised one of these dimensions disproportionately, because it corresponds to his parents' comprehensive conceptions, he is nonetheless raised to sufficient levels with respect to all of the other dimensions. Such a child, we might say, has been raised in an acceptably asymmetrical way. It is asymmetrical, because some dimensions of the human good have in his case been emphasised, but it is acceptably so, because this has not occurred in a manner precluding the development of other dimensions of his personality. Though oriented toward a certain conception of the good, he nonetheless comes to possess the wherewithal on the basis of which to make other choices.

A child is accordingly said to be raised in an unacceptably asymmetrical way if the latter condition is not met, that is, if he is raised with an emphasis placed on one aspect of human flourishing, but to the exclusion of all others. (To complete the picture of possible ways of raising a child, let us say that a child is raised in a symmetrical manner when he is equally oriented toward all possible forms of human flourishing. Presumably, this is the state that is aimed at by what I have above termed 'random' or 'objective' parenting, that is by parenting not guided by a comprehensive conception.)

[10] See James Griffin, *Well-Being* (Oxford, Oxford University Press, 1986); Martha Nussbaum, 'Aristotelian Social Democracy', in RB Douglass et al (eds), *Liberalism and the Good* (New York, Routledge, 1990).

If the parental right to orient children according to their comprehensive conceptions is to coexist with the child's right to an open future, that right must be interpreted as requiring of parents that they prescind from unacceptably asymmetrical parenting (but not that they abstain from acceptably asymmetrical parenting). To revert to Clayton's terminology, what matters is not that parents enrol their children into their comprehensive conceptions, even their religious conceptions, but rather that they do so in a manner that does not meaningfully undercut the ability of children to make meaningful choices. How is this to be achieved? That is the question that I will be turning my attention to in the next section.

III. Parenting Ethics and the Use of State Power

I have been operating thus far under the simplifying assumption that whether or not a child's right to an open future is upheld depends solely on the manner in which she has been raised by her parents. This is of course not the case. Children in fact undergo the influence of a wide range of institutional agents. These include parents, to be sure, but also civil society associations of various kinds, as well as educational institutions. Whether children whose parents raise them on the basis of a comprehensive conception of the good end up unacceptably or acceptably asymmetrically raised thus depends on the combined effect of all kinds of agents and institutions.[11]

The question arises, therefore, as to what the division of moral responsibility ought to be as between parents, civil society organisations such as religious institutions, and schools, to ensure that this right is satisfied. Now, there are at least two ways in which this question might be asked. It can, to begin with, be asked as an abstractly ethical question. On this construal, we want to know what the moral responsibilities are of parents, as well as the officers of civil society organisations and schools.

Another way of considering the question of the division of moral responsibility sees it as a question of political ethics. Here, the question is not how these different agents should behave, but rather how the state should use its enforcement capacity. The state is a peculiar kind of moral agent, after all. Its claim to the obedience of those who fall under its authority is backed up by the monopoly of legitimate violence. There can be uses of this power that strike us as morally problematic, even when they are carried out in the pursuit of otherwise morally legitimate ends.

[11] The short list compiled here is of course itself a simplification. For example, it has been shown that children's peer groups may have more of an influence on their development than parents do. See Judith Rich Harris, *The Nurture Assumption*, 2nd edn (New York, The Free Press, 2009).

So there are two kinds of questions we can ask about the role of parents in their children's upbringing. The first has to do with what they are morally duty-bound to do in order to ensure that their children are not unacceptably asymmetrically raised. The second has to do with the desirability of the state enforcing whatever duties we have ascribed to parents at the level of ethical analysis.

A theorist who has pleaded forcefully for a parental obligation to abstain from 'enrolling' their children in their own comprehensive conceptions of the good (whether religious or not) is Matthew Clayton. His argument is premised on three central arguments. The first is that to the extent that we think that the state ought only to use its coercive authority on the basis of norms and principles that all could accept, and therefore on norms of 'public reason' rather than on norms grounded in comprehensive conceptions of the good, we ought to think the same thing of parents, since the families over which they preside share three essential features with the state: they are involuntary, they are coercive, and their influence on the lives of those who grow up within them is pervasive.[12] The second, which flows directly from the first, is that parents should not seek to enrol their children in comprehensive conceptions, because children lack the requisite ability to consent to, or to reject, these conceptions. Finally, there are no countervailing arguments, acceptable to public reason, that would justify such attempted enrolment. Arguments grounded in intimacy and in autonomy in particular are seen to fail.

I do not want in this chapter to focus on the abstract moral question of how parents ought to deploy their parental power, or on the constraints that they ought to observe in deploying that power. Rather, I want to focus on what the state can do in order to ensure that the rights of children to an acceptably asymmetrical upbringing are enforced. Assume, for the sake of argument, that Clayton's conclusions are correct, and that parents ought therefore to prescind from enrolling their children in their comprehensive conception. Does it follow that the state ought to enforce that obligation?

It does not. Clayton clearly believes that his conclusions are of more than merely abstract ethical import. That is, he believes that they have implications not just for the way in which parents ought to behave toward their children, but also for the way in which the state ought to act toward parents. Though he does not elaborate on the point, he believes that the interest of children in autonomy warrants the state in ensuring that parents are disabled, by force of law, from raising their children in a way that detracts from their autonomy. His argument, he claims, 'has revolutionary implications for parents *and public authorities*'.[13]

The following argument shows that the political implications of the moral vew that Clayton defends do not flow as naturally as he suggests. The state's authority

[12] Clayton (n 8) 93–103.
[13] ibid, 102 (emphasis added).

over parents to protect children against egregious abuse is based in the moral claim that the role of parent is not grounded in 'natural' facts. Parents occupy a social role, one that is justly regulated by the state. That 'natural' parents get to parent the children to which they are genetically connected is a defeasible presumption, rather than something that follows from the natural order of things. That this presumption is viewed as only defeated in the most extreme of cases does not take away from the fact that people occupy the role of 'parent' (as opposed to that of progenitor) as a result of legal arrangements that rightly balance the interest of children with that of prospective adult parents.

The question is how the state ought to use that power. There are two sets of reasons that in my view militate strongly against the power being used in a manner that would warrant its sanctioning parents who engaged in unacceptably asymmetrical parenting. The first has to do with the ethical unattractiveness of a society in which the state possessed the monitoring capacity required in order to ascertain whether children were being parented in this way, and the authority to sanction those parents found wanting. Indeed, it is hard to see how it could fulfil this capacity without being able to disrupt the limited degree of intimacy that actually is required in order for familial goods to be realisable. It would also have to be able to collect information about the everyday aspects of family life that would lead to everyone, parents and children, operating as if they were constantly being watched and scrutinised. The self-consciousness on the part of all parties that would inevitably arise would be incompatible with the level of intimacy required for family flourishing to be possible. (Note that this would not be the case for the lesser oversight that the state needs to deploy in order to ascertain that children have suffered physical or extreme psychological harm.)

The second point is a more practical one to do with what one might term 'carrying capacity'. By this I mean the ability of the state to actually fulfil the roles and responsibilities that it sets for itself without an investment of material and human resources that would place other important state functions in peril. Many public policies that may be justifiable on independent grounds of political morality founder because of an inadequate reckoning of state capacity. Prohibitionist policies of various kinds (against drugs, sex work, alcohol, assisted suicide, and the like) fail because, even if one believes they are motivated by worthy goals, they require of the state that it do things that it is simply unequipped to do, at least at reasonable cost. Though imperfect prohibition does sometimes manage to reduce the incidence of the impugned behavior, that gain is most often outweighed by the losses inherent in not being able to regulate the range of that behavior that is not effectively deterred.

There are epistemic issues as well. Even if we assumed, *per impossibile*, that the state actually could monitor the intricacies of family life in order to ensure that children were being raised in acceptably rather than in unacceptably asymmetrical ways, and even if we set aside the ethical issues raised by a state having that degree of monitoring capacity and accompanied sanctioning power, we would have to wonder whether agents of the state could make the fine-grained judgments required in order to distinguish between acceptably and unacceptably asymmetrical upbringings. Once one puts aside the most egregious forms of brainwashing of the kind usually associated with cults, the line separating the two is likely to be very difficult to make out clearly, assuming for a moment that such a line exists. Worse, there are reasons to think that, where these judgments are made by members of the cultural majority, they would tend to identify failings with respect to the line more readily in the case of minorities than they would in the case of forms of parenting more familiar to the majority.

Now, were it the case that the kind of morally, practically and epistemically risky form of state action involved in monitoring parents for their violations of their children's right to autonomy was the only way of ensuring that children are not raised in an unacceptably asymmetrical way, then perhaps these risks would be worth incurring. But it is not. I return here to the claim made at the very beginning of this section of the paper: whether children end up being raised in a manner protective of their autonomy depends not just on whether their parents prescind from enrolling them in their comprehensive conceptions of the good life in a morally problematic way, but also on the role played by other actors that are also influential in shaping a child's upbringing. Simplifying somewhat, as I did above, we can say that the upbringing of children is the result of the combined efforts of three kinds of actors: parents, civil society organisations (including religious institutions), and the state. We have just canvassed some reasons to think that the state should be parsimonious in the way in which it governs the family. Need it abstain to quite the same degree when it comes to its regulation of the manner in which civil society institutions and schools contribute to the upbringing of children? It is to this question that I will not turn my attention.

IV. The Regulation of Civil Societies

By civil society institutions, I refer to the organised social life that occurs, as it were, 'between' the private sphere of the home (where, I have in effect argued that parents should be given a wide berth to raise children pretty much as they please, on condition that they abstain from visiting egregious physical or psychological harm upon them), and public institutions which are either part of the state apparatus, or that are operated or at least regulated by the state (think of health institutions in most countries, and as I will argue below, of schools). A useful way of identifying institutions of civil society is by the following two features: first, they are organised. By this I mean that they are not merely spontaneous associations, which might arise from the unstructured everyday encounters of individuals, but rather have at least the rudimentary structures that lend them a degree of permanence and decision-making capacity. Second, though they are more than spontaneous expressions of human interaction, they emanate from the civil sphere. By this I mean that even though they may elicit the regulatory activity of the state, it would be no part of the state's responsibility to bring them about were they not to emanate from the unfettered activity of citizens. This includes a broad range of the settings within which modern citizens of most developed societies lead their lives. Within this set we find trade unions and institutions devoted to artistic and recreational pursuits, such as musical societies and sports associations. We also find firms that compete on the economic market. And we find institutions through which citizens organise their religious and spiritual lives: churches, mosques, synagogues, and the like.

Part of the debate that separates liberals from libertarians has to do with the degree to which these institutions should be regulated by the state. Libertarians tend to believe that a free society is one that allows almost complete freedom of association, whereas many liberals feel that there should be limits on the (still quite substantial) freedom that civil society organisations enjoy.[14] It would require another paper (indeed an entire book) to settle that issue, but suffice it to say that only the most extreme libertarian would claim that civil society institutions should be exempt from regulations when it comes to the interest of children. For example, while there is debate about the age at which children should be allowed to play contact sports that put them at risk of concussions and other injuries, few (if any) libertarians would argue that they ought to be allowed to play such sports without protective gear such as helmets, or sit in the front seats of cars equipped with air bags.

Though children participate in civil society institutions (they do not spend the totality of their time in their parents' homes and at school), they are usually at least until adolescence in a sense not *agents* within civil society. They are for the most part guided in their path through civil society by parents. Parents decide whether they will participate in sports or not, whether they will sing in a choir, whether they will accompany them to religious services.

'Parenting ethics' should include the question of how those who are assigned the responsibility of bringing children up should conduct themselves not just at home but in their role as 'guides' of their children into civil society. 'Good' parents, we might argue, do not attempt to make their children as they would wish them to be, but listen for intimations of their children's own inclinations and dispositions as they choose the forms of organised social life in which their children will take part.

But as mentioned above, this is not an essay in parenting ethics, but rather in the ethics of the state as regards its responsibilities toward children. Our question is

[14] There has been a renaissance of libertarian writing about the role of unregulated intermediate associations in liberal democracies. See for example Victor Muniz-Fraticelli, *The Structure of Pluralism* (Oxford, Oxford University Press, 2014).

therefore not how parents should behave with respect to their children, but rather how (or whether) the state should regulate how children are treated within civil society.

Arguably, the state has more of a regulatory role in this sphere than they do in the regulation of the home sphere. The ethical, practical and epistemic worries that led me to hold that the state should be parsimonious in its regulation of the home dissipate, or at least do not apply to the same degree, where civil society organisations are involved. (Thus, to take a trivial but revealing example, the state prevents my children from seeing movies in cinemas that it cannot prevent them from seeing at home).

Theorists who believe that the state should protect the children against forces that would inhibit the development of their autonomy might concede that it would be inappropriate for state authorities to monitor the home so as to uproot threats to autonomy that might exist there. They might however argue that they should observe no such restraint when it comes to civil society. Thus, it might be argued that though parents cannot be prevented from involving their children in religious practices and rites in the home, they should be prevented from taking them to religious services, or to receive religious teaching outside of the home. Another option might be for the state to regulate the content of religious teaching in a manner that makes it more compatible with the development of autonomy in children.

There is prima facie plausibility to a role for the state in a way that there was not in the case of the state's putative regulation of the home. Protecting children from the autonomy-inhibiting impact of civil society organisations might be seen as no more problematic than the requirement that they wear helmets and mouth protectors when they play ice-hockey.

Despite this prima facie plausibility, several considerations militate against the state acting in this manner. These considerations are both ethical and practical. From the point of view of political ethics, there can be little doubt that intervening in the life of religious institutions (for example by prohibiting children from attending them before they have reached the age of consent, or by regulating the content of the teaching that they receive in religious institutions) strikes at the heart of liberal freedoms in a way that safety regulations in organised sports do not. Freedom of association and freedom of religion are not without limit. As we have seen, the intergenerational transmission of religion is part of the *point* of freedom of religion. It is situated at the core, rather than at the periphery, of the right. Given the centrality of intergenerational considerations to religious freedom, prohibiting children from attending religious institutions with their parents, or regulating the content of the communications they receive there, would be viewed as grossly disproportionate to the task of ensuring that religious life be compatible with the requirement that children receive an acceptably rather than an unacceptably asymmetrical education. Practically speaking, this means that the state might appropriately step in when places of worship engage in hateful or speech or in incitement to violence toward members of other groups. But it ought not to prohibit attendance of religious institutions by children or to regulate religious speech more strenuously than is required in order to block the promotion of hatred or violence.

Another consideration that militates against the state intervening to limit the impact that religious institutions might have upon children is that religions, by their very nature, have institutional dimensions. Contrary to those who, like Dworkin, would reduce religion to individual belief and conscience, religions have irreducibly communal dimensions. They link people not just diachronically but synchronically. People come together to worship. They form communities of faith. To tell parents that they can introduce children to their faith, as long as they do it in the privacy of their own homes, is thus in a sense to deny them the right to religious freedom altogether.

There are thus powerful ethical and practical reasons to limit the reach of the state into civil society organisations in general, and into religious institutions in particular, even for the sake of the protection of the future autonomy of children. These reasons might be outweighed were the regulation of religious (and other civil society) organisations the *only* way in which to protect children from unacceptably asymmetrical upbringings. But as I will argue in the next section, this is not the case. The state appropriately regulates education, and it can use its control over the educational sphere in order to ensure that children are not subjected to unacceptably asymmetrical education in a manner that frees it from having to intervene in the sphere of the family or of civil society to achieve this goal.

V. The Case Against Religious Schooling

I am going to make the simplifying assumption that in order for children to receive an acceptably rather than an unacceptably asymmetrical education, it suffices that one of the three agents which contribute to the upbringing of children be devoted to securing that objective. To put the assumption another way, my assumption is that the state's responsibility is not that *all* of the forces that shape a child into an adult conduce to her autonomy, but rather that *some* non-trivial force do. What the state must avoid is that parents, civil society institutions and schools conspire to create what one might term a 'totalising environment' for the upbringing of children.

My argument is that the best way in which to achieve this end is through the regulation of schools. Whereas there are reasons, grounded in a concern for the intergenerational and communal dimensions of freedom of religion, but also in the practical and epistemic limitations of the state's regulatory actions, for the state to respect the authority of parents in the intimate sphere of the family and to prescind from too much intervention in the domain of civil society institutions, these reasons do not obtain in the case of schools.

Many theorists have already argued that schools ought to promote the autonomy of children.[15] I do not wish to add to their arguments at the level of abstract ethics. What I want to suggest is that while it is theoretically possible to imagine the autonomy of children being secured in an environment in which parents or civil society organisations are the main agents ensuring that children are shielded from totalising environments, the regulation of schools (rather than of family life or of civil society) is most attractive as a matter of state ethics.

Begin by considering the fact that unlike purposes served by civil society organisations, the purpose served by schools—that of educating children—is one that the state would have to ensure were it not spontaneously served by civil society. Children will not be able to lead flourishing lives as adults unless they acquire a range of competencies, and in an environment that is both psychologically and physically healthy.

A state devoted to even minimal social justice must moreover ensure that *all* children receive instruction, and that they receive instruction of roughly the same quality. Even less demanding conceptions of distributive justice, ones that emphasise equality of opportunity rather than insisting upon egalitarian outcomes, will tend to claim that the (potentially unequal) outcomes of social competition can only be justified if all are roughly equally equipped to compete.[16] There is but a step from this minimal egalitarian claim to the requirement that at least rough equality obtain in the field of education. Educational equality is not likely to emerge spontaneously from an unregulated educational market. Parents are likely to evince partiality toward their children that might lead them to attempt to obtain competitive advantages for their children by providing them with better education. The already well-off might in particular be inclined to use their greater financial resources to ensure that their children be favourably situated at the starting line. If educational equality is to be achieved, it will therefore have to be through state action prohibiting parents from using their resources to advantage their children through educational institutions designed to create an economic, political, or social elite.[17]

Finally, the state has a legitimate interest in at least some of the contents that make up the school curriculum. Though care must be taken to ensure that the state does not engage in undue perfectionism through schools (by privileging controversial educational goals), liberal democracies must also avoid the paradox of being neutral relative to liberal democracy itself. Thus, liberal democracies

[15] See for example Meira Levinson, *The Demands of Liberal Education* (Oxford, Oxford University Press, 2002).

[16] Thus for example even Milton Friedman believed that the state has a role in equalising educational opportunity in a competitive capitalist economy. *Capitalism and Freedom: Fortieth Anniversary Edition* (Chicago: University of Chicago Press, 2002).

[17] For a magisterial account of the tension between parental partiality and the requirement of justice in the area of education, see Adam Swift, *How Not to be a Hypocrite: School Choice for the Morally Perplexed Parent*, (London, Routledge, 2003).

have an interest in equipping children with basic civic competence that will allow them to be active citizens of liberal democratic institutions. Civic competence seems as important a goal to invest in educational institutions as does literacy and numeracy.[18]

The state must therefore, for at least these reasons, be active in the educational sphere to ensure that all children receive education, and it must also regulate that sphere if all children are to receive a roughly equal education. We might add that the state must also be there to ensure that the quality of education that is provided to all children be as high as possible. The state can through taxation mobilise resources to this end, and it can also impose standards on the training of teachers to achieve as high an educational standard as possible for all children.

Thus, the state is necessarily present in the educational sphere in a way that it is not with respect to those other forces that constitute the environment through which children are brought up, namely the family and civil society. The first point I want to make in this section is thus that this necessary presence of the state in the education of its future citizens makes schools a natural locus through which to ensure that children are not brought up in an unacceptably asymmetrical manner.

How might the state achieve this end in the educational sphere? It can do so by exercising some control over curriculum. Simplifying for the sake of brevity, my suggestion is that whereas parents and civil society organisations act toward children so as to increase the probability that they will end up endorsing their parents' conception of the good (whether religious or not), for example by not exposing them as much as they might to other conceptions, or by disparaging such conceptions, though not encouraging hatred toward them, or by increasing the psychic costs associated with abandoning one's parents' conception, schools should offset this horizon-constricting dimension of upbringing by presenting children with as many such conceptions as practicable, and by presenting them in an eligible light, that is, in as positive a light as the conception into which the child has been raised at home and in civil society. It should insist upon a curriculum that does not transform the educational sphere into an extension of the home and of civil society institutions, whether religious or otherwise.

Whether this amounts to a ban on religious schools depends entirely on whether religious schools are able to cleave to the requirements very briefly laid out above. But it does amount to a very serious restriction of the role that religious schools have traditionally ascribed to themselves.

Does the state that promotes the autonomy of children by regulating the curriculum in the manner just suggested fall afoul of the strictures we described above in the case of the family and of civil society? That is, does it violate important principles of state ethics? Does it risk exceeding the 'carrying capacity' of states, or giving rise to self-defeating results? I don't think so.

[18] On this point see for example Stephen Macedo, *Democracy and Distrust: Civic Education in a Multicultural Democracy* (Cambridge, Harvard University Press, 2003).

First, the regulation of school curricula does not require the kind of constant, heavy-handed monitoring that would be required in order to ensure, say, that parents were acting in the way in which they bring up their children so as to protect their autonomy. As we have seen, children have to be educated in a tolerably equal way anyway, and we have suggested that this can only be done when the state organises education. The extra level of regulation that must be engaged in by the state in order to ensure that the curriculum that it sets up for children does not detract from their autonomy is infinitesimal, relative to the level of monitoring and sanctioning that it would have to engage in were it to attempt to steer families and civil society organisations toward this end.

Second, the regulation of schools, that might make it impossible for certain kinds of religious schools to operate as they did, strikes less at the communal dimension of religion than does the regulation of places of worship. While it is impossible to imagine a fully realised religious life that does not centre upon church, mosque, synagogue, etc, this is not the case with respect to schools. Prohibiting schools from being vehicles for the transmission of a conception of the good does not prevent that conception of the good animating the life of the home. Regulating religious schools does not prevent children from receiving confessional religious teaching through religious institutions, outside of school hours. Schools thus seem to belong to the core of religious freedom to a lesser degree than do religious institutions.

Even if we concede, as I think we must, that prohibiting religious teaching in schools does limit religious freedom, the argument developed in this chapter suggests quite strongly that it does so less than other restrictions that might be thought to be required in order to ensure that children are not educated in an unacceptably asymmetrical way. To claim that even this limitation would be disproportionate would in effect be to give the communal dimension of religious freedom infinite weight relative to the right of the child to a sufficiently open future.

VI. Conclusion

I have argued that the right to freedom of religion must include the right of parents to enrol their children in their conceptions of the good, as long as this is done in an acceptably asymmetrical way, one that secures the child's right to a sufficiently open future. I have also argued that as a matter of state ethics, the regulatory activity of the state should be focused on schools, rather than on family life or on institutions of civil society. The organisation of schools in a manner that promotes autonomy is the best way to make the parental right to freedom of religion and the child's right to an open future compossible, in a manner that does not breach fundamental principles of state ethics by forcing state agents to act in a manner that poses problems from the point of view of a plausible theory of state ethics.

I end with a caveat. This has been an exercise in what some might call 'ideal theory'. That is, I suppose a sufficient level of compliance with basic moral principles by the agents, individual or institutional, that I consider in this chapter.

What happens to my conclusions when one relaxes these simplifying ideal assumptions? We are familiar with the way the argument runs in the case of parents. When parents act in ways that detract from the realisation of their children's most fundamental interests, an obligation on the part of the state to act within the familial sphere might be triggered, culminating in extreme cases in the removal of children or even the termination of parental rights.

What about when the state does not fulfil its obligations in the educational sphere? There are at least two ways in which this can occur. First, it can itself use its power to organise schooling and to set curriculum to promote a perfectionist project, one that reasonable persons can disagree with. In this case, it would no more be contributing to the autonomy of children than would parents and civil society organisations invested with their own comprehensive conceptions. Second, the state can fail in its mission by providing children with inadequate education. The promotion of autonomy is, after all, not just about prescinding from the inculcation of comprehensive conceptions. It also requires that children possess adequate tools with which to face the challenges of adulthood. When states fail to provide children with these tools, either through lack of adequate resources or both, it fails them in the pursuit of autonomy just as surely as if it were to attempt to inculcate a state religion.

How do my conclusions change when the state acts in one or another (or both) of these non-deal ways? In such cases its claim to overrule parental preferences in the educational sphere diminishes. There may, therefore, be a non-ideal theoretical case against the state's claim to organise and regulate education. This case must be mounted contextually, on a case-by-case basis. Such an endeavour, however, falls well beyond the scope of this chapter.

11

'Open House'/'Portes Ouvertes': Classrooms as Sites of Interfaith Interface

SHAUNA VAN PRAAGH*

I. Introduction: Invitation to an Open House

Every fall, throughout Quebec, high schools invite prospective students and their parents to an 'open house', or 'portes ouvertes'. Eleven-year-olds in the sixth and final grade of their primary schools visit a range of public and private high schools during 'open house' season, taking advantage of the 'portes ouvertes' to learn more about academic programmes, classroom experience and extracurricular offerings. They can speak with older students, teachers of various subjects, librarians, guidance counsellors, and coaches. Most importantly, they can glean from the visit whether they can imagine themselves in that place as secondary school students from grade seven to grade 11. The open house is a mix of presentation and invitation: it provides each school the opportunity to present its unique combination of the content and form of teaching and learning, and at the same time serves as an invitation to each young person to consider eventual enrolment.

In the fall of 2015, one Quebec high school proudly opened the door to one of its classrooms in particular. The 'Open House' at Loyola High School, a private Jesuit institution, will no doubt have featured the school's litigation voyage to the Supreme Court of Canada and back—a voyage undertaken to confirm recognition of a Catholic version of the provincially mandated Ethics and Religious Culture (ERC) course. It is true that every high school in Quebec will introduce prospective students to its ERC classrooms and teachers during the season of 'portes ouvertes'. In the wake of its success at the Supreme Court, Loyola could do so confident that its students will participate in learning Ethics and Religious Culture

* Appreciation goes to two doctoral candidates in law at McGill for their related work and assistance: Rung-Guang Lin and Blair Major. This chapter is dedicated to the memory of my colleague H Patrick Glenn who, I think, would have enjoyed the metaphor of endless portes ouvertes.

from a perspective infused with the school's own faith-based identity and culture. It is not hard to imagine the 2015 version of 'portes ouvertes' at Loyola as not only a mix of self-presentation by the school and open invitation to students, but also as a meeting place: as a metaphorical site of encounter between religion in the form of the school's Jesuit mission and public authority in the form of provincial curricular requirements and Supreme Court of Canada interpretation of the Canadian Charter of Rights and Freedoms.

I start with reference to the open house circuit for two interrelated reasons. First, as suggested above, the Supreme Court of Canada's March 2015 judgment in *Loyola High School v Quebec*[1] brings the exercise of public authority in the domain of education into sharp and timely focus, in Quebec and beyond. A fictional entry through Loyola's open doors allows us to trace the impact of religious freedom claims on the contours of an educational programme aimed at all young students within one jurisdiction. Second, and more broadly, I use the metaphor of 'portes ouvertes' to structure the methodology and substance of this chapter in a book collection dedicated to religion and the exercise of public authority. I aim to illustrate—through an imagined open house that juxtaposes diverse institutional settings—how the encounter of religion and state changes shape across classrooms and through corridors. In other words, I add the classroom to the more classic repertory of courts and constitutions, charters and codes as focal points of legal analysis and learning. A metaphorical 'portes ouvertes' event invites us to observe, listen, and insert ourselves into the very places at which traditions meet (interfaith) and the ways in which students and teachers participate (interface).

We know that education is a fruitful substantive terrain for investigating the coexistence, sometimes marked by conflict, of religion and state. Individuals and institutions of faith may claim exemptions from expectations or requirements found in state law and policy. In this vein, it should come as no surprise that the realm of education deserves its own analysis in any examination of the place of religion in Canadian law, such as that most notably and recently provided by Richard Moon.[2] Education is also a significant source of lessons: lessons for state law about religious authority and, conversely, for faith-based communities about state norms. Given the ways in which teaching the next generation is key to the sustainability of both religious communities and entire societies, education is an especially rich site for comparing 'law's religion', in the words of Benjamin Berger,[3] to religion's rules and structures.

[1] *Loyola High School v Quebec (Attorney General)* 2015 SCC 12 (*Loyola*).

[2] Richard Moon, *Freedom of Conscience and Religion* (Toronto, Irwin Law, 2014).

[3] Benjamin L Berger, 'Law's Religion: Rendering Culture' in Richard Moon (ed), *Law and Religious Pluralism in Canada* (Vancouver, UBC Press, 2008). See also Benjamin L Berger, 'Religious Diversity, Education, and the "Crisis" in State Neutrality' (2013) 29 *Canadian Journal of Law and Society* 103.

Education is an obvious lens through which to scrutinise the exercise of public authority over or alongside religion. The 2015 Supreme Court judgment that carves out for Loyola High School a unique faith-defined space for teaching its students about ethical, cultural and religious approaches to human existence and experience, is the latest in a series of pronouncements by the Court on the scope of religious liberty in the context of education. Earlier education-related decisions had sketched the contours of an individual student's religious freedom grounded in sincerity of belief (*Multani v Marguerite-Bourgeoys (Commission scolaire)*),[4] and the limits of faith-based rights of parents to exclude their children from parts of a school's academic programme (*SL v Commission scolaire des Chênes*).[5] The *Loyola* judgment most notably complements the earlier jurisprudence by confirming a collective dimension to freedom of religion: the religious rights of an educational institution are found to be infringed by an obligation imposed by the provincial Department of Education to teach Ethics and Religious Culture from a faith-neutral perspective.[6] Taken together, the judgments, and others related to them,[7] indicate that schools and the people who constitute them are particular subjects of law in its engagement with religion.

In fastening on education as an important site for examining religion-state dynamics in twenty-first-century Canada, I acknowledge the significance of a constitutional narrative of religious diversity guided by charters and developed by courts. But I suggest that the formal narratives of law and religion are woven together with other less formal or explicit narratives that emerge through the activities of teaching and learning.[8] Indeed, those are the narratives that a fictional open house invites visitors to hear and understand. They are the narratives that turn education into a source, even more than site or category, for examining the relationship of religion to public authority. In order to appreciate the ways in which participants in the terrain of education can provide insight into the possibilities of interfaith interface, I draw on fiction, roundtable conversations, and imagined conversations just as much as on court judgments and constitutional interpretation. Unlike an actual open house, we are not asked to consider eventual enrolment. But we are indeed asked to learn by entering through the 'portes ouvertes' and imagining the everyday on the inside.

[4] *Multani v Marguerite-Bourgeoys (Commission scolaire)* 2006 SCC 6, [2006] 1 SCR 256.

[5] *SL v Commission Scolaire des Chênes* 2012 SCC 7, [2012] 1 SCR 235.

[6] For the Court's discussion of a collective dimension to religious freedom, see *Loyola High School* (n 1) paras 60–62 (majority) and paras 89–102 (minority).

[7] Related Canadian jurisprudence in which religion and education have been addressed include: *Chamberlain v Surrey School District No 36*, 2002 SCC 86, [2002] 4 SCR 710 (religion-based challenge to school books), *Zylberberg v Sudbury Board of Education* (1988) 52 DLR (4th) 577 (ON CA) (challenge to mandatory classroom prayer), *Trinity Western University v College of Teachers* 2001 SCC 31, [2001] SCR 772 (potential impact of religious teachers on young students).

[8] See Shauna Van Praagh, 'Sharing the Sidewalk' (2010) 8 *Canadian Diversity* 6 and 'Sidewalk Stories: Sites of Encounter and Coexistence' in S Azmi, L Foster and L Jacobs (eds), *Balancing Competing Rights in a Diverse Society* (Toronto, Irwin Law Books, 2012).

II. *Interfaith Interface* in Classrooms and Corridors

A. A Theoretical Backdrop to the Open House: Interdependence of Traditions and Interactions of Normative Sources

Naming the education setting itself as a source of lessons for law and religion shifts our gaze and concentration as jurists in unusual ways and directions. In doing so, I draw on the insights of two Canadian legal scholars not typically on the list of regular contributors to discussions on religion and public authority, but whose creativity and sensibilities provide guidance and inspiration. The work of both Roderick A Macdonald and H Patrick Glenn places them firmly within the study and critique of law's theory and practice. And yet they insist on questioning the parameters of law itself, enlarging the range of significant sources of law, familiarising multiple sites of law creation and drawing our attention to the persuasive possibilities of innovative methodologies. While both men passed away in 2014, their voices continue to resonate in ongoing conversations in comparative law and public law, and in any exploration of the systems that offer structure to our everyday lives. If we think of schools as places governed by a mix of such systems, including those grounded in state and religious authority, then the writings of Professors Glenn and Macdonald become principal reference points. They help us articulate questions and tentative answers in ways not obviously available within the framework characterised by constitutional and human rights law.

The terminology of 'interfaith' 'interface', as a way to capture the reality and potential of the encounter of religion and public authority in school classrooms and corridors, combines the contributions of Glenn and Macdonald. For Glenn, complex legal traditions cannot have mutually exclusive identities; that is, they are necessarily interdependent and indeed are in constant communication with each other. Common law, civil law, islamic law, canon law, talmudic law, chthonic law: all, along with others, have unique and complex histories, structures, vocabularies and methods for development. And all rely on the permeability of their boundaries. Glenn writes:

> Complexity and interdependence necessarily characterize the relations between complex traditions … Complex traditions are by their nature, and in their leading versions, non-universal and non-universalizing. They offer many grounds of accommodation with other complex traditions. The larger and more complex the tradition, the less dangerous it is for others.[9]

The law of a state in which many systems coexist, grounded in their various traditions, may be accurately described as polyjural. So too might the governing

[9] H Patrick Glenn, *Legal Traditions of the World: Sustainable Diversity in Law*, 4th edn (New York, Oxford University Press, 2010) 374–75.

law of a school. To see how any school in a particular place at a particular time might serve as an 'interfaith' meeting place, we should pay attention not only to the diversity of individual adherents to religious communities within the specific educational institution but also, and at the same time, to the interdependency of authoritative traditions that marks its past and future.

For Macdonald, individuals integrate within their own lives the interactions of many, always shifting normative systems. Any or all of those normative systems offer guidance, rules, norms and consequences. They come together in a dynamic way that is unique to each one of us. Referred to as critical legal pluralism, Macdonald's approach insists on plural forms and locations of law, warns against focusing solely on the state as significant generator and overseer of law, and underscores the constant interactions of spheres or communities to which we belong or within which we act. The approach goes even further in a way that invites us to identify the 'interface' potential of classrooms and corridors. From a critical legal pluralist perspective, individuals (students or teachers or administrators) are not only situated at any given time and place at a normative interface, but also exist *as* a human interface of normative systems. Those systems might be grounded in faith-based practices or classroom codes of conduct, in provincial education policy or teachers' unions, in lunchroom etiquette or sports team expectations. Macdonald points out:

> Individuals may feel bound to a web of multiple, sometimes conflicting legal regimes, whether by virtue of their affiliations with various social groups, by their own individual normative standards, through their interaction with institutions (families, clubs churches, schools, self-regulating bodies, corporations, communities, etc.) that reflect, reinforce, and implement these standards. Law emerges, then, through these interactions and relationships and not through coercive means.[10]

He adds, '[e]ach person is forever deciding the relative weight of rules, processes, and values amongst the multiple legal regimes that attract, invite, or demand loyalty and commitment'.[11]

An examination of religion and the exercise of public authority directed by Macdonald's critical legal pluralism would acknowledge that religion could operate in someone's life as a source and set of norms. Authority on the part of the state, in its many forms and processes, would interact with those norms and others. Thus, the best places to listen and learn as jurists would be the interface encounters that shape the lives of individual actors. Informed by Glenn's insights, on the other hand, the analysis might start by interrogating the features of a jurisdiction marked by the coexistence and potential clash of religion and public

[10] Roderick A Macdonald, 'Custom Made—For a Non-chirographic Critical Legal Pluralism' (2011) 26 *Canadian Journal of Law and Society* 301, 324.

[11] Roderick A Macdonald, 'Legal Republicanism and Legal Pluralism: Two Takes on Identity and Diversity' in M Bussani and M Graziadei (eds), *Human Diversity and the Law* (Brussels, Bruylant, 2005) 50.

authority. Education might be an ideal place for exploring the mixed complexity of any particular jurisdiction, in its mixing of private and public, faith-based and secular, local and national. Educational institutions and programmes, just like their human participants, can embody a complicated interfaith reality.

The preoccupation of Glenn as comparative jurist for the interdependence of traditions, and the preoccupation of Macdonald as legal pluralist for the interactions of normative sources and systems, together help us navigate through the open house of educational encounter. Indeed, the open house metaphor might resonate with both of them for methodological as well as theoretical reasons. Glenn might enjoy thinking of his own comparative work on legal traditions of the world as a series of tradition-based open houses, inviting readers into the nooks and crannies of each one in turn. Macdonald would fully approve of a fictional or literal visit to classrooms as a way to discover, see, study and practice law. Both would like the fact that a school's open house can never be a complete representation of the reality of being a student there. In other words, the open house described below, in which we move through the playground to preschool, and on to primary school and secondary school as sites and sources of interfaith interface, is necessarily limited and partial. For jurists like Macdonald and Glenn, uninterested in a quest for certainty or clear models, a scholarly project should muddy the terrain and challenge the imagination. It should surprise us in its juxtaposition of sources and texts. Finally, while it might include references to courts and codes, it should never fail to go beyond those artifacts of state law or public authority to better grasp the fragile equilibrium of human traditions and the dynamic flux of human interactions.

B. An Empirical Plan for the Open House: A Roundtable Discussion on Religion and Education

Preparation for the task of leading readers through an imagined open house includes more than theoretical justification. It also benefits from empirical knowledge-gathering and the resulting preliminary picture of interfaith interface in educational settings. This explains the organisation, in anticipation of the writing of this chapter, of a roundtable discussion at McGill University's Faculty of Law in the fall of 2014 that brought together teachers and youth workers from a broad range of faith backgrounds and education-related experience.[12] All were educators in Montreal, keen to recount their stories of dealing with religious diversity of young people, bringing their own sets of beliefs to their work, teaching

[12] 'Religious Diversity in Childhood Education—A Roundtable Discussion', 29 October 2014, Faculty of Law, McGill University. The roundtable was supported by the McGill Centre for Human Rights and Legal Pluralism and the Université de Montréal; participants included doctoral candidates in Education and Law, teachers in public and private religious schools, and professionals engaged in youth and family intervention and support. No formal questions were posed to participants; rather it was a forum for sharing practices, questions and experiences related to religion and education.

about religion in public and private schools, and considering requests for particular accommodation. The roundtable drew inspiration from a project on religious diversity in Western Canadian education that gathered together school administrators, teachers and parents of various religious backgrounds to discuss issues of religion in public schools.[13] That project focused specifically on perceptions of individual space for the spirituality of adults involved in public education. Our roundtable made its central preoccupation faith-related exchanges with young people in a range of institutional contexts.

Recounting even a handful of the comments, observations and questions that arose around the table shows how the discussion helped give form and content to the open house framework. A secular Jewish teacher had spent a year at a Hasidic Jewish school and now found herself in a highly diverse public kindergarten where even very young girls turn up wearing hijabs, like their mothers. Another, a youth worker, wished aloud for stronger communities to which young people would feel connected, within schools and beyond. Another, calling herself double-blessed as the daughter of a Baptist Christian and a Sunni Muslim, was responsible for all levels of the Ethics and Religious Culture programme at a public high school and was working on a dissertation on how to effectively teach religion. Still another, a guidance counsellor, described a student's innovative project of creating a designated prayer space at his high school for a week. Finally, one talked about training student teachers to be prepared to take on Ethics and Religious Culture; she appreciated the supportive intervention of a child psychologist who spoke of the high level of mindfulness and reflection required by those teachers.

The circuit detailed below is thus the result of actual conversations combined with fictional narrative and significant case law. Not surprisingly, the difficult issues identified around the table of people involved in education are the same as those identified in policy discussions, litigation, religious communities and school administration. While the principal features of the open house are shaped by the religion and law context of early twenty-first-century Quebec, and indeed the cited sources are only fully understood against a backdrop of jurisdiction-specific language, society, culture and politics, the open house includes references from beyond the province in which it is imagined. Reader-visitors are invited to create their own endless variations.

C. The Open House Circuit

i. The Schoolyard

The initial religion and law stop on the education open house circuit is just outside the front door. A sign on the wall reads: *Stop 1—Individual Beliefs and School*

[13] Kimberly Franklin and Harro Van Brummelen, 'Religious Diversity in Western Canadian Education: Presumptions, Provisions, Practices, and Possibilities' in F Salili and R Hoosain (eds), *Religion in Multicultural Education* (Charlotte, Information Age Publishing Inc, 2006).

Rules. Gurbaj Singh Multani comes to greet us, and nods assent when asked if he is wearing his Sikh kirpan tucked into his clothes. For visitors familiar with the Supreme Court of Canada judgment that bears his name, that is the expected response: as a young devout Sikh, Gurbaj can carry a symbol of his faith that otherwise resembles the kind of weapon explicitly prohibited by the school's code of conduct. But, when asked whether he agrees with the Court's assessment of the meaning of the kirpan—that is, as suggested by the accepted testimony of a Sikh chaplain, 'a religious symbol which signifies mercy, kindness and honour'[14]—he slowly shakes his head. That isn't exactly how he understands it, he mumbles; it's more complicated and it depends whom he's talking to. But as long as there's space in the schoolyard for him, and acceptance of how he gets dressed every morning and presents himself to his peers and teachers, that's what matters.

What lessons can we learn from this initial meeting with a young person who belongs both to his faith community and to his public school? The very fact that we are prepared to stop and engage in a conversation with him distinguishes our understanding from that conveyed by a final judgment by the Supreme Court. The face-to-face encounter forces us to struggle to appreciate the complexity of this student's individual experience and ongoing relationships with those around him. Gurbaj Singh is clearly what critical legal pluralism would name a legal agent, whose reflections and actions exist at the interface of the circles in which he lives and learns. As legal agents, people are 'actively engaging in law-making endeavors',[15] constructing 'their own law, their own regimes of governance'.[16] And there is always 'an element of construction or creativity by the subjects of collective narratives when they are confronted with internormative conflicts'.[17] From this perspective, Gurbaj's own obedience to rules, whether those of his religion or school, is not simply dictated by authority. Instead, it is the result of interaction between authoritative mandate and his own, frequently submerged, reflection and decision-making. In his mind and experience, that obedience might feel shaky and less than permanently demarcated.

Depending on the questions we ask, we might learn from him that his co-religionists speak of the kirpan in ways that range from aggressive to peaceful, that some but not all of the teachers have been supportive in helping non-Sikh students respect his beliefs and practices, and that the school commission has occasionally invited representatives from religious communities to collaborate on the drafting and implementation of codes of student behavior. In the years before and after the original Gurbaj Multani was a young teenager, the Sikh tradition in Canada has absorbed lessons from the legal traditions of the state, and vice versa: 'Sustaining

[14] *Multani* (n 4), para 37.
[15] Macdonald, 'Custom Made' (n 10) 323.
[16] ibid, 324.
[17] Martha-Marie Kleinhans and Roderick A Macdonald, 'What is a *Critical* Legal Pluralism?' (1997) 12 *Canadian Journal of Law and Society* 25, 44.

diversity means accepting (not tolerating) the major, complex legal traditions of the world (all of them). It means seeing them as mutually interdependent … It means seeing all traditions as one's own, in some measure, since each is dependent on the others'.[18] That reality of interfaith interdependence is developed on a daily basis as Sikh students come to school with their kirpans worn so as to comply with appropriate conditions.

Finally, as we watch Gurbaj with his peers, we might be reminded that the actual trajectory of the *Multani* litigation started with agreement between the school and family: that is, accord based on interpersonal interaction. The issue grew into a major conflict between religion and public authority as it moved further and further away from the schoolyard all the way to the Supreme Court of Canada. This visit asks us as jurists to pay attention to the consequences on the ground for Gurbaj then and now.[19]

ii. Preschool Space

Once inside, the next stop is in the preschool or daycare wing, designed for young children from six months to four years old. Here, the sign that invites us to visit reads as follows: *Stop Two—Intersecting Images and Identities*. The babies and toddlers are busy developing their abilities to move and communicate; they are figuring out shapes and colours, using all of their senses to experience the world around them, and learning to name things and people and phenomena. Perhaps most strikingly, at a very young age, they are making connections to adults other than parents. Early childhood educators, then, take on a special role in the lives of these children. They prepare them for peer relations and for their eventual transition to school. They are the key people to talk to in this corner of the open house.

On one side of the daycare, we find the room in full Hallowe'en mode: pumpkins and bats and witches' hats in orange and black construction paper. The teacher explains that Hallowe'en is her favourite time of year, a moment when all of the toddlers in her public daycare classroom celebrate together. They all have different backgrounds, but at least they all enjoy putting on costumes for Hallowe'en. Last year, she notes, she had a tough time understanding why one of the children was kept home from the festivities. His mother had explained that Jehovah's Witnesses do not favour Hallowe'en participation, and therefore that her son had to be excluded. On the other side, the daycare displays its December decorations: a mix of snowflakes and stockings, Christmas trees, Hanukah dreidels, Kwanzaa colours, Diwali candles. Regardless of the actual identities of the children, the

[18] Glenn, *Legal Traditions of the World* (n 9) 378.

[19] See Howard Kislowicz, 'Sacred Laws in Earthly Courts: Legal Pluralism in Canadian Religious Freedom Litigation' (2013) 39(1) *Queen's Law Journal* 175, for a legal pluralist analysis of *Multani* and other cases grounded in empirical methodology (interviews with the litigants involved).

room embodies the diversity of the society in which they are growing up. Here, the teacher shares her excitement over the bright and festive space. But she worries about which storybooks are appropriate, whether parents should be allowed to come in to share their holidays and customs, and what she should say if one of the three-year-olds in her care asks about Baby Jesus.

Both modes of engagement with religious identity in an educational setting represented here are firmly planted in soil understood, in a range of ways, as secular. In the Hallowe'en display, we find assumptions as to the inclusiveness of a particular holiday, challenged by the possibility of self-exclusion on the basis of religious identity. In the Christmastime version, we find the representation of a spectrum of holidays, none of which is underscored by an explicitly faith-based narrative shared with the children. Indeed, the Quebec Daycare Directive,[20] an example of public policy guidelines for the place of celebratory symbols in public preschool classrooms, specifies that signs of various cultures and religions enrich appreciation of diversity on the part of very young children. On the other hand, however, the Directive prohibits what it refers to as teaching of any particular religious belief or practice in those classrooms. A Christmas tree is fine as decoration, but the angel on top must not act as trigger for a lesson on the religious significance of the holiday. The preschool classroom as interfaith forum may be more symbolic than substantive.[21]

As we prepare to move on, a young Muslim woman wearing a hijab walks in and introduces herself as one of the daycare educators. While the Daycare Directive in Quebec is an example of a state's transparent interest in the place of faith at a stage of education when young children are learning about themselves, it is also an example of wariness with respect to religious, ethical and cultural visions conveyed in early education classrooms. That wariness can extend to explicit signs of religious affiliation on the part of public daycare teachers, and the proposed but never adopted Charter of Quebec Values[22] would have expected Muslim women to remove their hijabs when at work with young children. Instead, as this teacher reminds us, she arrives at the daycare every morning with her head covered, and her young charges with whom she interacts simply absorb her hijab as one of her

[20] Famille et Aînés Québec, 'Directive: Activités ayant pour objectif l'apprentissage d'une croyance, d'un dogme ou de la pratique d'une religion spécifique dans un centre de la petite enfance ou une garderie subventionnée' (December 2010). In the spring of 2015, the Quebec National Assembly introduced a Bill that, if passed, would replace the Directive and incorporate its terms into law: Projet de loi n°62 (Loi favorisant le respect de la neutralité religieuse de l'Etat et visant notamment à encadrer les demandes d'accommodements religieux dans certains organismes).

[21] See Shauna Van Praagh, '"Inside Out/Outside In": Co-Existence and Cross Pollination of Religion and State' in René Provost (ed), *Mapping the Legal Boundaries of Belonging. Religion and Multiculturalism from Israel to Canada* (Oxford, OUP, 2014) 121, for further discussion of the Daycare Directive in Quebec.

[22] Bill 60, Charter affirming the values of State secularism and religious neutrality and of equality between women and men, and providing a framework for accommodation requests, 1st Sess, 40th Leg, 2013, Quebec (first reading) [Charter of Quebec Values].

distinguishing features. She continues by saying that she personally draws a line between the hijab she wears and a niqab, that would cover her face and body. She's not sure how she would react to a rule banning a niqab in educational settings, although she was impressed with the way in which a group of Quebec parents came to the impassioned defence of their children's niqab-clad private daycare educators in the summer of 2014.[23]

iii. Religious Primary School

Our next stop is at the primary school level, and the sign announces a very different setting: *Stop Three—The outsider teacher inside a religious community*. This is the primary school classroom of an ultra-Orthodox Jewish girls school in Montreal, described in the novel *Hadassa*.[24] Grounded in the actual experience of author Myriam Beaudoin, the novel tells the story of Alice, a French teacher for a year in a class of 11- and 12-year-old Hasidic girls. Not unlike Alice in Wonderland, this Alice is thrown into a world of characters, rules, relations and expectations with which she has no familiarity. Young Hadassa, for whom the novel is named, stands out given the close relationship that develops between her and the very different French teacher. As visitors to the classroom, we watch through the windows and listen to snippets of contemplation and conversation.

> I was dressed according to the terms of my employment contract that prohibited sleeveless blouses, above-the-knee skirts, pants, shiny fabric or tight styles. In the midday sun, I was wearing a dark dress down to my ankles. My hair was rolled into a bun; I stood still, nervous, my arms held close to my sides. Turning and laughing around me were hundreds of young girls in blue uniforms, coming closer in pairs or groups to examine my outfit, my pewter bracelet, my shy smile, and then running off to play before coming back again. I had been warned not to think that I could ever be their friend or trusted confidante.[25]

Here we see Alice, dressed as expected for her new post, the object of curiosity and amusement, the young teacher from the outside waiting to find out what lies ahead. And then we meet Hadassa—11 years old and already figuring out how to assert herself and trace her own relationship to the French class in which she is expected to learn from Madame Alice.

> I remember … the 11-year-olds, who wanted to know everything about me in return for sharing their secrets. I remember the test days when Hadassa Horowitz, frail and charming, became curiously ill…
>
> 'Miss, I don't feel well. Can I go home?'

[23] 'Parents support niqab-wearing daycare teachers', *CTV News* (21 November 2013) http://montreal.ctvnews.ca/parents-support-niqab-wearing-daycare-teachers-1.1553521.

[24] Myriam Beaudoin, *Hadassa* (Montreal, Bibliothèque Québecoise, 2010).

[25] ibid, 13 (author's translation from French).

> 'No, Hadassa. Today there's a test on verbs. It's very important'.
>
> The little girl sadly returned to her seat…
>
> Five minutes later, she was back:
>
> 'I'm going to start crying, my eyes are all red. I'm going to cry because I have a stomach-ache'. …
>
> Hadassa knew how to insist and, from time to time, I would give in.[26]

The intricacies of the relationship that develops between the girls and their French teacher are beyond full articulation. But they show their knowledge of and assumptions about each other in their informal conversations.

> Walking between the groups, I bent down to Yitty and Malky:
>
> 'You're lighting the first candle tonight?'
>
> 'How do you know?' asked Yitty, surprised.
>
> 'I learn by reading books from the library'.
>
> 'You can read about that too? They talk about us in the books you read?' She was stunned.
>
> A twelve year old passed behind us, closed the door then came back.
>
> 'But you know, Miss', said Pearl, her hand on her hip. 'Nechama's father knows much more than you do … There are lots of things you can't understand … because you're not Jewish'.
>
> 'Miss!' cried Tzirl, a girl with glasses bigger than her face. 'Do you know what this is?' she asked, holding up a toy near the window. I went over, and she handed me a wooden four-sided top. 'It's a draydel. It's for Hanukah. Do you celebrate Hanukah?'
>
> 'No, we have another holiday', I answered.
>
> '*Chrissssst…*' she started.
>
> 'Don't say it!' interrupted Nechama.[27]

Finally, as the story and her teaching contract ends, Alice and her charges reflect on this period in their lives. The teacher will leave the girls behind to continue on their paths within their community; the girls will no longer have access to the books and other less tangible symbols of non-Hasidic life that their young French teacher had shared with them.

> For nine months, five days a week, in a Hasidic neighbourhood, I had shared my life with eighteen bright faces … My time with the young daughters of Israel was coming to an end. I explained to them that I needed a break.
>
> 'Because you're getting married?'

[26] ibid, 40–41.
[27] ibid, 104.

'No, not yet'.

'But who will get us books at the public library? Who will buy us new Smurf books ...?'[28]

This is a setting very different from that in which Gurbaj Multani wears his kirpan and preschoolers are introduced to ways in which people present themselves and celebrate their holidays. A private religious school shapes its own community of students, families and teachers; it insulates itself to a great extent from the diverse society in which it exists. But, as the story of Alice and Hadassa shows, the world of this school and its pupils is never truly isolated.[29] It is a world into which Alice, the outsider to this faith community, is welcomed, albeit in a necessarily partial way. It is a world that cannot escape completely the attention of the province's authority over education, particularly language education as symbolised by cartoon books in French in the hands of young Yiddish-speaking students. The intersecting spheres of state, religion, neighbourhood, family and classroom all shape the learning experiences and vulnerabilities and projects of the individuals who live at their interface.

The Supreme Court of Canada, in its 1996 judgment in *Ross v New Brunswick School District*, underscores the significance of teachers in the lives of their students and communities:

> Teachers are inextricably linked to the integrity of the school system. Teachers occupy positions of trust and confidence, and exert considerable influence over their students as a result of their positions. The conduct of a teacher bears directly upon the community's perception of the ability of the teacher to fulfill such a position of trust and influence, and upon the community's confidence in the public school system as a whole.[30]

Alice and Hadassa may be fictional characters, but they provide striking lessons on the beliefs, actions, roles and responsibilities that form a web of teaching and learning, and of the weaving together of traditions and the individuals who carry them forward.

iv. Prayer in the Library

As we walk by the library, we're invited to take a quick look around before continuing. The sign on the wall reads: *Stop Four—Making and marking space for faith.* A longer visit to the library of any school could provide extensive information as to the place and influence of religious affiliation. A private religious school like the one we just left might have a very limited range of books on the shelf; a public school might be expected to have a much wider selection, including books

[28] ibid, 208–09.

[29] For a discussion of the permeability of the boundaries surrounding a Hasidic community and its schools in the US, see Shauna Van Praagh, 'Changing the Lens: Locating Religious Communities Within the U.S. and Canadian Families and Constitutions' (1998) 15 *Arizona Journal of International and Comparative Law* 125, 130–33.

[30] *Ross v New Brunswick School District No 15* [1996] 1 SCR 825, para 43.

on a spectrum of faiths and their histories and features. A librarian might be able to tell us whether past clashes of parents with school authorities, particularly with respect to religious values, have been factored into the choice of available books for the student body.[31] But for now, as we move through our open house, we simply step in to get a sense of the library atmosphere.

In a far corner, next to a window, Sarmad and Naman are rolling up their prayer mats after completing the 10 minutes of daily prayers that they undertake as Sunni Muslim young men. The two students used to attend Webber Academy in Calgary, a non-denominational and private high school, and subject of a 2015 decision of the Alberta Human Rights Commission.[32] But there, they tell us, their request for time and space to pray each day was denied. Now that Webber's decisions and actions have been found to violate the human rights of these Muslim students, Sarmad and Naman will be receiving monetary damages for the experience they've been through. But they won't be going back to that school. They remind us that they had never asked for a permanent designated Muslim prayer room; indeed, tomorrow they won't pray in the library, but instead in the nurse's office after she's gone for the day.

The temporary use of the school library as Muslim prayer space, a use overlapping with its other functions, underscores the tenuousness of any attempt to fix the precise contours of the interfaith forum provided by the school. Today, the prayers take place in the library, tomorrow in another corner of the school where the boys' beliefs and actions won't interfere with others. The necessary flexibility of the students and the school is precisely what emerges from the decision of the Alberta Human Rights Commission, combined with an appreciation of how the exercise of faith can be anchored in the everyday. Not every religious student has to stop to pray; indeed, there will be variation within each religious community as to the understanding of individual obligation, and ongoing arrangements made to share space and facilitate learning.

v. Ethics and Religious Culture—A Secondary School Classroom

Our final stop is an Ethics and Religious Culture (ERC) classroom in a high school in Quebec: a classroom in which teacher and students are discussing the recent Supreme Court of Canada judgment on ERC itself. This last sign reads *Stop Five—Variations in the teaching and learning of religious diversity.* Ethics and Religious Culture is the name of an academic programme, mandatory in all Quebec schools since 2008, focused on the coexistence of related but distinct ways of thinking about religious, cultural and ethical sources and issues. No matter their faith or cultural heritage, all Quebec teenagers are expected to participate in ERC courses to gain awareness and knowledge of a spectrum of

[31] See eg *Chamberlain v Surrey School District No 36* 2002 SCC 86, [2002] 4 SCR 710.
[32] *Amir and Nazar v Webber Academy Foundation* 2015 AHRC 8.

approaches to human existence and interaction, and to develop empathy, respect, and critical thinking. Since its inception, ERC has become a site of high hopes and sharp sensibilities, and a symbol of the shaping of the future of Quebec society.[33] The in-class study of the decision in Loyola High School is an obvious addition to the curriculum.

The teacher reminds the students and the visitors of the issue that took ERC and Loyola High School all the way to the Supreme Court of Canada. Loyola had requested an exemption from the official programme approved by the provincial Minister of Education, suggesting instead an explicitly Catholic version of the course to be taught at the Jesuit school. When the government representative refused the request, Loyola stood its ground. After conflicting decisions in the lower courts, the Supreme Court directed the province to recognise Loyola's distinctive faith-based approach to teaching ERC. As mandated by government policy, academic attention and real respect must be offered to all approaches to human existence, grounded in different faiths and cultures and illustrating different ethical standpoints. But the discussion of Catholicism in an explicitly Catholic high school can be steeped in the sources, traditions and structures of the religion itself.

What are the key lessons from the Court's judgment for high school students enrolled in the very programme at issue? First, they learn that religious freedom is important not only for individuals but also, even if differently, for institutions. A school characterised as religious will have an interest in presenting at least its own faith from an internal perspective, and that is precisely the interest protected by the Court's interpretation of freedom of religion as guaranteed by the Canadian Charter of Rights and Freedoms.[34] We can imagine an intense discussion over variations in teaching and learning across ERC classrooms in Quebec. If a classroom is anchored in and infused with one faith, what does it mean to treat, and teach about, other religious traditions and communities with respect? Is it possible to confine a faith-based approach to the teaching of only one faith? What are key differences and similarities between individual and collective religious rights?

The teacher follows up with a related question: what do the students think is implied by neutrality in the teaching and learning of ethics and culture? As we watch and listen, it becomes obvious that the particular backgrounds of the students in this group, combined with the particular teacher and the collective character of the school, naturally colour the ideas and arguments put forward. One student shares his family's mix of Greek Orthodox and Muslim traditions; another compares her family's Reform Judaism to the more Orthodox version

[33] For how the conversation around ERC represents a reflection on the identity of today's Quebec and the ways in which the society can move forward together, see Shauna Van Praagh, 'From Secondary School to the Supreme Court of Canada, and Back: Dancing the Tango of "Ethics and Religious Culture"' (2012) *Fides et Libertas* 102.

[34] See *Loyola High School* (n 1), paras 61–70.

described in the course materials; the teacher shares insights from a conference she recently attended on teaching religion. Another ERC classroom discussion down the hall might evolve in very different directions. An ERC teacher at Loyola High School itself might celebrate with his students the success of the school in its claim against the Quebec government. At the same time, given the Supreme Court judgment's concern over unacceptable indoctrination, that teacher might acknowledge the less than clear-cut task of making revisions to the content and pedagogy of the course in order to demonstrate concrete respect for all faiths and ethical perspectives.

The second lesson from the *Loyola* decision for this group is that of cooperation. Students can appreciate from the litigation story interwoven with their own ongoing participation in ERC that government regulations and regulators in the context of education must show openness to variation. At the same time, all schools, including those labelled as religious, must participate in the collective endeavour of teaching, learning and shaping citizenship. The programme in which these young people are studying ethics and religious culture has become a lesson in itself on the interactions of exactly those elements of our collective existence. The consequences of the *Loyola* judgment will require imagination, dedication, cooperation and respect on the part of the people who act with authority for government, schools and religious communities. Perhaps the students in the ERC classroom in our open house can show them the way.

This last stop displays interfaith interface in both form and substance. The ERC programme can be conceived as a high school version of Patrick Glenn's work on legal traditions of the world; it gives students an opportunity to study the history and structure and systems of one tradition after the next. They compare, they contrast, and they notice the interdependence of traditions in their own classrooms, schools, neighbourhoods and society. As Glenn emphasises:

> They [major legal traditions] all represent truths—ecological ones, religious ones, ethical ones, rational ones—and each represents enormous effort over a very long period of time to give effect in human lives to these truths … They each remind us of something important … they each provide social ordering in the world which the other traditions may be unable to provide; they each contribute to necessary diversity.[35]

The discussions that form the backbone of the programme reinforce Roderick Macdonald's pluralist vision of relying on ourselves to learn about and sustain law. As he suggests: 'As agents, legal subjects understand the normativity of law as originating in their own actions and interactions; that is, they learn about law, first and foremost, from themselves'.[36] What are the beliefs and norms that govern our lives and choices and actions? A successful ERC programme asks students to reflect on exactly that question and to draw on their interactions with others to

[35] Glenn, *Legal Traditions of the World* (n 9) 376.
[36] Macdonald, 'Custom Made' (n 10) 311.

come up with meaningful answers. The result, as suggested by our visit to the classroom, necessarily overflows the lines and limits articulated by any judgment. The Supreme Court can't design the course or direct the conversation. Instead it offers a framework for governing an educational programme: a framework given content and lasting power by the *interfaith interface* reality of the ERC classroom itself.

III. Conclusion: *Portes Ouvertes* and Everyday Education

The Open House comes to an end, but the doors stay ajar. Visitors are invited to notice the envisaged renovation projects, and indeed to take note of the fact that the building is under constant construction. At some open houses of schools undergoing structural work, visitors would be assured of an end date to the noise and dust and traffic. At this open house, however, we receive a guarantee that there is no end date in sight. The work will continue for the foreseeable future, as additional sources are unearthed, new questions asked, and partial answers keep being modified.

The relationship of religion to public law and authority in any jurisdiction at any time can be conveyed through the context of education. But that doesn't mean that the resolution—whether in school courses or corridors, codes of behavior or courts—of issues of inclusion and exemption, accommodation and curricular content establishes in any permanent way the interfaith interdependency of authoritative structures and institutions or the interface interactions of normative systems and circles. As we have seen, we can weave together the lessons of Patrick Glenn's creative comparative law and Roderick Macdonald's critical legal pluralism to appreciate the dynamics of Canadian classrooms. The reverse is also true: we can visit real and imagined classrooms in order to appreciate the interweaving of theoretical perspectives on legal norms and traditions in our lives and understanding of law.

As jurists engaged in a never-ending exploration of the Canadian landscape of religion and state, we are expected to listen with care, to look in unexamined places, to refine our understanding of law's potential and limits, on one hand, and of religion's authority and constraints, on the other. Perhaps particularly in the context of education, it is clear that both the state and religious communities perceive themselves as sources of identity and citizenship and as principal investors in the wellbeing of future generations. Appreciating that sense and scope of responsibility taken on by both public authorities and institutions and their religious counterparts is not a simple task. In this chapter, I have approached that challenge by combining fiction, roundtable conversations, court judgments and imagined conversations. To most effectively grapple with religion and public authority, I suggest, we can read novels together with Supreme Court reports; we can analyse administrative decisions together with classroom lesson plans.

Everyday points of interface between an individual and her faith, between the school and the provincial ministry of education, between a teacher and his students are necessarily hard to capture with any certainty. But they are perhaps precisely the sources that inform the fragile equilibrium of identity, authority and tradition that characterises religion-state interaction in contemporary Canada. And they are exactly what we find when we open doors to sites of teaching and learning that reject insoluble conflict in favour of complicated coexistence. As we leave the open house, we find a last message, signed by Patrick Glenn, posted next to the exit sign, and encouraging us to celebrate the complex messages and lessons of the visit:

> What the proponents of incommensurability would ultimately have to establish is the impossibility of human communication, radical untranslatability, and this is denied by all human experience, and possibly by the very idea of being human.[37]

[37] Glenn, *Legal Traditions of the World* (n 9) 47.

INDEX

www.ingramcontent.com/pod-product-compliance
Lightning Source LLC
LaVergne TN
LVHW052318200926
848481LV00002B/599